Ain't No Harm to Kill the Devil

The Life and Legend of John Fairfield, Abolitionist for Hire

Ain't No Harm to Kill the Devil

The Life and Legend of John Fairfield,
Abolitionist for Hire

by

Jeffrey S. Copeland

PARAGON HOUSE

First Edition 2014

Published in the United States by
Paragon House
1925 Oakcrest Avenue
St. Paul, MN 55113

Photo acknowledgements:
Slave Chains: Abraham Lincoln Presidential Library and Museum
Wanted Poster: Maryana Britt
John Fairfield image: Suzanne Lowe Birdwell

Library of Congress Cataloging-in-Publication Data

Copeland, Jeffrey S. (Jeffrey Scott), 1953-
Ain't no harm to kill the devil : the life and legacy of John Fairfield, abolitionist for hire / by Jeffrey S. Copeland. -- First edition.
pages cm

Summary: "Literary nonfiction account of the history and legend of abolitionist John Fairfield, one of the most successful conductors of the Underground Railroad before the American Civil War. A master of disguise and subterfuge, Fairfield used extortion and violence, when necessary, to deliver slaves to freedom in Canada"-- Provided by publisher.

ISBN 978-1-55778-913-6 (paperback : alkaline paper) 1. Fairfield, John. 2. Abolitionists--United States--Biography. 3. Tricksters--United States--Biography. 4. Underground Railroad. 5. Underground Railroad--Canada. 6. Fugitive slaves--United States--History--19th century. 7. Antislavery movements--United States--History--19th century. I. Title.
E449.F15C67 2014
973.7'114092--dc23
[B]

2014014375

The paper used in this publication meets the minimum requirements of American National Standard for Information Sciences—Permanence of Paper for Printed Library Materials, ANSI Z39.48-1984.

Manufactured in the United States of America
10 9 8 7 6 5 4 3 2 1

For current information about all releases from Paragon House,
visit the web site at http://www.ParagonHouse.com

For my daughter,
Crystal Lynn Ford

And for those who dedicated their lives to
carrying the torch of freedom

Contents

Author's Note

THE LIFE AND LEGEND OF JOHN FAIRFIELD have both long been shrouded in mystery. In this story, I've attempted to pull back the curtain and offer a new view of this remarkable warrior in the fight for equality and freedom for all. In doing so, I spent more than a year conducting the background research for this book. I visited with dozens of historians who shared with me little-known information about the Underground Railroad and the abolitionist movement. Each interview proved to be rewarding in its own right, but every time I found what I was positive was an undeniable fact about one of John Fairfield's adventures, other information would invariably pop up—and the accounts would be different. In some cases accounts varied to a small degree; in others, the differences were quite great.

It didn't take me long to discover that when it came to John Fairfield's life and work, the "historical record" was often blurred, at times, no doubt, on purpose and by design. Why? First, because of the incredibly large bounty ("Dead or Alive") on his head, which would translate into nearly half a million of today's dollars, he had to keep details of his personal life as secret as possible and known to only the closest of friends and associates. Second, because he was a wanted man, he had to create false "cover" identities for himself to carry out his work for the cause of abolition. In the balance between keeping his personal information private and the manufactured information that came to light as he lived the part of his "cover" identities, a shadowy figure appeared —a man of mystery—one trailed by rumor and innuendo.

In the end, after all the background research was gathered, I chose to go with the "facts/legends" which were most frequently reported and validated by those who knew John Fairfield. I've done my best to "stay the facts." However, Horace Greely probably said it best when describing what to do about stories of individuals of this type: "When it comes to a choice between writing the facts or the legend—always write the legend." What follows is both the life and legend of John Fairfield.

It should be noted the time period involved was compressed to allow the story to unfold as presented. For the obvious reasons, some of the names have been changed, and other characters are composites of several. I've given additional information about this in the companion e-book, *Finding Fairfield: The Behind-the-Scenes story of* Ain't No Harm to Kill the Devil: The Life and Legend of John Fairfield, Abolitionist for Hire.

—JSC

Chapter 1

The Trackers

May 7, 1855, West Liberty, Kentucky

Sheriff Sam Sullivan jerked hard on the reins, his horse rearing back and nearly bucking him off as he wrestled it to a halt. He raised his left hand and motioned his posse to veer left and stop next to a thick stand of birch trees. As they did so, one of the group belched loudly, and another jumped from his saddle and ran behind a tree to relieve himself. The other six members of the posse were either laughing or reaching into their saddlebags to pull out bottles of whisky.

Sheriff Sullivan's deputy, Marcus, eased his way forward, shrugged his shoulders, and said, "Saloon posse. What'd you expect?"

"I always expect better, but you'd think I'd know better by now," Sam replied. "Bar-flies, whiskerandos, and downright drunks. But, I guess they're better than nothin'. Look around. How many of the good citizens from town are with us? I'll tell you how many. Exactly none. At least these saloon rats rode along."

Stubby Jennings, the saloon sweeper, spittoon shiner, and a member of every posse to ride out of town for the past two years, yelled out, "What we stoppin' for? Let's keep goin'! Them robbers can't be far ahead now!" He drew his gun from its holster, cocked the hammer, and aimed it just over Sam's head.

"You shut up and listen!" Sam shot back, his voice firm, commanding. "And put that away before you shoot yourself. Just calm down. Marcus and I are goin' up ahead first. We'll let you know when we need you."

Sam, moving forward, pointed to a blazing campfire in a clearing below them and said to Marcus, "Funny place for a fire, wouldn't you say? They couldn't have stopped already. Nobody's that stupid. And besides, that's right in the middle of the trail we're following. Makes no sense. None at all. We better see what it's all about."

Turning to the posse, he ordered, "Stay here. All of you. And keep quiet. No talkin' above a whisper, and no more rotgut. Put those bottles away right now. If we're gonna to catch 'em, we're gonna to have to surprise 'em. We can't do that if you're back here wakin' the dead. Keep your mouths shut and your eyes straight ahead. And take those spurs off. Put 'em in your saddlebags. The way y'all are staggerin' around sounds like you're rattlin' pails of nails. Sound carries on a night like this."

When the men, grumbling quietly at first, had finally removed their spurs and quieted down, he said, "I'm taking Marcus with me to check out that campfire up yonder. If you hear shots, get to us fast as you can. Otherwise, stay out of sight. I don't want to see you, and I especially don't want to hear you."

Charlie Adams, part-time gambler and full-time trouble-maker, staggered forward and said, "And miss all the fun? I didn't ride all this way not to stretch a rope or two. Just let me get my hands on 'em. We won't have to worry about draggin' anybody back to town."

"There'll be none of that," Sam barked. "They didn't kill any-one, so our job is to get 'em back to justice. That's all I want to hear from you or anybody else. You better get that through your thick skulls or you might be stretchin' a rope yourself soon enough."

Sam dismounted and faced the men. "Right now they don't know how many we are. If they're hiding out in the trees down there and we come ragin' in, that campfire will show 'em our strength and make us easy targets. That ain't smart. Keep 'em guessin', keep surprise on our side long as we can."

Charlie belched loudly again and sat heavily down on the ground, crossing his legs under him in the process. "Then what in the Sam Hill did we come for?" he said to no one in particular.

Sam tapped Marcus on the arm, "Let's go. Tie the horses over there, and we'll walk down along the tree line. Keep close— and watch where you step."

As they crept forward, Sam ran the events of the early evening through his mind again. He was still full of questions, still couldn't make much sense of what had happened. Just as dusk was settling in, the bank in West Liberty, one of the largest banks in eastern Kentucky, had been robbed by a group of men who had managed to get in and out of the bank, taking the main cash box with them, without being noticed. Yet, they had then whooped and hollered and shot up the town as they made their getaway, drawing full attention to themselves. Each man wore a white hood and long, white gloves so that no part of his skin could be seen. Bystanders couldn't even agree on their number. Some said there were four, others five, and still others said they were absolutely positive there were six or seven.

In Sam's long experience—he had been West Liberty's sheriff now for seventeen years—most thieves weren't all that bright, but what had happened this day seemed to border right on the edge of the cliff of stupidity. Not only had the robbers called attention to themselves, but they had taken so much time to shoot up the town that several storekeepers were able to gather their guns and fire off a fair number of shots. At least two of those shots found a mark, as indicated by separate areas of blood drops found at the edge of town. As Sam and Marcus now inched forward, Sam still wondered to himself, "What were the thieves thinking?"

When they were just over twenty yards from the clearing, Marcus leaned toward Sam and whispered, "Why, there ain't nobody there. No men, no horses, no nothin'. Just the fire. What's it all about, Sam?"

"Take a look behind the fire," Sam replied. See that big pile of rocks. What's that on it? That what I think it is?"

"I see it now," Marcus said, raising a hand to block the glare of the fire. "Why, that looks like the bank's cash box. I can make out the golden eagle on it."

"Cover me," Sam said as he walked ahead, stopping only long enough at the mouth of the clearing to glance left and right before ducking down slightly and running over to the pile of rocks. The bank's cash box was, indeed, wedged between two of the larger rocks. There was also a piece of paper stuffed through one of the box's side handles. Sam removed the paper, unfolded it, and moved closer to the fire. In a beautiful, flowing script, it said,

> We made a mistake. We're just not thieves, and we're not cut out for this. We're sorry for what we did. We don't expect you to forgive us, but we're hoping by leaving the money behind you'll find some charity in your hearts and let us go. We give you our word we won't do this again. We hope you can believe this. Yours most sincerely, we that are signed below:

There were seven X's drawn in an irregular line at the bottom of the note.

Sam pushed his hat back, sat down at the base of the rock pile, and read the note again. And then a third time, just to make sure he hadn't missed something. He then opened the box and saw the cash inside; it appeared nothing had been touched. He finally exhaled deeply, shook his head, stood up, and called for Marcus to come over to him. When Marcus arrived, Sam handed him the note and said, "What do you make of this? Ever seen anything like it before? I sure haven't."

Marcus soon started laughing and pointed to the moon in the western sky. "Sam, I told you the other night. You know what they say: 'Crescent moon, all crazy come soon.' I'd say that's the case here, sure 'nough. Those crooks must all be crazy. Crazy as loons on a Sunday. What do you think?"

"Maybe," Sam replied. "But then again, just maybe they're crazy like foxes. Don't you think this all more than just a shade strange? By the time we rounded up the men and got everyone saddled up, those thieves had a good thirty-minute head start on us. If they had made their way just a mile east of here, we never would have been able to track them through the rocks and broken ground there. We never would have seen them, or the money, ever again. No, something just ain't right here."

"Maybe it's like the note says," Marcus said, holding it out for Sam to read again. "Maybe they just bit off more'n they could chew. They coulda just been down-on-their-luck cowpunchers who thought they'd grab a stake in a hurry—then realized they didn't want to go through with it. Or, they coulda been whiskey-bold and just now sobered up. We've sure seen enough of that in our time. Anyway, that'd be my thoughts. That's what I reckon."

"Well, whatever the truth is, they're probably way ahead of us now," Sam said, peering beyond the fire and off into the distance.

"We goin' after them—them hardcases?" Marcus asked, breaking into laughter again.

"I don't think so. We got the money back, and they don't pay me enough to risk my life over something like this. And besides, I'm sure our good citizens back in town would love it if most of us got killed in a gun battle with our thieves. They could not care less about us until some of their precious belongings get stolen or shot up. No, I say we head back. Still, I'd like to catch 'em, if nothing else than to find out the truth of all this. Beats anything I've ever seen. Oh well, I won't lose any sleep over it. Let's get the men and get the hell out of here. That is, if they aren't all passed out by now."

"And if they are passed out?"

"I'm half tempted to shoot 'em all and say the thieves did it. We'd be rid of the dregs of the town, and nobody would question it or care. What do you think? Think we should?" Sam asked, a thin smile forming across his lips.

"If I thought we could truly get away with it...," Marcus replied, laughing softly.

"Well, maybe we won't do it now," Sam said. "But I certainly won't rule it out for the future. And anyway, I'm too tired to dig graves tonight. Let's get back to the jail and sleep what little's left of the night. And, just for meanness, let's not tell anyone we got the money back. At least not yet. I'm sure all our good citizens are still at the hotel trying to figure out what they'll do if they don't get their precious money returned to 'em. Let's let 'em stew, leastways for the rest of the night. It'll be good for 'em. Go round up what you can find of our posse and get 'em mounted. That is, if they can still ride. I'll put out this fire and be there in a minute."

As Marcus picked up the cash box and started back, Sam grabbed his arm and said, softly, "That note was written awful pretty. Just who do you suppose they were?"

Marcus didn't answer. He just shook his head, turned, and started walking away.

Sheriff Sam Sullivan stood before the fire, looked one last time off into the distance, and repeated, "Just who do you suppose they were?"

....

At the same time Sheriff Sam Sullivan and his posse were turning back, one of the holdup men, John Fairfield, was just a few miles from reentering the town of West Liberty. An hour into their getaway on a course directly to the north, John, as was the plan, parted company from Tasby and Henry, his two partners in the robbery, and made his way directly east through a shallow creek that ran a good three quarters of a mile that direction. He had initially urged his horse ahead slowly, so as not to splash water along the bank or leave other signs of his departure from the group so that, he hoped, his new trail wouldn't be noticed by a fast moving posse. When he had traveled just over a mile in the new direction, he came to a logging road that ran back south toward West Liberty. There, he urged his horse to full gallop and headed for the Silas plantation, which formed the eastern boundary of the town and where he was to begin carrying out the second phase of his plan.

As John continued back toward West Liberty, Tasby and Henry kept moving north and did their level best to leave behind a trail a blind man could have followed. They broke branches every chance they got and even dropped scraps of cloth and paper along their path. They wanted the posse following them and not following John. Tasby and Henry, their skin color hidden by hoods and gloves from the frightened gaze of the townsfolk during the robbery, were both former slaves who had fallen in with John Fairfield, a man resolute and firm about the evils of slavery. On this night, they were proud to help carry out his plan and grateful for the trust he had shown them.

The first part of their plan had been for Tasby and Henry to lead the posse exactly another half hour farther north from the spot where they had split with John. At that point, they were to build a fire in an open space where it couldn't be missed, leave the money they had stolen from the bank along with a note John had prepared before the robbery, and then move on quickly just in case the posse decided to continue their pursuit. Robbing the bank had not been their true goal; it had been merely a ruse to draw attention away from the real purpose of the night. If Tasby and Henry were able to carry out their part of the plan without a hitch, enough time would be bought for John to be back in West Liberty—two hours behind the posse—and allow him the freedom he needed to set in action their true intent.

Part one of their plan had worked—perfectly.

....

CHAPTER 2

Preparing for Freedom

AFTER SPLITTING OFF FROM TASBY and Henry, I made my way fast as I could back toward West Liberty. I hadn't met a soul on my journey, and I felt confident I hadn't been followed. As I neared the town, I heard the rushing of a small spring just off the trail and decided to stop. Time was of the essence, but I needed to make the time to water my horse and, more importantly, clean my wound. I had been shot in the shoulder during our getaway—by Tasby, one of my own men. It had been an accident, pure and simple. In all the excitement as we did our best to rile up the town, he had lost his balance, nearly slipped from the saddle, and fired wildly, one of his shots striking me in the meaty area between the shoulder and my neck. As the bullet struck, I was more stunned than in pain, but my reaction paled in comparison to the look of sheer horror that spread across Tasby's face when he realized what he had done. Then, just as he started to say something to me, a bullet from one of the shopkeepers grazed him on the outside of his upper thigh. He immediately winced in pain and dropped one of his revolvers. The shots kept ringing around us—many more than what we had anticipated—so we yelled to Henry it was time all of us made good our getaway.

Once we were out of immediate danger and had slowed our horses to an even gallop, Tasby couldn't control himself any longer, begging me over and over in his low, deep voice to forgive him. However, I wasn't going to let him off that easy. I finally interrupted him and said, "I can't believe you shot me! I'll swear to Heaven it was on purpose! And just look at my new coat. Blood all down the back. Paid twenty dollars, and now it's ruined. I'll have to bury it!"

He protested with all his might, repeating over and over it was all an accident, but I put him off by reminding him we had a close schedule to keep and that our thoughts should be first and foremost on the job at hand. Still, for miles I could hear him muttering softly, "Didn't meant to do it. Honest, I didn't." Henry, realizing what I was up to, pulled down the brim of his hat to hide his smile. I winked at Henry, and then lit into Tasby again, shouting, "You did it on purpose! It's because of that five dollars I owe you, isn't it? Thought you'd take it out of my hide, didn't you!"

Tasby seldom did anything wrong, so I just had to carry this for all it was worth. At that point, he raised his eyes, mumbled something to himself, and urged his horse to sprint ahead of us. He was miserable—and I enjoyed every minute of it.

....

At the spring I slowly dismounted, eased off my coat, and carefully pulled my shirt over my head. I didn't think I was hurt that badly, but my left arm was already starting to stiffen. So much blood had caked on my back that at first I couldn't tell if the bullet had gone all the way through. I ripped a strip of cloth from the bottom of my shirt, dipped it into the spring, and pressed it to my shoulder. The cold water was soothing, and I felt better instantly.

As I did my best to clean the wound, I finally felt what I was hoping to discover, a small hole on the back of my shoulder where the bullet had exited. Relieved and not wanting to waste any more time, I slipped my shirt and coat back on, mounted up, and was back on my way.

Not more than five minutes later, I came over a small rise and saw the Silas plantation directly in front of me. One thing could be said about Tasby: he was a first-rate mapmaker. The directions he had prepared for me could not have been more to the mark.

I had chosen this location as our gathering point for the second part of our plan because the area was relatively isolated, and Mr. Silas, a widower, lived alone. That is, he lived alone if one didn't count the seventeen slaves he kept to do the work needed for his cotton and tobacco crops. On this night, he had already been away for a week and, if his plans held true to past form, would likely be gone for at least another several days. In my days spent in town prior to the robbery, I had learned he made a journey to Chattanooga each year at this same time to visit relatives and purchase two new slaves, one for field work and the other to take care of what he described as his "personal needs." According to his neighbors, who were only too happy to pass along gossip about him, he favored the darkest-skinned on the auction block, especially in relation to the slaves he kept for his personal pleasure.

Mr. Silas' absence fit nicely into my plan as his plantation, with the massive tobacco barn on the edge of his property in particular, was the perfect location to gather together the souls I'd be taking north to their freedom. Plus, the irony of using his plantation was just too good to let pass by: while he was away purchasing new slaves, we were taking north with us three currently serving under his whip.

Robbing the bank was not our true goal—far from it. It was simply a false trail designed to throw the scent away from our real intent—and to get the law as far away from us as possible. It would also keep the town buzzing about our exploits for days to come, allowing our real work to go unnoticed. From the very beginning, our main purpose had been to deliver from the bonds of slavery eight souls from plantations in the area: three from the Silas plantation, two from the Oglethorpe plantation, and three from the Anderson plantation.

My actions this night were inseparably intertwined with my life's calling, which was to help to their freedom as many of those as possible still living forcibly inside the evil institution of slavery. I had chosen this calling much to the horror and disgust of my family, most of whom had disowned me long ago. To my family, who had both tolerated and propagated the enslavement of the Negro, I represented the evil in this world. I represented a way of thinking that would lead to the ruin of the lives they had worked so hard to achieve. To them, I was right up there with Satan himself. I was now shunned, a complete and utter stranger to them, one who would never be allowed to cross the thresholds of their homes again. My heart was saddened by this irreversible divide, but the true overwhelming sadness within me came from the fact my very own family could see no other views but their own—and didn't want to try, even for a moment, to understand what I was trying to do with my life or the cause I supported.

To this point, my journey in life was not typical of those in the brotherhood of abolitionists. I was the son of slave own-ers. I grew up in Hampshire County, Virginia, son of William and Susan Fairfax. Father, a proud and successful businessman, made our lives in every way secure and comfortable. We owned seventeen hundred acres put in with cotton and tobacco, and the profit earned from each year's harvest was invested, always wisely it seemed, by Father in a multitude of business concerns in Richmond. These investments ranged from the exportation of cotton to England to the building of new dry-goods stores where settlers moving west could provision themselves before their journeys. Father was so skilled in the ways of business, a fact not unnoticed by those in the local towns and villages, that he became something of a financial weather vane for others wishing to increase their own fortunes. As such, he was both admired and respected by all.

Father also had another business that was not accorded much publicity but was, nonetheless, highly profitable: the sell-ing of human lives. He needed an inexpensive labor force to tend his fields and carry forth the day-to-day workings of a large plantation. To this end, our family owned, at any given time, somewhere near thirty slaves. I could not keep up with an exact accounting because bodies came and went with the regularity of the seasons. And, with each of these moves, Father increased his yearly profits. Slaves were sold off in the same way crops were sold each year. Families were routinely divided, never to see each other again. Father also allowed, and even encouraged, marriage within our community of slaves.

On the one hand, the slaves were grateful for his support of their relationships, which made for a relatively happy community at times. On the other hand, most of these marriages produced a goodly number of children. Some of the children were kept, and others, mainly those not deemed strong enough for fieldwork, were sold off. When the parents moved beyond the childbearing age, they, too, were sold off to become domestic servants all throughout the South. The slaves seemed to understand this was the way their worlds would unfold, and protests, even when their own children or parents were sent away, often seemed not overly wrought with high emotion.

Of course, their tolerance may also have been because of our overseer, Toliver Brown, a brute who loved doling out punishment more than anything else in the world. It took little more than a sideways glance at Overseer Brown to call up torture of the worst type—brandings, whippings, and in the most severe of cases, the splitting of feet with an axe, an action that crippled but still allowed for enough movement so that the unfortunate victim could eventually return to field work. Overseer Brown always stood just to the right of Father when sales were announced, and his presence alone may have been the cause emotions were kept in check. Quite often, the only sounds of grief were low sobs late into the night that came from the small slave cabins in the canebrake down by the large creek that ran through our property. As much as I try, I can never get those sounds out of my mind. They marked me, marked my soul.

At first, while a young boy, I turned deaf ears and blind eyes toward this segment of Father's commerce. Just like my father, I saw slavery as a matter of business—nothing more, nothing less.

Having slaves also meant I didn't have to work the fields myself, so I accepted the institution out of pure selfishness and sloth.

At the same time, each Sunday our preacher talked about the equality of all men. I heard this while singing hymns of devotion and looking through the church window at slaves cultivating long rows of tobacco plants across the road. I heard this while watching slaves curry the horses and ready our buggies before church service ended and we all started our journeys back home. I heard this message when Reverend Simmons spoke of how all men are God's children and part of the same family. For the longest time, I never questioned what I'd been brought up to believe. I looked the other way, believing exactly as all around me did, until three events that would forever change my heart.

The first came as the result of one of our field workers not picking cotton fast enough to the end of a row. Overseer Brown tied this young man to a nearby oak tree, uncoiled the oily leather whip he kept cinched at his waist, and lashed the man fifteen times so hard the tip of his whip snapped free during the last strike. When the young man, who had passed out after the fourth lash, was cut down and crumpled to the ground, he was ordered to get up and resume his picking unless he wished another taste of the whip. He didn't have to worry any more about getting stripes on his back. He was dead. Overseer Brown was not disciplined for this act, for this senseless taking of a human life. I asked Father about this later that same day and was told that an overseer could never be punished, at least not publicly, or the slaves would not feel the same degree of fear that kept them hard and fast to their work. The lesson that day was simple enough: the work to be done and the cash from the crops were more important than life itself. The lesson was one I would never forget—one I couldn't forget.

The second event took place on a Friday in July during the hottest summer of my youth. The twelve-year-old daughter of Paul and Grace, two slaves we had owned for as long as I could remember, was sold to a business acquaintance of my father.

Paul, in a tone of voice that I could only describe as hauntingly hushed, begged my father not to let her go. Paul never raised his eyes while imploring my father to change his mind. I'll never forget his tears that dripped steadily to the soft earth below. I'll also forever hear my father's reply to him. "There, there," my father had said, moving forward and placing a hand on Paul's shoulder. "You know this is the right thing to do. Mr. Jacobs is taking her to be one of his breeders. Why, your blood will run forever once she starts, which will be soon enough. So don't you worry. This is the natural order, the Lord's will." Paul and Grace then knelt to the ground together, wrapped their arms around each other, and didn't move for what must have been a good hour. My father, so genuinely and matter-of-factly, had said taking a child from her parents and breeding her like an animal was natural and the Lord's will. From that day forward, I never felt the same toward my father again.

The final event that tipped the scales in my heart, the one that branded my future, happened just barely a week after my eighteenth birthday. My father had been away on business for quite some time, and when he returned, he asked if there wasn't some type of special birthday present he could provide for me. For several months before that birthday I had been practicing the speech I was going to give if he made such an offer. When I was five, my uncle, Thomas Fairfax, bought two small boys from a plantation near the North Carolina border. One of these boys, Bill, was my age, and I took an immediate liking to him. We became constant companions and went everywhere together. My uncle even agreed to "loan" Bill to my father and allow him to live with our slaves so I wouldn't have to keep riding to his plantation to see Bill.

Whenever Father cautioned me not to get too close to the "property," as he often called slaves, Bill and I offered up a ruse where I pretended to scold him something terrible, using as many wicked words as I could get away with, in front of witnesses. At other times, I took him in the barn and had him scream loudly while I turned a whip on a slab of timber holding up the loft. These displays of discipline seemed to satisfy both my father and my uncle, so I was allowed to continue my time with Bill. As we grew into young men, our visits diminished as I was often taken to town with Father to learn, first-hand, his business skills—and Bill was schooled in the various forms of field work on my uncle's plantation. Still, we saw each other as often as time permitted.

As my eighteenth birthday approached, I was planning to ask my father to purchase Bill for me so he could be my manservant. I knew this would also keep Bill away from the fields and far from the whip of overseers. When Father returned from his business venture, I worked up enough courage to ask him about Bill. I did my best to show no outward emotion when Father informed me my uncle had made an agreement to sell Bill on their recent trip and that a representative of the new owner would be arriving in a few days to complete the transaction. As I stared blankly ahead, my father repeated, almost word for word, what had become his standard explanation when slaves were sold: "This is the natural order, the Lord's will." He may have believed it, but by then, I did not.

I may never know or completely understand the exact reasons this event struck so powerfully to my heart, but that night I vowed I wasn't going to let Bill be sold off. I went to my uncle's plantation the next day, took Bill from the tobacco field, and told him two things when we were out of earshot of all around. After telling him how he had been sold, I informed him, with as much boldness in my voice as I could conjure, how I was going to take him to Ohio where he'd be a free man. Bill immediately reached out to embrace me, but I drew back sharply and told him to act as if nothing had happened, to keep up with his best work until I came back for him.

Three nights later, Bill and I helped ourselves to two of my uncle's best horses and set out for Ohio. Four days into our journey I left Bill in Hanover at the home of a Dr. Robertson, a man whom I had heard favored the cause of abolitionism and provided shelter for those making their way to freedom. Dr. Robertson's support of the cause turned out to be true, and he took Bill into his home. After Bill and I made our heartfelt good-byes and promises to meet again in the future, I began the long journey back home.

As I did so, I worked on several stories I thought might help keep me from at least some of the trouble I knew would be waiting for me. One of the stories I came up with had me stealing away in the middle of the night to go see a young woman—and taking Bill along as my servant. Then, while I courted the young woman, Bill just up and ran off. In another version I had Bill playing the part of the hero. This tale had the same young woman at the heart of the story but, in this one, Bill and I were attacked by highwaymen during our travels. In the resulting struggle to save ourselves, Bill had been killed shielding me from the robbers, and I had to bury him along the side of the road. In still another, and the one I thought might be the easiest to believe, I decided I'd simply explain while on my own "business" trip, a trip I had made to try out the new skills I had learned from my father, I had found a better offer for Bill and had sold him to slavers who intended to take him to Louisiana. In this version, I'd have to say the purchasers promised to have the funds sent to our bank in Richmond. Then, while we waited for funds that would never arrive, I figured Bill would be able to make his way far enough north that he'd never be recaptured.

As it turned out, I didn't get a chance to make use of any of the stories. Just a day's ride from home, I stopped for a meal at a Shopwith's Tavern on the outskirts of Front Royal, a town frequented by my father and uncle. There I overheard a table of men talking about how my uncle had asked for a warrant to be sworn on his very own nephew—for stealing one of his slaves! There had always been a stream of coldness dividing my uncle and me, but I never thought he'd have the law on me, no matter what the circumstances. I didn't relish the thought of being sent to jail, so

I decided upon another course of action. The next night I snuck back to my uncle's plantation, gathered up nine of his slaves and horses to match, and again started the long journey to Hanover. Word came later that my uncle had posted a reward for my capture, but I didn't let the news bother me for long. I had already decided I was never turning back.

The die had been cast. I was a fugitive from justice. I was also, according to the measure of my father and uncle, just another "rotten, low-down, stinkin' abolitionist." I was also, for the first time in my life, full of purpose and determination. Oh, I was going to be a businessman, same as my father, only I was not going to be like my father. I'd be handsomely rewarded for my work, only my compensation would be of a type my father and uncle never could have understood. That didn't matter to me. My compensation would be the satisfaction I gained through helping slaves escape their chains. I knew, if successful, I could make a difference in the lives of many. I had long needed a North Star, a beacon for my life, a reason and purpose for my existence. Whether it all happened by chance, circumstance, or by Divine Will didn't matter to me at that point. Finally, I was completely resolved.

This resolve was fueled because I knew, as did those who owned slaves and those who did not, that a network of abolitionists existed that helped slaves north to their freedom in Canada. Working with these abolitionists seemed like a logical place for me to begin my new life, so I returned to Ohio and never looked back toward Virginia again. The risks of such an enterprise were many, including the very real possibility of ending up at the end of a rope tied hastily to a tree. For me to succeed in this venture, caution would have to be the watchword—and cunning would be my game. I was ready for it. At least in my youthful bravado, I thought I was.

Those events happened what seemed a lifetime ago. Today, cunning was still my game. The bravado? That was tempered by the harsh realities of the brutality I'd seen in my work. Yet, above all, I was resolved—more so than ever before—to make my mark in the fight for freedom for all men.

....

I was thinking of my family when the Silas plantation came into view. Lucius, pistol at the ready, was guarding the door to the tobacco barn when I rode up. The moment I laid eyes on him, I felt myself relax, felt a wave of safety wash over me. The fact he was standing there told me our plan had been successful to this point.

Lucius had been with me from very nearly the beginning. Broad of shoulder, strong as an ox, and a natural-born woodsman, he was the type of man I needed with me as I began my new life. I had met him in Hanover when I took my uncle's slaves to Dr. Robertson. Lucius was working at the Spread Eagle Tavern, a depot on the Underground Railroad, but his usefulness there had just about run its course; he had been there so long his face was becoming too recognizable to slave catchers roaming through the area. He wanted to stay with the cause, but he also badly needed a change of scene.

Dr. Robertson introduced us to each other one evening, and in no time we grew to be fast friends and confidants. Lucius was one of the best men I'd ever known—and a man devoted to the elimination of slavery. In his younger days he had helped put together a network of depots to help runaways from Georgia and Tennessee reach Ohio and the first leg of freedom. He had even built a secret room in the barn on his own property to shelter runaways who needed a temporary place to hide as they passed through on their way to the next safe haven on the route.

However, once while he was away helping establish another depot, several runaways showed up at his home in the middle of the night. His wife, feeling she couldn't turn them away, hid them in the barn. The next morning, slavers hot on the trail of the runaways forced their way into Lucius' home and questioned his wife. Although she did not betray the runaways, the slavers still found them. That is, they found all but one, a young boy who had decided to hide in the nearby woods—and who later relayed the horrific events of that day to Lucius. In an act obviously meant to serve as a warning to others, the slavers set fire to the barn and the house. What they didn't know was Lucius' two infant daughters were sound asleep inside the house. Just as Lucius' wife ran in to get them, the roof collapsed. Lucius, upon his return and after burying his family, vowed revenge against all slavers. Two weeks after laying his family to rest, he caught up with the men who had destroyed his family—and introduced them all to their own final resting places. He had found his revenge, but it wasn't enough.

He was still against slavery, but he was now a man on a mission of another type: to destroy as many slavers as he could. Most other abolitionists would have nothing to do with him because of his advocacy of violence, but I saw this as an asset, rather than a liability. His hatred was the kindling that stoked the fire in his soul. I knew I could, if it ever came to it, trust him with my life.

As I stepped down from my horse, Lucius smiled and said, "'Bout time you got here. Sure took your sweet time, didn't you?"

Then, noticing the blood on my coat, he voiced his concern. "Whoa there—you okay? Better let me look at that."

"I'm fine. We don't have time to worry about it now. Everybody here? We ready to go?"

"How 'bout the posse?" Lucius asked, moving closer to look at my shoulder.

"All worked as planned. Smooth as cat hair. That posse should be just over two hours to the north and west, which means if we stick to the original plan and head east right now, by the time they get back and figure out what's going on, they'll never be able to catch us. And, if the maps Tasby scratched out for us are half accurate, not even a backwoods trapper could find us with that much of a start on 'em. But we need to get movin' quick as we can. We can rest up later. According to Tasby, we'll come to some caverns about daybreak where we can hole-up, have a quick meal, and sleep an hour or two. Then we'll have to push north at a good pace to meet up with Tasby and Henry in two-days' time across the Ohio River at Jackson. This time of year the river's always up at least some. If we can't cross there, we'll have to try at Worthington, and that will cost us valuable time, time we don't have."

Lucius, seeming more interested in my wound than in the details of our plan, shook his head and said, "By the look of you, by sunup you're going to need more than a meal and a short rest. That is, if you don't lose all your blood before then. Take off that coat and let me take a look."

"Later," I said, stepping back. "What I want now is to have a few words with our passengers. You think they're ready?"

"I do. They're scared right down to their toes, but they already know what'll happen to 'em if they turn back now. I don't think we'll have any problems with this group. None at all."

"Did you tell them I'm the one they have to worry about now?"

Lucius smiled and said, "No. I always save that little pleasure for you. I think you'd actually miss it if you didn't get to scare the Johnny-B-Jiggers out of 'em."

I gave him a quick glare but didn't say anything because he was at least partly right. Whenever we prepared a group for escape, it was my job to remind them what would happen if we were caught. Most of them knew this anyway, but I figured it didn't hurt to emphasize just how horrible their deaths could be if the plan failed.

"Well, let's get it over with—then let's get a move on."

As Lucius followed me into the barn, I heard shuffling above my head and saw hay fall from the mow.

"You can come down now," I said sternly. "Hurry up. Let me take a look at you."

All eight of them, in rapid succession, climbed down the ladder and fell in line in front of me. Over the past week, while Lucius and I investigated the town and made plans for the robbery, Tasby and Henry, under the guise of being freedmen working as peddlers with items for sale to slaves, had met with each of our passengers at their plantations. During those meetings, our passengers learned that their relatives who had already found a way to freedom had sent us to bring them north and reunite them with their families. They had also been told, in the strictest manner possible, the importance of secrecy; they were to tell no one, not even their closest and dearest friends. Finally, after the meeting day and time at the Silas plantation had been established, Tasby and Henry moved along to the next plantation before any suspicions were aroused.

As our passengers now stood before me, all were breathing heavily, all appeared as frightened as any group I'd seen before. To break some of the tension, I began, "I want to know who you are, but I first want you to know something about me. As you are putting your lives in my hands, I suppose that's only fair. I go by many names—I've gone by many names—but to your former masters, I am the Devil, plain and simple. To others, I'm a murderer. Whether that's actually true or not is open for debate. Others call me the worst kind of criminal who walks this earth, one who is trying to bring down the walls that separate those who are white from those who are not."

I paused, then added, smiling, "And to still others—and just a handful—I might be known as a giver of freedom."

Here Lucius cleared his throat loudly and closed his eyes.

"See," I said. "Even one my dearest friends wouldn't go that far in describing me."

Turning as serious as I could, I continued, "Whether I'm saint or sinner isn't what you need to know. What you do need to know is I'm the man who is going to take you to another life, a life where you'll no longer have to answer to anyone but God. Our journey won't be an easy one, and some of you may die along the way. If you do, we won't have time to bury you; your body will be hidden the best we can in the woods. That's the truth of the matter, and you have a right to know it. At the same time, if any of you give up along the way or do anything to hold the rest of us back, I won't hesitate to shoot you dead."

To a person, our passengers looked up from the ground, and their eyes met mine. They didn't blink. Neither did I.

"We're going to rely on each other—you upon me, and me upon you. Together we can make it. If we don't, I'll be strung up, and you'll be tortured—and then killed as well. You know what that means? It means we're going to fight to our last breath if necessary, and you better understand that now."

There was no doubt I had their full attention now. "Look at me and listen closely. I'm going to give you arms—some will get rifles and others pistols—and along the way we're going to teach you to use 'em. I know most of you believe it is a sin to kill. You listen to me now and never forget this: Slaveholders are devils, and it's no harm to kill the Devil. You keep telling yourself that every step you take toward your freedom."

A tall, lanky man on the far right spoke up, "Massah, I got to ask you somethin'...."

I cut him off, and shouted, "If you call me or any other man 'Massah' again I'll cut your tongue out! From now on, from the minute we leave this barn, you're a free man. Nobody will ever be your 'Massah' again. You can call me Mr. Fairborne, just plain Mister, or Sir, but that's all, and I mean it. You understand me?"

"Yes, Suh," the lanky one replied, smiling weakly. "What I want to know is, where we goin'?"

This was most often the first question groups of passengers asked. I knew I couldn't tell them the truth in case someone got captured, so I had finally come up with a story I knew would sound both exciting and full of adventure to give them something to hold to.

"We'll be eventually going west to Missouri," I said, matter-of-factly. "Along the way we'll go over the most beautiful mountains you could imagine. From there, we're taking a boat up the Mississippi River to free territory. That's all you need to know for now. I'll let you know more when the time is right. Any more questions?"

There weren't any, so I went on, "I said before we're going to help each other along. That means I need to know who you are and what type of work you did before tonight. We'll start at the end of the line and work our way across. Tell me quickly because we can't waste time. We have to be moving within the half hour."

One at a time, I asked each to step forward and provide the information. On the far left was a plump young woman I guessed near thirty. Her name was Lucy, and she said she had been a cook in the main house.

"That's good," I said. "You'll help Lucius prepare our meals. He's a horrible cook and, believe me, he needs your help—more than he'll admit to anyone." She smiled, nodded, and stepped back.

To my surprise, the next three, at the same time, stepped forward. When I raised an eyebrow, the oldest spoke up. "We brothers and sister. I Toby. He be Thomas. She be Alta. I take care the horses. Thomas a field hand. Alta a field hand—good with a hoe. She chop the head clean off a rattler last month."

"You'll all be important on this trip," I said, motioning them to step back in line. Addressing Toby, I said, "I'm putting you in charge of the horses, starting the minute we leave tonight. And Alta and Thomas will help us gather any food we come across in fields along the way. So, if you find something good for us to eat, you grab it up and let me know."

A short, bag-of-bones boy near to fifteen stepped forward and said, "I'm Mumphry. I was in charge of the chickens. Can pluck one faster'n a whip-snap."

"You're now our official chicken liberator, chicken stealer. If we come anywhere near a coop, I want you to catch our dinner for us." He nodded, smiled, and stepped back in line.

Before I could motion the next to step forward, an older man with graying hair advanced. "I'm Elijah. My Mass...." He cut his word short and sucked in his breath before continuing. "I mean, I used to do huntin' for the family when meat was short. They let me have the rifle, 'cause I hit what I aim at. You give me a rifle, I sure nobody get us from behind."

"Then you shall have a rifle," I said. "And you'll take up the rear guard with one of my other men when we meet up with them. Glad to have you along."

The next introduction came from Delia, a beautiful young woman with skin the color of coffee cut with an ample portion of cream. She spoke softly and stuttered. "I-I-I aaam D-D-Del...ia."

When I asked her to speak more clearly, Alta leaned forward and said, "It's okay, child. Won't have to take care of that man no more."

From the look on her face, I had a notion what Alta was talking about. I moved forward, raised Delia's chin so that she could see my eyes, and said, softly, "You're going to help Lucy with the cooking. Can you do that?" She didn't respond, and I didn't press her.

The last to step forward—the tall, lanky fellow on the far side—said, "I'm Walker. Got the name 'cause I can walk anywhere faster than anyone else. I go places. I do errands."

"If we need a message sent forward, you'll be our messenger," I said, motioning him to step back. "I have the feeling you'll be very important to us."

With the introductions completed, I asked for their attention one last time. "I know you're afraid," I began. "I always am, too. But I've done this thirty-seven times before—this will be thirty-eight—and I'm still here. A little worn down, I grant you, but I'm still fighting, and I intend to see thirty-nine, forty, and more after that, Lord willing. You just listen to me and Lucius, and chances are good you'll make it just fine."

Lucy interrupted me and pointed to the blood on my coat before saying, "You won't be doin' this much longer, like as not, if you don't take care of that. Let me look...."

"Not now. It's nothing. I'll have you look at it later—after our first rest."

Turning to Lucius, I said, "Bring around the horses. It's time." Then, facing the group again, I asked, "How many of you can ride?"

All but Delia had experience, so I instructed her just to hang on as best she could. At the same time, I asked Toby to ride beside her and hold her reins until she learned enough to be on her own.

When we had all mounted and were ready to begin our journey—myself, Lucius, our eight passengers, and with two packhorses trailing—we were quite a sight to see. A group of this size and composition wouldn't be difficult to follow. Therefore, I didn't bother with the instructions I normally gave about how to best conceal tracks and prepare false trail signs along the way. Instead, I chose to focus on something I felt more important with this group.

"Take a look above," I said, pointing to the cloudless night sky. "Look over here, to the left of the moon. See that star, the one that's brightest of all? That's called the North Star. Keep your eye on that while we travel. After we go east for a spell, we're going to use that North Star to guide us to freedom and worlds you've only seen in your dreams. That star, your hope, will guide our journey."

I motioned to Lucius, who said, loudly, forcefully, "Well, what are ya'll waitin' for? This way—this way to freedom!"

He then led us all away from the barn as the North Star shone brightly above.

....

CHAPTER 3

Night Flight

TASBY'S MAP SKILLS HAD ONCE again been perfect. The caverns came into view just as the sun started creeping above the horizon.

The first leg of the journey had been uneventful. Our group of relatively inexperienced riders had all somehow managed to keep in the saddle, even Delia, who gripped the horn of her saddle as if her very life depended upon staying upright. We also marked up a very distinctive trail as we moved along, but I wasn't all that worried about being followed.

Every quarter hour or so, I had sent Toby, the most experienced rider of the group, ahead to meet up with Lucius so that both sides of the trail could be scouted. We saw no one the whole time, and I hoped with all my might we hadn't been spotted by anyone off in the dense woods around us. Traveling as far east as we were and coming so close to the Virginia border brought its own danger. Slave catchers coming back from northern states often followed the Ohio River across the upper border of Kentucky in the chance they'd come across runaways looking for a shallow spot to ford the river. Then, near the eastern tip of Kentucky, the slavers often dropped straight south to hire out again to those posting rewards for their fugitives. Lucius and I were both aware we had just entered this area.

From the many caves that pocked the bluffs around us, Lucius and Toby found one with an opening large enough for us to lead our horses inside. We were finally able to stop for a much needed rest. But first, I assigned duties for everyone. Toby was to feed and care for the horses. Lucy and Delia were to fetch our food supplies from the packhorses and prepare a simple meal. I assigned Mumphry and Elijah to lookout duties at the left side of the cave opening and Thomas and Alta to the right. Walker was to go several hundred yards up the trail to look for signs of recent travelers and then to come back to report.

We couldn't risk a fire in case we were being followed—or in case slavers were in the area—so I instructed Lucy and Delia to prepare for each of us some cured ham slices and hardtack biscuits.

"Can do better'n that," Lucy replied, smiling broadly. She opened a small cloth sack she had been carrying with her and withdrew some square, golden slabs.

"Is that what I think it is?" I asked, my mouth dropping open.

"Can't have ham without we have cornbread," she said, continuing to pull even more slabs from her sack.

"We'll eat high today," I said. "We better. It might be some time before we stop again, so I want everyone to have something, even if you don't feel hungry."

Lucy handed the stack of cornbread to Delia and walked over to me. She pointed to my shoulder and said, "You say my life in your hands. Won't be worth shucks if you dead."

She had a point. While my shoulder didn't actually hurt, it was starting to stiffen more and more as the hours drew by. I eased out of my coat, pulled my shirt over my head, and let her examine the wound.

After she poked and prodded me, she pointed to the ground and said, sternly, "You sit. Got to make a poultice. I be right back."

I had barely had time to sit down and start to rest when she returned with a handful of wild onions in one hand and a large but thin oval rock in the other. She placed the rock on the floor of the cave and started mashing up the meat part of the onions on top of it. Then she walked over to Delia, who was slicing the ham, and returned with a sliver of ham fat. She mashed the ham fat on top of the onion meat, and the result was a sticky, white paste.

At this point she called over to Lucius, "Gunpowder!"

She pointed to his powder horn and held out her hand as he walked toward us. After he poured a small quantity into her hand, she mixed it in with the paste, which made it instantly turn black.

Lucius smiled at me and said, "Oh, this is a sight I won't soon forget. I hope this burns—and bad."

"Thanks," I said, dryly. "Maybe if I pay Tasby back that five dollars I can get him to shoot you next time."

"Hush now," Lucy scolded me. "This may gonna' bite."

As gently as she could, she spread the paste first over the front and then the back of the wound. She next ripped a strip of cloth from her skirt, soaked it with water from one of our canteens, and draped it over my shoulder so that both areas were covered.

"Keep that covered up—and keep it watered. Maybe you stay alive," she said, turning abruptly to go help Delia with the food.

I grabbed her hand and stopped her. "Thank you," I said. "That was most kind."

"Weren't nothin'," she said, smiling. "Just you keep that watered." She patted my good shoulder, and walked off.

"Poultice," Lucius said with a tone clearly indicating he was skeptical. "And with gunpowder." Here he started to laugh. "Good thing we don't have a fire. If we did, you'd like as not fall in and blow us all to Kingdom Come!"

I started to jump up to give him a swift kick in the behind, but I winced and sat back down instead. I knew I needed the rest, but it would have to be a short one. We had to keep moving.

"Here," I said handing him my coat. "Take the pistols out and put 'em in my saddlebags. Then go out back and bury this somewhere nobody'll find it."

"You sure?" he asked. "You'll be mournin' loss of this 'un. Best you ever had. Why, there must be on to five guns in all them pockets—and loops for knives, too. Make you like an army your-self. You for truth want it buried?"

"It's bad luck to keep a coat marked by a bullet," I replied. "I'll get another made when we get back. Just make sure you put it deep. Don't want anyone to know we were here."

"Okay," he said, shaking his head. "I'll find a hole for it. Shame. Damn shame."

By the time Lucius returned, Lucy announced our meal was ready. I told Lucius I'd take the first watch while he joined the oth-ers. He didn't argue. I stood by the right edge of the opening, the spot with the best vantage over the trail running below. Nothing was moving, which was comforting and unsettling at the same time. I glanced back and saw that our passengers had sat on the ground and formed themselves into a tight circle. Lucius, already gulping down his cornbread, was sitting by himself a good four yards away from them.

"What's this?" I asked, pointing my rifle barrel toward their small circle. "Lucius, don't you think you ought to join them?"

He shrugged his shoulders, got up, moved over to them and sat down between Mumphry and Alta. The others put down their food and stopped eating. They just stared at Lucius and suddenly appeared they didn't know what to do next.

"What is it? What's the matter?" I asked, perplexed.

After an uncomfortable and awkward silence, Toby finally spoke up, but not before first looking around the circle.

"Well, Suh—it be this way. We ain't never took meals with white folks 'afore. Don't rightly know what to do."

I sighed and shook my head. "You put food in your mouths and chew. From now on you aren't different from anybody else unless you make yourselves different. You get to make that deci-sion now. I hope you'll eat with us, but I have to admit I likely wouldn't blame you if you didn't want to after all you've been through in your lives. I consider you my brothers and sisters, and I hope before long you'll feel something of the same toward Lucius and me. But, that's up to you."

I turned and again faced the trail below. Behind me, I heard Lucius ask someone for another slice of ham. The color of skin wasn't going to ruin his appetite. When I heard Lucy reply, "You eatin' too much," I knew all would eventually be fine.

I figured I had lectured them enough for the time being. After all the groups I had taken to their freedom, I still couldn't put myself enough in their places to understand what those first moments of freedom must have felt like. At the same time, I knew they were frightened and unsure of the future. I couldn't blame them for that. The best I could do would be to give them time to let their minds catch up with their emotions. I'd have to wait them out. Freedom wasn't something they could understand until freedom was actually wrapped around them. And that wouldn't happen completely until we set foot in Canada, which was still a long way off.

To my surprise and relief, Elijah soon came over and volunteered to stand watch while I ate. He reminded me he was the best shot on his plantation, and I reminded him he was not to shoot at anything below unless he first received permission from me. A gunshot in this terrain would carry for miles and instantly reveal our position.

The minute I sat with the group, Alta quietly asked me, "Suh, why you doin' this for us?"

Lucy glared at her and started to say something, but I stopped her. "No, Alta's question is a fair one, and you deserve a fair response. There are two answers to that question. The first is the easy one to explain. You eight were chosen because I'm being paid to take you to people who love you and want you with them. It's fair you know I'm not doing this just out of goodness of heart. I'll have gold in my pocket when I get you to freedom. I make no apology for that—and never will. Freedom comes at a dear price. I use the gold I earn in my own way, for my own work in the cause."

They stared blankly at me. I could tell they didn't understand what I was trying to say, but I also knew they'd fully understand what I was about to offer next.

"The second answer has to do with something I know you've been wondering about since I first spoke to you in the Silas barn—that you are being taken to your loved ones."

Here I paused, got their complete attention and, above all, their silence. I cautioned I didn't want to hear any of them cry out, didn't want to hear any loud displays of emotion. I reminded them we were in a cave, a location where sound would magnify and cascade below. With that admonition, I began.

"Lucy, you probably don't remember much about your father because he was sold away from you when you were quite young. He's now a free man, a blacksmith, in a place far, far away from here, and he asked that I find you and bring you to him. And, Lord willing, that is exactly what I intend to do."

She immediately pulled up the edge of her skirt and buried her face in it. I could hear her sobs of joy through the cloth. I stood up, walked over to her, and put my hand on her shoulder.

I then addressed Toby, the oldest of our group. "Your father's brother, Harrison, came to his freedom a long time ago. He works aboard a ship and has saved enough money to get you to him. He told me he made a promise to your father that if he could ever do it, he'd send for you. He's a good man—and true to his word."

Toby raised his eyes and said, softly, "Praise, Jesus." He covered his face with his hands and cried softly.

Alta, Thomas, and Mumphry were already holding hands and inching closer to each other when I stopped in front of them. They looked up at me, their eyes already wet with anticipation.

I had only said, "Your mother...." when they all three let out a high-pitched wail and closed in to hug each other tightly. I urged them to remain as quiet as they could, then continued, "Your mother was taken away from you when Thomas was near to ten-years-old. You three were able to stay together, but I can only imagine the hole in your hearts that must have grown over the loss of your mother. She is now a free woman who has part-interest in a general store. You'll be working right at her side in no time."

Mumphry broke loose from his brother and sister long enough to say, with words crowded by pure joy, "Thank you—thank you—bless you."

"Don't thank me," I said. "Thank your mother. She's a good woman, one who loves all of you very much."

Walker and Elijah were both at the mouth of the cave and keeping watch on the trail below. "Both of you have fathers who are free men now and who work together. They've been making plans to get you to them ever since they set foot on free land."

Both looked shocked, incredulous. "Your fathers ran off at the same time and somehow, I never did get the story straight, ended up partners in a livery they built together. They'll have to tell you the whole story. And that'll be soon enough."

The last of our group, Delia, had backed slightly out of the circle and had drawn her knees up to her chest. Of all our passengers, I was worried most about her. It wasn't that she appeared physically fragile, which she actually did. It was more than that. She often had a wild, back and forth glance in her eyes, as if she were waiting for someone to jump her from behind. She also stammered terribly when she spoke. Many times as frustration set in, she would simply bite her lip, clench her fists, and look to the ground.

She was rocking gently back and forth when I began, "Delia, when we get to the free land where I'm taking you, you are the only one in this group who is going to have a very different type of choice to make. It's one that you won't want to make lightly, so I'm going to explain this to you now so you have time to think about it before you must make your decision."

She stopped rocking, looked up, and almost met my eyes. Tears were already spilling down her cheeks.

"I - I - I - I hhhaaavvv no no one," she cried, again covering her face with her hands.

"That's not true," I said, kneeling next to her and placing my hand on her shoulder. The second I touched her she spun away and fell over to the ground, her face crashing on the hard rock.

As I pulled her back up, she struck at me with clenched fists. I drew her to me and wrapped my arms around her, tightly. Delia continued to sob uncontrollably. I motioned for Lucy to come over and try to comfort her. As soon as Lucy sat down, Delia quickly swung her arms from me to her.

Gently stroking Delia's hair, I said, "Someone says he cares for you, enough to risk a great deal to get you to him. You should at least listen to this so you can make up your mind what you want to do. You might owe him that much."

I didn't know how much Delia could hear through her sobs, but I knew Lucy, who it was obvious cared for her deeply, would help her through the information later. Therefore, I began again, "Many years ago you lived on a plantation owned by a Mr. LaBelle. Remember him?"

Delia raised her head from Lucy's shoulder and nodded. "Part of the reason he sold his place and moved north was he felt he could no longer live in a country where so many men and women were owned by others. He didn't believe in slavery, but he also didn't know how to fight it. He's ashamed of it now, but rather than find a way to fight, he just up and left after selling his place and his slaves to his brother. Apparently, he had taken quite a liking to you—and he says he still has those feelings. He's the one paying me to bring you north, and he wanted me to tell you this as soon as I could. He also wanted me to tell you this: as soon as we get to free territory, you're free to go your own way if you want to—with his blessing. On the other side, if you want to come be with him—as a free woman and not his slave—then he'd more than welcome that, too. Above all else, he wants it to be your decision."

I studied her face carefully. "He owns a tavern and says you can work there with him if you wish it so. That is a decision you'll have to make, but you'll have to make it quickly when we get there because I'll be moving on almost immediately."

I was waiting for some type of reply from her when Elijah threw a small rock at my feet. I looked over, and he had ducked down slightly and was pointing down the trail. Before I could move, Lucius leapt to his feet, grabbed his rifle, and was already on his way to the mouth of the cave.

At almost the instant Lucius took his position, he whispered back to me, "It's slavers. Sure of it. I can see the chains draped over the packhorses. Looks to be three of 'em. At least that's all I see."

"Nobody move!" I said, louder than I should have. Then, lowering my voice I said, "Toby, get up now and walk quietly to the horses. Keep 'em from being spooked. Lucy, keep low, but gather up our foodstuff and pack it back in the saddlebags. The rest of you stay where you are—and keep quiet. If they see us, you know what will happen."

I didn't need to emphasize just how much danger was right at our feet. They knew.

Lucius came over and handed me his rifle as I gave him the pistol I kept tucked under my belt. "I'm going to work my way down along that line of rocks," he said. "They won't see me. It doesn't look like they know we're here, but if they do spot us, I can do more good down there if they rush us. If they do, I'll try to pin 'em down while you and Elijah try to pick 'em off from here. If nothing else, I'll be close enough to shoot their horses. They won't be able to follow after that."

By the look in his eyes, I knew what he was really saying: if he had to shoot their horses, that would be the signal for us to mount up and make our getaway—and leave him behind. I nodded I understood and reached out to shake his hand for luck. He looked at my hand and laughed. "We'll shake later. Got things to do now." With that, he was off, easing slowly from rock to rock down the side of the hill.

The slavers moved deliberately, glancing from side to side as they followed along the trail. Then, when they were almost out of sight, they stopped. The lead rider stepped down from his horse and pawed at the ground, finally picking up a handful of dirt and flinging it to the side. He turned to face the others while pointing back to the ground. He had spotted our tracks.

Lucius and Toby had done their best to destroy evidence of our group leaving the main trail and moving up the rocks to the cave. As I watched the lead slaver talking to his partners, I could see their confusion by his hand gestures. He had found the beginning of a trail, one that just appeared suddenly before them. But where had it come from, and where were those who had made it? With as many tracks as we had left before Lucius and Toby covered up our last movements, I guessed the slavers were powerfully confused by what they'd just discovered—and were also mighty suspicious.

My guess, unfortunately, was correct. The other two slavers dismounted, and the three of them started poking around the brush and trees behind them, obviously looking for signs. One finally disappeared into the trees on the other side of the path. Another walked farther up the trail in the direction we'd come from. The last, the lead man and the one who appeared to be in charge, started up the rocks toward us.

Elijah raised his rifle and started to take aim. Quietly and slowly, I waved him back, indicating I wanted him in the shadows behind the mouth of the cave. At the same time, I whispered, "Wait—Lucius is down there. If this man gets too close, he'll take care of him. Stay out of sight for now."

I wasn't sure where Lucius was hiding, but I was relatively certain the slaver had already gone past his position. With two others lurking down below, I knew Lucius wouldn't make a move unless he was sure we'd been spotted. This was no time for a fire-fight, especially, with us holed-up in a cave that offered no means of retreat. Our best course of action was to keep ourselves concealed. I'd been with Lucius long enough to know he was likely thinking exactly the same thing.

Soon, the leader was so close to the mouth of the cave that I could have easily struck him with a rock. To their credit, the members of our group remained absolutely silent and moved not a muscle through fear, and, I suspected, more than a tad of courage.

Just as the leader broke through the scrub bush ringing the mouth of the cave, his man who had been retracing our trail let out a "Haaaallllooooo!" that diverted his attention. After one last glance into the darkness of the cave, he turned and started back down the hill as quickly as he could, small clouds of dust rising each time his boots touched the ground. Once he was back to the bottom of the hill, his man pointed back to the west and said something that obviously caught the leader's attention. All three then remounted and headed west at a gallop.

"What did he see?" I muttered, staring intently that direction. I didn't know, but I did know we were at least of the time being safe. Turning to our group, I said forcefully, "Make yourselves ready. As soon as Lucius gets back, we have to move."

Lucius, out of breath from the climb back up the hill, handed me my pistol, caught his breath, then smiled broadly. "You've got to be the luckiest trail-bum I've ever seen. Know what they were after? Food. I bet they haven't eaten in days. Game's scarce all through this area."

"And?" I asked, hanging on his words.

Lucius chuckled, "The one down our trail saw two good-sized does jump off into the timber. They'll probably never catch 'em, but it looks like they're goin' to try. Now's our chance. Let's get out of here before they get any more curious about what made our tracks."

"I was thinking the same thing," I said, motioning everyone to the horses. Elijah, still standing guard at the mouth of the cave, whispered, "Don't think so. You better come look."

Lucius and I stepped ahead, then ducked as we saw another rider directly below us along the same path.

"He's with them," Lucius said, his voice firm, positive. "He's their rear guard. They might be slavers, but they're not stupid. I'd have had a man back there, too."

He was much younger than the others, appearing sixteen, maybe seventeen-years-old. He dismounted, tied his reins to a dead branch wedged between two rocks, and stared our direction.

"When did you first see him?" I whispered to Elijah. "Was it as he entered the clearing or where he's now stopped?"

"Sorry, Suh," Elijah replied, softly. "Took my eyes off just for a minute. He already there. Coulda seen me, I sup'ose."

Lucius and I looked at each other at the same time. "We may need a diversion," he said, taking my pistol again. "I'll work my way behind him if I can, but you better figure out some way to keep him looking up here if need be. I'm not looking for any angel wings today."

"I understand," I replied. "Get ready. I'll think of something. If I have to, and it wouldn't be my first choice, I'll do what we did back in Calhoun, Georgia. Remember when I pretended to surrender—then Tasby got 'em from behind? Worked once—don't know why it wouldn't again."

"Let me try this first," Lucius said as he got to his hands and knees and started inching his way out of the cave. "If I can get behind him...."

"Toby—you've handled a gun before, right?" I asked, motioning him to come stand beside me.

"No," he whispered.

"That's ok. You take this rifle. If I call out your name, point the gun straight ahead and pull the trigger. You don't have to shoot anybody. It'll just be for diversion. It might get that slaver to raise his head some higher, and if he does, either Lucius or Elijah can pick him off."

I moved to the edge of the opening, pushed Elijah to the side, and readied myself in case I needed to walk out and be the diversion to attract the attention of the young slaver. Suddenly, from my left and before I could do anything to stop her, Delia stepped out of the cave and was nonchalantly waving a stick back and forth as she made her way a few feet down the rock path. The slaver instantly saw her and ducked behind a large boulder. At that point, Delia unbuttoned her blouse, slid it part way off her shoulder, and leaned back on a rock, as if taking in the early morning sun.

The slaver's head popped around the boulder, his eyes taking her in full view. He then dropped down slightly and started a slow and deliberate climb toward her. His movements were quiet but clumsy; he lost his balance once, and if he hadn't used his rifle butt to steady himself, he'd have gone down flat.

Delia lowered her blouse even more as she wriggled her back against the rock, as if scratching an itch. She next stretched her arms out wide, palms up, and appeared to yawn.

The young slaver couldn't have been more than twenty yards from her when his head disappeared again.

Other than Delia's, there was no movement, no sound, of any kind for a good minute. Then, from the same area where I'd last seen the slaver, Lucius' head suddenly popped up. He raised his right hand, extended one finger, and waved it slowly back and forth. That was the sign I'd been waiting for: one man dead.

I stepped through the mouth of the cave and into the light, ducking slightly as I did. "Delia," I called out as loud as I dared. "It's okay now. It's all over. Get back up here—fast!"

She pulled her blouse together and ran toward me. When she was close enough, I took her arm and led her back into the safety of the cave.

"Why'd you do that?" I asked, more curious than angry with her. "You could have been...."

This time it was Delia who cut me off. "I-I-I know hhhhow to...."

I pressed a finger to her lips. I knew what she was trying to say. I could see it in her eyes.

"Hopefully, this is the last time you'll have to. I pray it's so," I said. Then, my voice stern, I said, "We'll have more words on this later. No time now."

By this time Lucius was back. He nodded to me. "Let's send Mumphry and Elijah down there to fetch him before the buzzards start circling—and they will before too long. There's no food for anything around here."

Mumphry and Elijah both had been listening and didn't

wait for my command. By the time I had turned around, both were well on their way down the hill. When they returned, they placed the slaver's body on a ledge over to the left of the opening.

"Strip him clean. Take everything," Lucius commanded. When Mumphry and Elijah looked at me, I nodded.

"Everything," I repeated. "Those boots look about your size, Walker. Come here and try 'em on. And that shirt looks like it'll fit you, Toby. Take it."

Mumphry checked inside the trouser pockets and withdrew a small poke that jangled with the sound of coins. "I'll take that," I said, extending my hand. "Might come in handy later." Without opening it, I slipped it under my belt.

When I saw they had left his trousers on, I barked, "I said everything. I meant what I said. Strip him bare. And don't forget to pick up his rifle on the way down the hill."

"But he's so young," Alta said. "He's little more'n a boy."

"He was a slaver," I said. "Age don't matter nothin'. He would've clamped you in chains or shot you dead without a second thought. A boy? Hardly. When a person takes up slaving, he becomes the right hand of the Devil. And you remember what I said. It ain't no harm to kill the Devil. Now throw that body over in the corner and cover it up best you can with some of that brush. We've got to move."

"Mount up!" Lucius called out. "Be careful goin' back down the hill. Always easier to go up than down, so keep back in the saddle. Toby, you keep tight on Delia's reins. Don't want her horse boltin'."

"I'll take the lead," I said, easing my horse out front and down the narrow rock path. "Follow close and don't fall behind. Thomas, you grab that slaver's horse and tie it with the pack-horses. We can't leave it here in case the others come back, and we might need it later on if one of ours comes up lame. It's a stroke of luck, and we'll take all the luck we can get."

When we were all safely down the hill and ready to move ahead, I turned one last time to the group. "We've a long ride now, but the next time we camp you'll be in free territory. Hang your thoughts on that. You ready?"

The smiles and nods I received made me feel richer than any bucket of gold. If I ended up not making more than ten cents out of this journey, their faces were already payment enough. As my eyes went back and forth across the group, I felt a joy as wide as the Ohio. I couldn't show it outwardly, though. I couldn't let them see it. We were still too far from freedom for anyone to stop being diligent. So, I did what I should have done in the first place. I pointed at Lucius and commanded, "You—take the lead. Toby, hold back, cover up our tracks best you can, and watch to the rear. Take that slaver's rifle with you. The rest of you, keep close to me. Let's move out."

And we did—with freedom enticing our hearts and minds.

....

CHAPTER 4

Spider and Fly

May 10

WILSON TAGGART ENTERED THE SALOON and eased his way to the far right end of the bar. There he stood slightly sideways, so his back would not be toward the door. He was left-handed, and by positioning himself so, he'd have a clear, unobstructed draw if he needed to pull his gun.

He immediately asked for a glass and a bottle of whiskey. After pouring right up to the rim, he took small swallows as he started soaking up the conversations around him.

Moments later, his partner, Warren Lewis, roughly pushed his way through the swinging doors at the entrance. From experience, he knew exactly where Taggart would be standing and walked over to join him.

The two men didn't greet each other. Instead, Taggart asked him, "Any news yet? Find out anything?"

"Not sure. Could be," Warren replied while motioning the bartender to bring another glass. "Found out a white man, one of those traveling peddlers, with two manservants was here for about a week. Gone now. Can't find anybody who talked to him. Looks like mostly kept to himself, which seems powerful strange for a man in that trade. Stayed in his wagon outside town. Can't explain why, but I'd almost lay money it was him."

"Maybe," Taggart replied. "Then again, maybe not. Lots of peddlers come through towns these days."

"That's true, but how many let their Negroes have free run of the town and local farms? Could have been his scouts. He's used them before."

Taggart poured Warren a drink. "Take it and move to the other end of the bar. Keep your ears open. Find out something for me. I want some news, or I'm going to be very unhappy. Understand?"

Warren didn't need any other directions. He picked up his drink and moved away quickly.

Wilson Taggart had been chasing John Fairfield from state to state, from north to south and east to west, over the past four years. Their trails had crossed many times, often within mere miles of each other, but they had come together only once when, quite unexpectedly, both sides met in the middle of a large, dry wash just outside Jackson, Tennessee. As if by way of instinct, Fairfield and Taggart recognized each other, and a sudden and violent gun battle erupted. In the conflict, both ended up marked. A wild ricochet left John with a thin, crescent moon scar on his left cheek. Wilson was hit to the side of his neck, his wound resulting in a permanent S-shaped ridge just below his ear. Each also lost two men in the initial volley of shots, so both sides chose to retreat briefly and tend to their wounds before continuing battle. When Taggart finally rallied his remaining men and tried flanking Fairfield, he and his men were gone. Taggart followed him for two days before the trail grew stone cold. The encounter had been deadly for both groups, but both Fairfield and Taggart felt the cost worth it. Each man finally knew the other's face, a face neither would ever forget.

This skirmish, bloody and costly as it had been for both sides, wasn't why Taggart was so hell-bent on capturing Fairfield. For Taggart, it was more a matter of pride of the worst form. John Fairfield was the only abolitionist of his ilk—a conductor who traveled with the runaways and helped them every step of their flight to freedom—Taggart had tried to capture but could not. Every single attempt to this point had ended in failure.

Other slave catchers throughout the South agreed Taggart had the best knowledge of the network of abolitionists devoted to helping with the cause. However, Taggart saw most of these men and women as benign creatures, mostly religious do-gooders, who merely supplied money and an occasional temporary refuge for the runaways. He generally tolerated their efforts and at times even downright appreciated them in a backward sort of way—for a practical reason. He figured out he could use them, figured out early on that if he kept men along the routes he had discovered connecting the depots on the Underground Railroad, he'd be able to catch a fair share of the runaways during their predictable movements. In short, he viewed such captures as akin to fishing a well-stocked stream—and the fish were the slaves he would return to their masters after capture.

John Fairfield, on the other hand, was as unpredictable as anyone he'd ever encountered. Chasing him had been like trying to run down a ghost, one that could change form and vanish at a moment's notice. Fairfield, a master of disguise, changed his physical appearance and his identity regularly to help him get close to and in the confidence of those who owned the slaves he was out to liberate. The disguises also made it easier for him to outwit those who were set upon his capture. At various times, he grew differing lengths and shapes of mustaches and beards, dyed and lengthened or shortened his hair, and walked with the aid of a variety of canes and crutches. At the same time, his attire, from hats to boots, was constantly changed to reflect the occupations he chose to imitate during his travels. To Taggart's knowledge, Fairfield had never repeated a look or an occupation twice in a row, a fact that made locating him even more difficult.

Taggart couldn't prove it, but he was still confident it was John Fairfield who had over the past several years put himself forth as a purchaser of slaves, a physician, a wealthy businessman sent to purchase cotton and tobacco crops, a land speculator, a surveyor, and—what bothered Taggart the most—a slave catcher. In each case, the false identity had allowed for easy and unquestioned movement among the local townspeople. Even the names Fairfield used changed regularly, adding yet another complication. Again, even though he couldn't be completely certain, Taggart believed that Fairfield had gone by the names Fairborne, Freemont, Felton, Johnson, and Travis.

The two men could not have been more different, yet there was a common thread of a type that tied them together: both were exceptional at their chosen professions. By results and by reputation, Wilson Taggart was the best and most feared slave catcher in the South. If that weren't enough, his physical presence alone most often made strangers he came upon lower their eyes and cautiously walk around him. A broad, sturdy man, he stood well over six feet tall. His long, unkempt dark hair framed a face with deep-set eyes and a perpetual scowl. His arms, muscled and deeply bronzed, were still nimble, so much so that his speed with a pistol had never been bested. Those who had challenged him were now in shallow graves marking the landscape from Mississippi to Michigan.

Just as he was superbly proficient with a pistol, he was equally adept at tracking down and capturing runaway slaves. In the past year alone, he had recaptured over thirty-five, on eight separate forays. Each capture was profitable and rewarding in its own right, but the chase—the matching of wits with the runaways—was the true excitement that stoked his soul. Always after the capture of a runaway, Taggart felt a deep sadness for the loss of the challenge, and he took these losses out on the unfortunate creatures he ran down. With a blazing-hot iron, he branded the letter "r" on the left cheek of the males and the right ankle of the females. The "r" marked them as runaways, but in Taggart's mind it served a much more important purpose than that. In the game he played, each slave was entitled to one attempt at freedom. However, if he caught the same slaves twice—which he had done multiple times—and found his mark upon them, he executed them on the spot—and took his time doing so to the point most eventually begged for the sweet release and peace of death.

Wilson Taggart had learned his trade from his father, Carson Taggart, a man many agreed to be one of the most skilled trackers of his generation. Taggart's mother had been lost in a Blackfoot uprising, and his father, without any other relations to call upon, started taking Taggart along and teaching him the signs in nature and the skills he would need to become an expert tracker. Father and son had grown close and developed a special bond forged by the excitement of the chase. However, this came to a sudden end when a runaway slipped his chains and, before making good his getaway, shoved a knife through Carson's throat. Taggart tracked the runaway for three weeks before deep snow set in and the trail was lost, forcing him to withdraw. Not catching his father's killer haunted him, drove him. He vowed he'd never give up on a search again, no matter how weak the trail grew or how much it would eventually cost him.

John Fairfield's trail, therefore, was one he was not going to let go. He couldn't let it go. Not now—not ever.

Wilson Taggart had little time for small-talk, so it was with great distaste he sipped his whiskey and listened to those around him sharing the everyday goings-on of the town. Mrs. Baxter's cow, missing for four days running, had finally been found with a bull in Johnston's meadow, a fact that brought high-pitched laughter all around the table next to him. Sheriff Sam Sullivan, while cleaning a rifle, had also dropped his new spectacles, smashing them to bits. Two men offered now was the time for someone to put a slug into the sheriff's righteous hide, a suggestion that brought nods and smiles from men Taggart measured as all bravado and not a fair ounce of courage in the lot. Mr. Shermer, the local dry-goods merchant, was suspected of altering his scales so that when items were weighed, several additional ounces showed in the final measurements, a speculation so petty to Taggart it caused him to refill his glass and gulp it down in one motion.

He'd heard enough and was just to the point of storming from the saloon when Warren signaled him over. Five men playing matchstick poker, a game designed to pass the time and in which no actual money was won or lost, were laughing and joking about what they were now calling the "I'm Sorry Thieves."

"Still just can't believe it," the oldest of the group, a man wearing greasy chaps and boots well worn past days of normal use, croaked. "Had to be loco. All of 'em. Why, that sheriff of our'n couldn't find a flower in a field. If they'd kept a runnin' with that money, they'd be livin' the life now, I'm tellin' you."

"Scaredy-cats—that what they were," another volunteered. "Musta thought they was up agin' pistoleros—and not that ruby we got for a sheriff."

All nodded agreement. Before any other thoughts could be shared, Taggart walked over and placed the remainder of his bottle of whiskey in the middle of their table.

"You gentlemen look thirsty to me." Taggart pulled up a chair and wedged himself between two of them facing the door.

"I've been on the trail for weeks now and haven't heard nothin' but snorin' from my partner there." He pointed at Warren. "I need to hear a good story. Somebody tell me about the—what did you call them? The 'I'm Sorry Thieves'?"

He called for the bartender to bring glasses for all at the table. "Drink up. There's plenty more to follow if your tale's to my liking. Tell me all about it now."

Each man, in turn, offered his version of the robbery, and each did his best to add to and spice up the particulars. By the time the story had almost made its way around the table, it was decided that there had been a good dozen robbers; they were all riding the most spirited and expensive of stallions; all were outfitted with gun belts, boots, and hatbands adorned with silver braid; and the amount of money they had taken swelled to the tens of thousands of dollars.

Finally, everyone looked at the old man, the last to have an opportunity to build up the details. He slowly poured himself a drink, gulped it down, set the glass back on the table, then said, simply, "That's the way it were."

Everyone howled and pounded fists on the table, causing the matchsticks to fly every which direction. That is, everyone howled but Wilson Taggart, who sat quietly, waiting for the laughter to play itself out.

"Now I believe all of you. I do," he said. "And that was a humdinger of a tale. No doubt 'bout that." He poured himself another drink, took a swallow, and placed his glass back to the table. "I have just one question. At the time of the great robbery, did anything else in or around town go missin'? Now think hard. Anything at all? Anybody report they lost anything?"

The matchstick poker players looked confused and turned silent while running the question in their minds.

"Maybe another drink or two will help," Taggart said, taking a fresh bottle from Warren and setting it on the table. "Think hard," he said again. "I know you'll come up with it if you try. There had to be something else that somebody complained about losin'. Try again."

The man directly across from Taggart suddenly sat up straight in his chair, then slouched again as he said under his breath, "Nah, wouldn't count."

Taggart picked up the bottle and poured the man's glass full. "Go ahead. What were you going to say?"

The man sipped half his glass, and said, "Well, that old miser Silas was sniffin' around town today. He got back from his travels to Chattanooga coupla days early, and he done had three of his darkies run off."

"You don't say," the old man said, slapping his knee. "Funny thing. Oglethorpe can't find two of his'n. Maybe they get up their own posse and chase that money. Wouldn't that be a goodun' on our sheriff!"

They all laughed again. This time, Taggart managed a weak smile before looking at Warren and motioning to the door.

"Thank you, gentlemen," he said, standing and nodding his head slightly. "Your tales have made me smile, and for that I'm grateful."

"You ain't heard nothin' yet," the old man said. "Sure you can't sit a spell longer? I'll tell ya 'bout when I found a gold nugget the size of a hen egg. Lost it, though...."

The others, who had heard the story too many times before, gave a collective groan and threw matchsticks at the old man.

Taggart didn't respond. He was already halfway to the door, Warren following close behind. Once outside, Taggart turned and said, "Let's see this fierce sheriff. I want to see if anything those liars said was even close to truth."

Sheriff Sullivan had just returned from another fruitless posse ride and was crawling into his bed when he heard the pounding on the door. When he pulled back on the handle and before he could say anything, Taggart wedged his foot in the doorway and said, "Sheriff, I have just one question. The men who robbed the bank—did you get a good look at any of 'em?"

"What? Why do you want to know? And who the hell are you, anyway?"

"Just a simple question," Taggart said, lifting his pistol from the holster and dropping it back in.

Sheriff Sullivan caught the motion out of the corner of his eye and asked, his voice growing bolder, "You threatenin' me?"

"Just a habit, I reckon. Do it when I'm in a hurry—or when I don't get what I'm lookin' for. Again, just one question. Anyone get a look at 'em?"

The sheriff looked first at Taggart, then at Warren. Not wanting a confrontation, especially after so many hours in the saddle, he replied, his voice emotionless, "They had masks, hoods. And gloves. Nobody saw a thing."

With that, he slammed shut the door and went back to his bed.

Taggart turned to Warren and said, "There's a hotel down the street. Might as well have a soft bed for the night. Could be the last one we'll see for a spell."

As they walked, Taggart spoke quietly to Warren to make sure his words weren't caught by the town gossips, some of whom had already left their matchstick poker game and were now sitting on the hitching posts in front of the stores. "They have too much of a head start on us. We'll never catch 'em now. Besides, we're too close to the Virginia border. Too many ways they could have gone. We'd be shootin' in the dark."

Scowling at the gossips perched around them, he added, "We were close this time. Close. I thought... I thought we might have him."

He shook his head and grew silent. Then, grabbing Warren's arm and pulling him into the shadows next to the undertaker's shack, he said, "I've decided—here's what we're gonna do. We might as well make some money while we wait for more news. Not quite a week back five slaves run off from the Matthews plantation down to Decatur. We done work for him before, remember? He pays good. Those Alabama darkies always head the same direction, right toward the Tennessee border. Must be the only route they ever heard of. If we head down there now, we'll likely be just in time to come across them at Signal Mountain. Probably just have to lead them right to the horses 'cause they'll be tuckered out by now. The bounty for the group's a thousand. You and I can do this by ourselves. Don't need none of the others. And don't you worry none—I'll pay you a fair share."

"Let's be at it," Warren said, his excitement building, but Taggart stopped him and continued, "Hold a minute. Not finished. Slow yourself. After we get 'em back to Matthews, we'll go to Chattanooga and take rooms at the Bristol Palace. I'm growing weary of chasing this man, so we're going to settle in there and do nothin' but drink, play some cards, grab a woman or two, and fill our bellies. Don't know how long we'll stay. Haven't decided yet."

Warren looked at him as if Taggart had completely lost his mind. This was not the leader he had come to fear, the man who couldn't stand to stay in the same camp more than two days at most.

When Taggart saw the unsettled look in Warren's eyes, he laughed. "I haven't gone mad. Leastways, not yet. I've got a new plan, that's all. My pap once told me that story of the spider and the fly. The spider puts out that web and just sits back and waits for the fly to come on in. We're gonna do the same. While we're in Chattanooga, we'll send men to different towns, from Nashville down to Montgomery—and some of the small ones, too. We'll tell 'em what to look for: someone new who'll show up with big plans for the money people there. If they spot someone, they'll get a message our way. Maybe, if luck shines on us, we'll catch us a fly."

"We'd have to be at the best side of luck for that to pan out," Warren said, shaking his head. "Long shot."

"I'm not finished," Taggart said, coldly. "That's just the first. I've heard too much about that settlement up to Canada. Not sure, but think it's called Elgin or somethin' close to it. Supposed to be where more and more runaways are taken, and we can't touch 'em there. For over a year now I haven't found any of his once they're north of Columbus. He has to be takin' 'em somewhere we can't go. My guess is there—to that Elgin."

"We goin' to Canada?" Warren asked, stepping back and falling against a post. "What for?"

"We're not goin', you knothead!" Taggart said loudly, too loudly. One of the gossips across the street leaned forward while pretending to be dusting his boots.

Taggart lowered his voice. "Remember our pretty boy, Mr. Boyle—close by to Ashville? The one who still hasn't paid us for bringing back three of his? I hear tell he's up to his eyebrows in gamblin' debts he'll never be able to make good. I want you to go have a visit with him. Tell him he's goin' on a trip for us. He's an educated man. We'll send him to Elgin as a land buyer so he can ask around and see if he can find him—or find out if that's where he disappears to when we lose his trail. Who knows, Boyle might even just catch us a fly himself."

"Why would he do this for us?" Warren asked.

"'Cause we'll tell him we'll forget what he owes us and will pay off his gamblin' troubles to boot. That'll put him on our side."

"And if it don't?"

"Then tell him we'll kill his family. He's got two little daughters and a son, right? And if I recall, a beauty of a wife. Tell him they might meet a bad end—or get sold to white-slavers. That oughta' bring him around."

"And you'll pay off all them debts he owe?"

Taggart smiled, lifted his pistol out of the holster, and let it drop heavily back in place. "What do you think?" he asked, his smile growing even broader.

"Just checkin'," Warren replied, shaking his head from side to side. "Was afraid for a minute you really had the madness. I remember Boyle's wife. I want that when we're done."

"Like hell!" Taggart shot back. Then, lowering his voice again, he said, "Okay, we'll cut cards for her."

"But I always lose—you always win," Warren protested.

"And I always will," Taggart said, staring coldly into Warren's eyes. "Don't you ever forget that."

Warren didn't reply. He just nodded weakly and followed Taggart to the hotel.

....

Chapter 5

River of Dreams

Worthington, Kentucky

AFTER LEAVING THE CAVE, WE rode through the day and most of the night, stopping only to water the horses as we came across streams—and that wasn't too often. To their credit, not a single person in the group uttered a complaint. Whether it was the thought of the freedom that lay ahead or the fear of slavers catching us from behind—or a combination of both—their resolve seemed as full of fire as ever. Oh, they were tired, all right. More than once I glanced back to see a body nearly slipping from the saddle, but the next rider behind always gave a little shout and snapped them back to purpose.

I was tired. Dog tired. My left shoulder was starting to tighten so much I could barely move my arm. Lucy kept begging me to have us pull up so she could make a new poultice, but we couldn't take that chance. Not just yet, anyway. We were drawing close to the Ohio River. Once across it, we wouldn't be completely safe, but we could, at least for a short while, stop holding our breath. "An hour more," I kept muttering under my breath. "Just an hour more."

In this part of the country, the Ohio River separated states that honored the institution of slavery from those that did not. The direction we were headed, the Ohio divided Kentucky, a powerful slave state, from Ohio, the first bastion of freedom for those coming north. However, even though Ohio was a free state, those who entered its borders did not instantly achieve freedom. The "Fugitive Slave Act," a Federal law, saw to that.

The Fugitive Slave Act made it legal for anyone to capture runaways in Ohio, or in any of the other free states, and bring them back south to their chains. Furthermore, the Act made it illegal—punishable by fine, imprisonment, or both—for anyone to help runaway slaves to their freedom. All white citizens had a solemn duty to help with the recapture of runaways—or face dire consequences if they chose not to. Offering even the slightest of assistance to a runaway could mean thousands of dollars in penalties, the confiscation of homes and property—and even months of prison time. Therefore, the help we would receive once across the river would come from those who ran the depots along the routes of the Underground Railroad, those who had taken up the cause, no matter the consequences to themselves. Because of the law and the harm they knew could come to them, others along the way simply could not be trusted.

The slave catchers used the Fugitive Slave Act to justify every corner of their behavior, from the torture of slaves they recaptured to the burning of the homes of white citizens found in the aid of the runaways. In truth, the Act gave slave catchers the freedom and the authority to do whatever they wanted, without, in most cases, reprimand of any kind. Those who were against slavery hated this Act just as much as they did the slave catchers themselves, but there was nothing they could do about it. However, outside the law they pursued many courses of action, including the financial and spiritual support of those who risked their lives by operating the depots providing safe haven. Abolitionists did this at great peril to themselves, but they did it nonetheless. They did it because the principles of abolitionism ran in their veins. Although I may have had other motives as well, I was still proud to be in that camp.

As our group neared the Ohio River, I knew we'd have to find a shallow section to ford. We were a month behind the peak time for a crossing. By this point in May, the snowmelt from the past winter had swollen the river in many places well above safe levels. Finding the shallows in May was more often determined by luck than by skill. I hoped the luck we'd had to this point would continue a little longer—to be exact, an hour and a half longer.

My thoughts of the river were suddenly interrupted by Lucy, who had urged her horse up next to mine. "I be curious. We lef a dead man back there. You ain't bothered?"

"No—because that wasn't a man. That was a slaver, and slavers are the devil. And it ain't no harm...."

Lucy reached over and touched the cloth covering my shoulder, rubbing it gently. "Ain't wet no more. Gotta wet it—now. If you don't, you lose that arm—or you die."

I was so tired I wasn't in any mood to argue with her. I called ahead to Lucius, who had already drawn back toward us, "We'll rest up for fifteen minutes and not a tick more. Get everyone dismounted and have Toby take care of the horses. Then you come back over here so we can talk. We're close. Very close. I swear I can smell it."

"Me, too," he said. "By my thoughts, Flatlands Ford is just a mile or two away and might be best to try. But we better keep close to the woods, just in case that doesn't work out and we have to try farther ahead. Many travelers come through this time of year. Don't want 'em to spot us."

As Lucius gave orders to the others, Lucy pointed first to me and then to the base of a large oak and said, "You sit. I be back."

With that, she pulled more wild onions and a slice of ham from a small cloth sack tied to her saddle. She had also brought her flat rock with her, so it wasn't any time at all she had another poultice ready for my shoulder. As she pulled the old cloth scraps way and the cool air swept under, a dull pain shot down my arm, causing me to wince and tighten my fist.

"Tole you," Lucy scolded, shaking her head. "Shoulda stopped long ago."

"Do the best you can," I said. "Thank you for all you've done."

"Ain't done much yet. We see first if you die." She quickly turned her head, trying to hide a shy smile.

"Well, if I do die, it'll like as not be the smell from that poultice that kills me. Where did you learn to do that—from some witch?"

"You hush," she said, her smile widening. "Too bad you mouth weren't shot."

Just as she finished wrapping my shoulder, Toby came up to us. "Suh, horses is ready. You just res up now. I keep watch."

"Thank you, Toby," I said, leaning back and closing my eyes. "I need just a minute...."

....

When I opened my eyes again, I could tell by the position of the moon I'd been asleep for hours and wasn't happy about it. Before realizing I was alone, I called out, "Who's responsible for this? We should have been across the river hours ago."

I looked down, and I wasn't against the oak tree any more. I was on a blanket behind a row of lilac bushes flanking the main trail. As I sat up, Lucius hurried over to me.

"I know what you're thinkin'," he said, trying to calm me with the tone of his voice. "But we had no choice. I went up to Flatlands Ford, and the river was way too deep, too swirly. So, I went on to Worthington. There's some bad rocks and some quick-mud, but I marked a crossin' we can try. Those who ain't tall will have to go horseback so water don't get in their nose, but I ain't looking for nobody to drown on us. I think we'll be okay."

He looked shocked I didn't scold him, then continued, "Besides, you need the rest. You've got fever, and it ain't good. I made the decision, and I'll stand by it. I swear there ain't nobody on this road right now, so we can still cross up ahead any time we like. Besides, I used the time you were sleepin' to learn 'em what I could about the guns. They all know how to aim and fire. Least they'd make a lot of noise now if we need 'em to. And that Delia— bet she could shoot with any man just by the look in her eyes."

He had been right to look for the secondary crossing, so I said, "Your decision was right, and I know it. But it's going to be close to daylight by time we get there. I don't know...."

He smiled, proudly. "Then if you ain't going to shoot me, I suggest we stay hid over beyond that tree line an hour or so more, then move on. "

"The others?" I questioned.

"Already put 'em up over there. Not sleepin', though. Too scared, I expect. But the rest is good for them, too. And givin' 'em time to pray, which I seen a lot of while you were snorin'. Looked like some of it might have been for you."

"Didn't you tell 'em I was too mean to die?" I asked.

"I did—but they don't know you enough to know it's gospel truth. Just told 'em to take it on faith."

Looking around me again, I asked, "Why am I here—and they're over there?"

"I wanted you here with me in case we needed to ride. We can always get more of them. I can't get no more of you."

"They had to know what you were doing," I said, looking over to the line of trees.

"No doubt they did," he said, spitting to his right. "Weren't no matter to me."

"And you say I'm the one going to hell," I said, shaking my head. "Well, at least I'll be in good company when I get there. Now get over here and help me up. I better walk over so they can see I'm not dead yet."

As Lucius gently helped me up, the pain ran down my arm again. I noticed my elbow had swollen considerably. Lucy had been right. We should have changed the poultice more regularly, but there are times *should* and *could* just don't meet up. Before we crossed to the trees, I turned again to Lucius and said, "I haven't had a chance to ask until now. There's something I want to know. Those slavers back there at the cave. You think there's any chance they belonged to Taggart?"

Looking deadly serious at me, Lucius replied, "No chance.

The boy didn't have a mark on him. He'd of looked like drawn through a thorn patch if he'd been one his. Taggart don't ride with milk-boys. You know that."

"I get your point," I said, relieved.

As soon as we were through the tree line and in view, all our passengers immediately stood up.

"That's another thing I want you to stop right now," I said, scolding them, but gently. "Never again will you stand for any man—unless it's something you want to do of your own accord."

Mumphry said, "That what we doin'. We jus glad you alive."

All gathered around me, each one touching my shoulder for what they said was some type of ritual of luck and good fortune. I thanked them—I figured it couldn't hurt—then asked all to circle up and sit with me. I wanted to prepare them for what was coming next, to ease some of their fears and give them as much hope as possible. As I looked at them, I could tell they needed both—badly.

"Listen carefully," I began. "Your lives will depend upon this. Mine, too." I was sure I now had their complete attention. "We're close to where we're going to cross the Ohio River. I've already told you what that means. That'll be your first touch of free soil, but you'll still be far from free. There's a law, a very unjust one, in this country that says any white people above the river helping those like you would be risking everything they have in doing so. So, here are three rules once we're on the other side."

All were leaning forward as I continued, "First, just because it's free territory doesn't mean all the whites you see are against slavery. Whether it be caused by fear of the law or whether they don't hold with freedom for all men, plenty would just as soon turn you in as look at you. So, if occasion comes up, don't talk to any white folks unless either Lucius or I tell you it's okay."

"Second, you're all still my responsibility until we get where we're going. That means you do what I say, without question—and as soon as I say it. All it takes is one person out of harness and we could all go down. I'll get us through, but you have to follow my orders exactly. Understand?"

All nodded they did. "And finally, number three—and most important of all. By looking at you—all of you—it appears you believe in the good Lord above. Draw upon that faith now. Hold fast to it, and don't let go of it for even a second. These next miles of our journey could be the most dangerous of all. Just as we're on this trail to keep ourselves hidden, others are using it for the same purpose. Outlaws, killers, those on the run from who-knows-what. And then there are the slavers. They know many take this route, so sometimes they just sit and wait for bounty to cross by."

They were anxious. Toby was now using a stick to draw small circles in the dirt at his feet. Alta pressed her hands against her cheeks. Even Delia squirmed and re-crossed her legs. They needed at least a thimble full of reassurance. "But I have a few tricks up my sleeve. And as I said, this isn't my first time along this trail. We'll make it. We will make it. You just listen to me and Lucius and do what we say. And, while you're doing that, you keep your thoughts with the Lord above. Anybody have a question?"

Delia asked, "Wwwwhen wwwe ffffiii...nlly get ... there?"

I knew someone would ask this. Groups always did, so I was prepared for it. "We have several stops up ahead, and we'll likely take rest and food at each. You may even have to stay hidden for days at a time. Can't tell now. How long it takes us to get where we're going isn't important. What is important is to survive each day. Then, when we do finally get there—when all of you are with your families again—the time you spent along the way won't seem like anything. It never does."

"Let's mount up, and let's get movin'," I said. "I make it not quite an hour to the crossing. We'll stop there, and Lucius will tell you what to do to get across."

None of them moved. "You don't want your freedom?" That got them up instantly. All were in the saddle before I was.

I sent Lucius and Toby out to keep watch ahead of us. At the same time, I ordered the others to keep in a tight line behind me and ride as close to the woods as possible in case we needed to dart in quickly. I told them not to talk, not to make any other sounds, unless absolutely necessary. I had a nagging feeling we were being followed, so after what must have been a good quarter hour, I asked Walker to keep us in sight but to drop back and watch our rear.

As many times as I'd crossed the Ohio, the last minutes beforehand always made my heart pound. I wasn't afraid of the actual crossing. I'd had some close calls, but I'd never lost anyone to drowning—yet. It wasn't the river, although a healthy dose of fear of a river as dangerous as the Ohio isn't necessarily bad. I had no idea why, but when I saw the Ohio, images of those I had seen perish in the bonds of slavery always reentered my mind.

One such image, one that I couldn't forget no matter how much I tried, was of a young man I saw on the auction block in Charleston, South Carolina, while I was there pretending to be a broker of slaves for plantation owners in Georgia. For those whose plantations I was visiting to locate my passengers, I made dramatic show of participating in the auction. I was cautious never to end up with the winning bid, but I made sure my actions seemed great sport to those watching me.

Near to the mid-point of the auction, a young, proud-looking man, tall and strong of limb, was brought forth and tethered by chain to a rail at the front of the block. As the potential purchasers examined him closely, inspecting his teeth and muscles, he jerked back, his chains snapping. Suddenly free, he jumped from the block, the crowd falling back in horror before him, and tried making his escape down the main road. He hadn't gone but a dozen or so steps when a shot rang out. Then another. Then still another. The slave stopped, turned to face the crowd, raised his hands, fell to his knees, then flopped forward to the ground.

It was over quickly and had absolutely no lasting effect on the crowd. Almost immediately, the organizers held a mock-auction for his remains. The bidding was long, the bid increments only a few pennies at a time, much to the approval and applause of the onlookers, many of whom were lunching and taking drink. When I could stand it no longer, I called out, "Two dollars!"—which was followed by a roar of approval. The auctioneer immediately slammed down his hammer and screamed, "Sold!" Again, around me were nothing but smiles and laughter. Inside, my heart screamed as I began thinking of ways to have his body moved for proper burial.

As long as I walked the earth I'd never be able to forget the looks on the faces of those next to be sold on that same block. To my great surprise, their spirit had not been shattered by those horrible events. On the contrary, I saw the angry fire in their eyes they would not let be destroyed—no matter what the future held for them. From then on, images of that day seemed to appear whenever I felt need for extra courage. The Ohio always called them forth, and I was once again glad for it.

My thoughts came back to the present as I saw Lucius and Toby making their way back toward us. Lucius pulled his horse up beside me and said, "Just around the bend there. Need to get 'em ready."

"Any time you want," I replied. "You're the leader."

He smiled and called over the others. "Look here," he began. "Don't want nobody to float downriver, so here's what we do. Can't all ride across. Too many rocks. Horse take a bad step, rear back, and throw you right off—maybe drown. Lucy, Alta, and Thomas—you're not big as the rest of us, so you have to stay in the saddle. Rest of us will walk and hold your reins, too."

"Water's up to about here," he said, holding his arm straight out just below his shoulder. Over the head of you three. If any get throwed, rest of us will be there to fetch you. Only about a hundred yards across, so we can go slow—and be safe. On the other bank, pull them horses out fast so they don't fall back in."

Then, turning to me, he said, "I'll go first off. 'Bout half way, I'll change us more to the left and downstream to miss the quickmud. When we turn, hold the horses tight so they don't scare. Water'll be swiftest there."

He walked over to one of our packhorses. "We've got one more thing to do before we're off. We need to make some 'danger stakes.' If anybody's following us, the stakes just might buy us a whole day—or more."

Lucius was referring to a trick we had used many times in the past. Where we were to enter the water, we'd place in the ground a long row of stakes with red strips of cloth attached. These "danger stakes" were used to warn fellow travelers the area was rife with quicksand and unsafe to cross. Lucius had discovered the area before us was the only safe place to cross within several miles, so I should have felt at least some guilt about deceiving the families that would soon be traveling by and looking for a place to ford. However, I felt none—no guilt at all.

Lucius reached into one of the saddlebags and drew forth the rolled-up strips of red cloth we'd brought with us. I then ordered Thomas, Elijah, and Walker to round up as many small but sturdy branches they could find so we could tie the strips to them and place them in the ground.

When the last of the stakes had been planted, I motioned to Lucius it was time to start the crossing. "Mount up!" he called out. "And follow my lead."

Then, before we moved forward, he turned and said, "Just one more thing. If your body floats down river, it could give all us away. So don't."

By the silence that followed his warning, I guessed they'd taken all to heart.

Shielded by cover of darkness, we entered the water slowly, cautiously. The water still held the cold from winter's snow, but the current close to the bank was easy and smooth. I held tightly to my own reins and Alta's. Not five yards out the water came close to neck-level for those of us walking, but, to our relief, it soon dropped again below our shoulders. At one point, Lucy's horse, a large bay, stumbled slightly and stopped in its tracks. Lucy looked around, her eyes pleading, until Lucius reached back and jerked the reins; her horse bobbed its head several times, snorted, and then again moved slowly ahead.

Almost halfway between banks, Lucius pointed to his left and said, quietly—so as not to spook the horses or the riders—"Follow close—quickmud over there. Don't get in it."

No sooner had the command been given when Mumphry, just a few feet from me, took a step and instantly disappeared below the surface. Alta let out a low scream, and I slapped her hard on the leg to quiet her; even the softest of sounds could carry miles across water. Just as I took in a breath, held it, and prepared to dive below, his head popped back up. He was choking and gasping for air. I drew him to me and held his face near my shoulder to mute the sounds. When his breathing returned to normal, I whispered to him, "Fine time for a bath."

He wanted to laugh softly, but covered his mouth before I could do it for him. I just shook my head and motioned him to move ahead.

Thankfully, the rest of the crossing went smoothly enough. When Lucius reached the shoreline, he gave his horse a good kick and urged it to climb up and over the bank. He tied off his horse and ran back down to help pull up the others. Each, in turn, made it to the top of the bank. Those on horseback climbed down and joined the rest of us when I motioned everyone to move in close around me so that I didn't have to speak loudly.

"See that," I said, pointing back to Kentucky. "Know what that is?"

I didn't give them time to reply. "That's your past. You'll never forget it, but, hopefully, you'll never have to experience anything like it again. Bend down and take a handful of dirt and roll it between your hands. Know what that is? It's your future, and like that dirt, Lord willing, just maybe you'll be able to shape it some as you see fit."

What came next took me completely by surprise; no group had ever done so before. Together, our passengers first circled round and hugged me, then moved to Lucius and did the same. No one said a word. They didn't have to.

Silently, we all mounted and rode into the darkness full of promise and hope.

....

Chapter 6

The Interlopers

Center Station, Ohio

SHORTLY AFTER CROSSING THE OHIO, we made our way directly northeast through countryside with few towns or farms along our route. Still, we weren't yet far enough north we could let down our guard, not even for an instant. We finally came to an old hunting trail that Lucius and I had used many times before—and one we knew would serve as the shortest route to our meeting with Tasby and Henry. The wide and even trail made our forward progress much easier, which provided great relief for our passengers. At the same time, I knew we still needed to cover our tracks as best we could. With the sun starting to climb over the horizon, I knew it would be safe to continue for no more than an hour more. Then, we'd have to find a safe place to pitch camp and rest ourselves for the better part of the day.

Even amidst the constant threat of danger, the first hour of travel after dawn was always a wondrous time for me, and this particular morning it was especially so. The landscape around us, highlighted by the emerging rays of the sun, glistened in the morning dew, and I found myself, at least momentarily, caught up in the majesty of late spring. The flowering dogwood, rosebud, and crabapple trees still held their fragrant blossoms. Just off our path, starlings and robins flipped over leaves in search of a morning feast. Bees buzzed our faces before settling to the wildflowers at the base of trees. Creeks still flush with spring rain gurgled as we passed. Trout lily pleased our senses, and even skunk cabbage, nature's blend of the acrid and the beautiful, reminded me that summer was just ahead.

Sadly, these moments of bliss were always fleeting. Even a moment without diligence could have dire consequences. The smoke of a campfire off in the distance could belong to slave hunters. The sharp snap of a twig farther into the trees could be warning of an impending attack by highwaymen. The sudden rustling of a bush at the top of a ridge could signify a posse ready to spring upon us. I was well aware I had to maintain and keep sharp the keen senses of the hunted. Our lives depended upon it, so the beauty around us faded to the background.

However, it was now becoming more and more difficult for me to keep alert as I needed to be for the safety of all. The poultices Lucy prepared for my shoulder offered some relief, but a sharp throbbing had settled into my left arm, and I found it difficult to keep a tight grip on the reins. The sweat on my brow also told me my fever had worsened. I knew I had to have rest or I wouldn't be any good to anyone, so it was with relief I saw Lucius riding toward me.

"All clear to the north," he said when he pulled along side. "No cabins. No crossings. Just ahead of that stand of trees up yonder is a small stream back off the main path. I think that'll do for now. Good cover—in case we need it. Good place to camp."

"That sounds fine," I replied, reaching over to pat him on the shoulder. As I extended my left arm, I winced. He noticed immediately and said, "You have to rest—now—and take care of that. You better not die on me."

"Well," I replied, smiling weakly, "that's a thought we both share. Just get us hidden and bedded down. Rest'll do us all good."

The first order of business was to take care of the horses and find soft patches of ground among the trees where we could spread our blankets. Lucius said he'd stand the first watch to the north, and Walker volunteered to keep a watchful eye on the path behind us. No one spoke as we prepared our camp. All were too tired and ready for the temporary, and badly needed, peace of slumber. Once all was readied, it didn't take long before most of us fell into a sound sleep.

When I finally woke, I tried to stand up too quickly, supporting myself with my arm, and immediately fell back to the ground. Lucy ran over to me and said, "You ain't ready—not by a pig's eye."

She pulled my shirt to the side and readjusted the bandage covering my wound. "I don't know," she said, shaking her head. "Looks sepsis to me. Don't know how much more I can do."

"I'll make it," I said, weakly, again trying to stand. Lucy pushed me back down and wagged a finger in my face. "You not goin' nowhere. Least not yet. Time for new poultice, so you just lay yourself back to restin'."

I was so dizzy I didn't put up much of an argument. I lowered myself again, my teeth beginning to chatter, and covered up as much as I could with the blanket. Lucius soon walked over and asked Lucy how I was getting along. She motioned him to follow her a short distance away, and the two stood talking and gesturing, first pointing my direction, and then at the road up ahead. I couldn't hear them, but the looks on their faces told me they were not in agreement about what to do with me.

Finally, Lucius held up his hand, as if indicating to Lucy their conversation had run its course, and said, loudly enough this time for me to hear, "Get that poultice ready, and make him comfortable as you can."

He then walked slowly over to me, sat down, and said, his voice gentle but firm, "If we push ahead right now, we might be able to meet Tasby and Henry by next morning. I'll allow you there'd be some danger to it. Don't like travelin' through here in daylight, but I've scouted ahead and nothin's movin'. I just have a feeling...."

Lucius' feelings were almost always right, so I didn't fight him. Instead, I asked, knowing full well what his answer would be, "Do you think you should leave me here? You could probably make better time if you didn't have to worry about me."

We played this game every time one of us received a wound, no matter how small or how serious. It was not only gallows humor.

"Well, I'm half tempted," he replied, trying to make his face more serious. "You're the one with the price on your head, but it's 'cause of that I guess I'll jump a risk and keep you around. After all, I could sure do my fair share of whoopin' it up with that kind of money, so if you decide to leave this earth along the trail, I'll just flop your sorry carcass across them packhorses and find a sheriff. I can see that pile of money right now."

"Don't go spendin' it just yet," I replied. "I don't see any buzzards circling, do you? And besides, you're about my height and weight, so if you get thrown and hit your head or get snakebit, I'd get great pleasure convincing a lawman—and you know I could do it—that you are the notorious John Fairfield. Then who'd be rich?"

"And I just bet you would," he said, reaching over and poking me right at the center of my wound, which caused me to wince and step back.

"You know I would," I said, grabbing the handle of my pistol.

At that point, we both laughed and shrugged. We hadn't realized it, but our passengers had witnessed our exchange. Most were now either laughing softly or shaking their heads. All, that is, but Lucy, who called out, "If you knock down that poultice, I skin both you. I want the freedom, and I need you show me the way. So why we jawin' here?"

She had a point, so I said to the group, "You heard her. Let's get about it."

In short order we were all saddled and ready to continue the journey. I wasn't overly happy about traveling in the late afternoon, so I decided to double our guard, sending Lucius and Toby ahead and Walker and Mumphry behind. I stayed with the others and led them along as close to the trees as possible.

Just before dusk, Lucius sent Toby back to let us know two wagons were coming our direction. Lucius had asked him to let me know those in the wagons looked like settlers making their way back east. No matter who they were or where they were headed, we couldn't let them see us. I had everyone move as quickly as they could well back into the trees and find places to hide until the wagons rolled by. Then, turning to Toby, I said, "Go find Walker and Mumphry and tell 'em to get themselves hid. Go—now!"

I then eased my way a fair distance into the woods to join the others—and waited. It wasn't five minutes later the wagons, each pulled by a team of longhorn steers, rambled past. Lucius had been right; they did look like settlers, and I felt no immediate danger.

That is, I didn't until Delia sneezed.

In one motion, the man in the lead wagon immediately yanked back the reins and pointed his rifle our direction. I didn't move—and hoped and prayed the others wouldn't panic and would keep absolutely still.

"What's it about?" the man guiding the second wagon called out.

"You hear that?" the first responded. "Not sure what it was, but it sure as rain came from over there." He pointing almost right where I was standing.

"Was it game?" the second asked. "The children have the sour belly and could sure use meat."

"Maybe. Then again, maybe I was just hearin' things. Or maybe just an owl. Can't say for sure."

"Well, I'm all for lookin'. Won't hold us up to make a shucks. I'll go."

He handed the reins to his wife and said, "Mind the team. Don't let 'em wander. Won't be long."

He jumped from the wagon, rifle held to his chest, and slowly made his way into the trees before me, his eyes sweeping left and right as he came forward. The dense cover around us was good, and the group was farther back than I was. If they stayed quiet, there was a chance he wouldn't be able to see them until he passed by me. "Please stay put—and stay still," I thought to myself, looking back to the group.

I was standing behind a thick maple with low-hanging branches right at the edge of an animal-trot heading deep into the woods. Because of my covered position, I was sure the man couldn't see me and had no idea his every movement was being watched. At the same time, he was now far enough away from the wagons that I felt sure his traveling companions had probably put their attention elsewhere.

He suddenly picked up his pace, moving quickly right past where I was standing. As fast as I could, I stepped out behind him, cocked the hammer of my pistol, shoved it roughly to the middle of his back, and said, calmly, deliberately, "Move again or make a sound and you're dead where you stand."

He froze. I grabbed the back of his shirt and pulled him behind the tree so we were both out of sight. Once there, I reached around and took his rifle, propping it against one of the lower branches. I then grabbed his shirt again and held firm in case he decided to bolt.

"I won't kill you... unless I have to," I said, evenly. "So you just stand yourself still for a minute and listen to me."

After all the years of being chased, there wasn't much I hadn't experienced. I'd been in close quarters with pursuers many a time, and through experience I knew it was often more to my benefit to keep someone alive than to blow a hole through him. This man wasn't a pursuer—by his dress I judged him to be a farmer—but he still presented a danger, the danger of potential discovery of our party. Even so, I judged he might be of service if allowed to keep his life.

"What name do you go by?" I asked, tightening my grip on his shirt.

He arched back and replied, his voice cracking, "Ned. Name's... Ned."

"Ned what?" I asked. "How are you called? And where are you headed?"

"Ned Funk—and we're off to Baxter Junction. We-We-We bought us a homestead there," he stammered.

"Well, Ned Funk of Baxter Junction, I now know your name and where you can be found. You think hard on that. If you ever were to cause me any harm, my brothers—and I'll make sure they know all about you—will come kill you and your whole family. You wouldn't want to see your children after they'd be done with 'em."

"Please, Sir..." he interrupted. "Mean you no harm. Just lookin' for game. Please let me go."

"I'm thinking on it," I said, dragging out the words. "But before I decide, I want you to know something."

Again, through years of practiced deception, I had a passel of stories to draw from for nearly every situation I could imagine falling before me. In that time, I had also learned nothing turned a captive to an ally faster than pretending to enlist the person in a cause of justice.

I pushed the barrel of my pistol even rougher against his back. "I want you to know something, and heaven help you if you ever decide to cross me on it. I'm here laying for that rotten skunk Ebenezer Trowbridge. Know him?"

I didn't wait for his reply. "He killed one of my brothers. Shot him in the back."

I paused and poked him repeatedly with my gun. "Shot him for no reason. None at all. Murder was what it was, and the law is after him with a rope—but I aim to get hold of him first. You see anyone camped back where you came from? Anyone at all? You see Trowbridge?"

When he didn't respond, I said, "Speak up. You see him back there?"

"I-I-I didn't see nobody—all day. Nary a soul. Swear to you I didn't."

"Not a soul? No one camped along the trail?"

He didn't speak, nodding instead. Just then, one of the horses snorted. The man started to look that direction, but I quickly jerked him to the left.

"Never you mind my horse," I said, gruffly. "Best you know nothin' 'bout me. You know why that's so, right?"

Again he nodded.

"I shouldn't, but I'm inclined to let you go. It ain't you I'm after. It's that Ebenezer Trowbridge. Ever seen a man skinned alive? That's too good for him, but that's what I expect I'll do. He's a murderer; that's good enough for him. You agree?"

"I-I-I do," he said, panting now. "Please, Sir, let me go. I swear if I come to any sign of him, I'll get word back to you. I swear it so. I hope you get up to him."

"If you're willing to help me, then there'll be no harm in letting you off. Now don't you move. Stand right still while I give you back your rifle."

I let go of his shirt, picked up his rifle, and drove the barrel end of it several inches into the dirt in front of his feet. "If you pull that trigger before you hone the earth out that barrel, it'll blow up. Don't look back this way. Right now, you don't know my face. If you see me, I'll have to shoot you down—and then go for the others. Nod if you understand my words."

He did. I slipped the rifle in his hand and said, "Now be off. And don't forget your sworn promise. If you see that mangy Trowbridge, I expect you'll let me know. I'll be right here all night and into tomorrow. Now go. And don't you turn around."

It had been a long time since I'd seen a man move that quickly in thick brush. And, all the way back to his wagon, he kept his neck stiff, never coming close to looking back. When he finally reached the wagon, in one motion he handed his wife the rifle and climbed back up to his seat.

"What'd you find?" the man in the first wagon called back. "Any game 'round?"

"Weren't nothin'," he replied. "Musta been the w-w-w-wind. We're wastin' time. Let's be off b'fore we grow roots here."

"Okay," the first man said. "But I coulda swore...."

With that, they were again rolling slowly down the trail. When they were far enough away I was sure I couldn't be heard, I called over to the rest of the others. "And who was that who sneezed?" I asked, already knowing the answer.

Delia stepped forward into a small clearing ahead of the tree she'd been behind. She dropped her head and stared at the ground below.

"Why, you hear that man stammer?" I asked, loud enough for all the group to hear. Then, directing my words to Delia, I added, "I don't suppose you two are related?"

She raised her head, and for the first time I saw her smile, if only for an instant. Lucy stepped from her hiding place and scolded me, "Now you stop. Leave this child 'lone." She pulled-Delia close and hugged her.

"We best be off," I said, motioning the others to come to the clearing to join us. "And besides," I said, smiling, "that nasty Ebenezer Trowbridge might be lurking somewhere in these woods."

"Ain't right to lie so," Lucy said, shaking her head. "Heard the whole thing."

"Maybe not, but I'd bet we'll never see the likes of him again. And, we also found out—and I believe him—we don't have to worry about anyone camped ahead of us. I'd lie any day for information like that, and I'll never feel a bit sorry for it. And, he'll talk—sure as shootin'—to anyone they meet coming from the east, and they'll think twice before they pass along where someone set on murder is laying off in the woods. That'll keep what's behind us at bay for a spell. No, guilt won't ever get the best of me, least not for a lie. Never."

"Maybe you truly be the Devil," Lucy replied. "Why, the words that come out your mouth...."

"Some would say you're right," I said. "There are days I'm not so sure myself. Now, let's get moving—back to the trail."

Just as we were clear of the woods, Toby, Walker, and Mumphry came into view. I waved them over and said, "Toby, you get to Lucius and tell him we're fine—and that the road ahead is likely safe. You understand?"

"Yes, Suh. I let him know."

"Then be off," I said. "We can cover many more miles before morning if we push ahead."

When I turned back to the group, they were already mounted and ready.

"So far, so good," I said to myself. "Now if our luck will just hold out...."

With what lay ahead, we'd need every bit of luck we could get.

....

Chapter 7

Rendezvous

Jackson, Ohio

As it turned out, Ned Funk of Baxter Junction had told the truth: we didn't come across a single camp or traveling party the rest of the evening or throughout the night. Because we didn't have to stop to conceal ourselves, we pushed ahead as fast and as hard as I dared. Other than short stops to water our horses and stretch the tightness from our legs, we didn't leave the saddle.

A couple of hours before sunrise, we came to a large, natural spring surrounded by dogwood trees a short distance below Jackson, Ohio. This was the landmark we'd been pushing for. Just over the rise and no more than half a mile to the east was what was left of the Turner home, our point of rendezvous with Tasby and Henry.

For those moving through the area, the pile of ash and half burned logs now scattered about the ground where the home of Zachariah and Deborah Turner once stood represented the climax of a cautionary tale—and a dire warning for those who might have a notion to follow in their footsteps. For years, their home, nestled in the rolling hills of central Ohio, seemed little different from any other in the valley. They'd always had a fair grouping of tobacco fields and a lush, narrow meadow their livestock ambled along for grazing. Their home—a wide, low cabin that sat next to two barns, one for the drying of the tobacco and the other for their horses and chickens—was ringed by dense stands of oak and maple trees, which were harvested as needed and sent to the lumber mill in Jackson. To those in town, the Turners were simple, God-fearing souls who kept fairly to themselves, save for their Sunday morning buggy rides to worship service or occasions when they helped a neighbor raise a barn or dig a well. They had not been blessed with children, and many of the area felt they carried a deep sadness with them because of that.

The townsfolk of Jackson, therefore, fell to complete disbelief when they discovered the true passion at the center of the Turners' lives: their work with the Underground Railroad. Their home, known to a select few in the cause as the Turner Depot, was one of the last stops on the route passing through to Columbus. Over the course of fifteen years, the secret room below their livestock barn had seen well above two hundred slaves sheltered, fed, and clothed being sent again on their way to freedom.

Their work came to a sudden halt just over three years before when two runaways who had been re-captured attempted to save their own skins by betraying the Turners' secret. Despite the information they provided, the slaves were still tortured and hanged. The slave catchers—many believed Wilson Taggart among them—then rushed to the Turner home, walked Zachariah and Deborah to the woods behind their cabin, shot them both, and set fire to their buildings.

Some months later, several families of the area inquired about purchasing the property, but the officials in Jackson, a town divided nearly equally on the issue of emancipation of runaways, refused all overtures. Half believed the Turner homestead should be kept in permanent state of ruin as a reminder of the fate that could befall those who provided any aid to those in flight. The other half believed the ruins should not be cleared so they'd serve as a symbol of the sacrifices made by many and of the work yet to come before all men could be free. The beliefs of the two sides may have been as far apart as the sun and the moon, but the final result was still the same: the Turner property was forbidden ground for all in Jackson, a situation that made it, ironically and sadly, a perfect meeting place for those carrying forth the Turners' work.

Tasby and Henry had been able to elude the posse and keep to schedule. They would be waiting for us in the woods just south of the cabin ruins. After watering our horses and dipping our aching feet and ankles in the cool spring, I called Lucius over to me.

"I'll stay here with our passengers while you go find Tasby and Henry. I still can't bring myself to go there. The Turners were dear friends. Saved my wretched life once, and they saved yours, too. They were so kind, so generous—to everybody. I get sick to my stomach every time I think of them resting in those unmarked graves. If it's the last thing I do, I'll get proper markers put up there. And you should help me. You owe them, too."

"They're dead," Lucius replied, looking off into the distance. "Markers won't make a lick of difference. They knew the chances they were takin'. Same as all of us. They just got caught. That's all."

"How can you be so cold about them?" I asked, my tone clipped, scolding.

It was at that moment, and before he could respond, I suddenly remembered why he never wanted to talk about the Turners. His own farm had also been torched by slave catchers, so I was sure the thought of riding to the Turner homestead brought to the surface images he'd rather not ever see again.

I was the one being selfish for not wanting to go there. "I'm sorry. I wasn't thinking. I should do it. Besides, with my arm as it is, you're better suited to stay and protect the group."

I started for my horse when he took my arm and held firm. "No," he said, "I'll go. I need to. I...."

He didn't finish the thought. He didn't have to. "I understand," I said. "I'll get everyone behind those rocks. We'll be right there when you get back."

"I know you will," he said, swinging into his saddle. "Make

sure all their guns are loaded. Might need 'em. And try not to get yourself shot again."

Without another word, he was off.

I called for the others. "Toby, take the horses behind those trees over there and stay with 'em. Keep 'em quiet. The rest of us will get behind the rocks. Lucius will be back soon with the other men, and then we'll decide when to move out. The rest of you, follow me."

As we started moving toward the rocks, Lucy said, "Suh, I'd like to ask somethin' if you don't mind."

"What is it you'd like to know?"

"Well," she said, lowering her voice, "when do we get to that Miss'sippi River and them boats?"

"You tired of riding already? That why you want to know?" I asked, smiling.

She frowned, put her hands on her hips, and shot back, "I'd ride to Kingdom Come to get the freedom. All us jus want to know how far is all."

I didn't answer her right away. I knew I still couldn't tell them about our destination, so I decided to put focus on the journey ahead, hoping this would at least partially sate their curiosity. Once we were behind the rocks, I called them together again, had them sit down, and tried to explain the workings of the Underground Railroad as best I could, without sharing information that might cause everyone harm if put to the wrong hands.

"There are a few things I'd like to share with you, so move in and gather 'round. We're headed toward some depots, each one about a day's ride apart. These are also known as safe houses, places where we can rest and take our meals without worry of being hunted. The good people who own these homes believe in the equality of all. Even so, they're all not the same, and I want you to know this because we'll be putting our lives in their hands while with 'em. Some believe in the cause through their religion. Others simply believe we are all born equal, with the same rights to master our own lives."

I looked around the group. All were leaning forward, the looks on their faces deadly serious. "And there are those who provide aid for money. At the end, though, all do have two things in common. No matter their other motivations, they share a heartfelt desire to destroy the chains that keep you from lives of choice. They also do this at risk to everything they own and their very lives."

Here I paused and pointed toward where the Turner cabin once stood. "We're less than a mile from where a man and his wife, two of the kindest souls I've ever known, were murdered by slave catchers because it was found out their home was a depot. What they sacrificed isn't known to many. Still, it's our duty to make sure they're never forgotten. They, and the others like them, are the ones you need to thank most when we get to where you're going. Not those like me. I do this for the money it brings. You're my passengers—I'm your conductor. That's all. I get paid, and well, even if you don't make it. It's fair you know that, too. I sincerely hope you do make it, but if you don't...."

Here Lucy spoke up. "You ain't be that hard, Suh. Can't make me believe so. You just might on to be confused at times, I say."

"No, I'm not confused. I know what I want. I'm just thankful your freedom and my desires are along the same path. I'll get you to your freedom—and maybe someday I'll find what'll bring mine. For the time being, I do what I can."

I chose not to explain further. Instead, I went on, "The Underground Railroad has many routes, many destinations. Because of the Fugitive Slave Act I told you of before, many of these routes end up a long, long way from here—even as far as Canada. And what of those, like yourselves, who follow these routes? Some decide to stay at the depots along the way—knowing full well they risk their new freedom and being captured—so they can help others who will come behind 'em. Others make new lives wherever they end up. I understand the desire in both. This is a virtue of freedom. You have the power to choose."

I was about to continue when, off to my left, I saw riders

coming over the hill. Instinctively, I motioned for everyone to move in closer to the rocks. Just as I pulled my revolver from my belt, my heart pounding, I saw these riders were not foes but friends: Lucius, Tasby, and Henry.

"Stay here and keep low," I said to the group. "It's Lucius coming back with the others. I need to speak to them first."

I walked over to greet them, and Tasby was the first to dismount. "You still alive?" he said, shaking his head. "Thought you'd be six feet down by now."

"Not hardly," I said, raising my arm and wincing. "But if I recall, you sure did your best to make it so. Still can't believe you shot me. And on purpose, too, I imagine. But, no matter. I feel like a spring chicken now."

"You never goin' to let me forget that, are you?" he said, coming over to shake my hand but at the last minute circling his arms around to embrace me. "Maybe I just put another bullet in you and finish you off. Then I won't hear 'bout it no more."

"Good to see you, too," I said, backing away and pointing to his leg. "And what of your wound? Really thought you'd have no blood left. And don't I note you're limpin' more than just some? Think you might make it through the day—or should we get to diggin' a shallow grave?"

"That'd be a good laugh," he replied, "if you could use that arm to lift a shovel. You the one who should be skittish 'bout a grave. Looks like you got one foot in it already."

"Let me look at that wound," I said. He turned away from the others and carefully lowered his trousers until I could see the wound, which was starting to fester with pus. I didn't say anything for fear of frightening him more than he already was. Instead, I just shook my head. He needed a doctor—soon—and we both knew it.

Henry walked over, but he didn't offer to shake my hand. Instead, as was his usual custom, he just stood there, nodded, and smiled. If the Good Lord had put a more shy man on this earth, I'd yet to meet him. Henry was short of stature—but more than plenty big of heart. The top of his head didn't reach my shoulders and we teased him his arms were nearly skinny as willow branches, but what he lacked in size he more than made up for in his ability to write, a skill not allowed by law for our dark brothers, but one he possessed just the same.

Henry had been sold at age twelve to an elderly, very gentle man, Martin Kessens, who was the proprietor of a small printing shop in Birmingham, Alabama. The elderly gentleman's eyes were dimming, so he decided to teach Henry to read and write so he'd be able to set lines of type and operate the printing machines when needed. After first swearing Henry to secrecy and explaining the importance of never letting anyone find out about what they were set upon doing, they began what would become daily lessons: the print work in the morning, the study of words in the afternoon. Henry was quick to learn and in just over a year was conducting most business brought into the shop. However, Mr. Kessens passed in his sleep one night, and Henry was then sold to a plantation in the northeastern part of the state. Because of his size, he wasn't fit for fieldwork, and he was too clumsy for house duties. It wasn't long before his new owner, frustrated by his apparent lack of skills and abilities, sold him to a slaver passing through the area.

I was that slaver.

At least I was thought to be a slaver by the plantation owner, who I've no doubt was taken quite by surprise when the bank draft I provided him in exchange for Henry turned out not to be worth the paper on which it was printed.

While in the area to secure other passengers, I'd stayed a few days as guest of the plantation owner. One afternoon, while entering his barn to saddle my horse for a ride to the nearby town, I surprised Henry, who was studying a newspaper I'd been carrying in one of my saddlebags. When he saw me, he immediately backed away, his eyes wide with terror, and dropped the paper to the ground. He had then fallen to his knees and begged, "Please don't beat me. Just lookin' at the drawin's, Suh. That be all."

At the moment I had caught him with the paper, I noticed his lips moving as his eyes went side to side, so I was fairly certain he had been looking at more than the drawings. "Just get my horse saddled," I said, calmly bending down to retrieve the paper. "And don't let anyone catch you with this again, understand?"

I knew if he could read, I could use his help in my line of work, so I immediately inquired whether he was for sale. His owner was so happy to get rid of him he let me purchase him for the sum of $50, which was about ten times below what a male slave of his age should have brought in that part of the state. However, the price didn't matter; I'd have paid $500 or more if need be, especially because I had no intention of making good the bank draft anyway.

Once we were to free territory, and after Henry came to feel he could trust me, he shared knowledge of his skills. For a long time I'd been seeking a printer sympathetic to the cause who'd be willing to prepare false bills of sale for those I spirited to the north—and false documents of freedom for those I brought to the Elgin Settlement in Canada. Those documents, while not absolute guarantees of security, did help many in their quest for new lives, both in Canada and back in America. I asked Henry if he'd be interested in making his mark as a printer of these documents, and he readily accepted the challenge, even though such work, if discovered, carried with it a death sentence in most places we'd travel.

Upon our return to Elgin, I provided him with enough funds to construct a small print shop, with attached living quarters, on a small parcel of land at the west end of the main road through the settlement. In exchange for this, I asked only that he help prepare such documents as would help during my excursions. At the same time, I promised him a small share of my profits when the documents helped the success of one of my ventures. After I purchased the necessary equipment and machinery, Henry began his work, work that was beyond the skills of any I'd ever known in that profession. Of necessity, we kept most of his work secret, but he was soon taking in other orders from those in the settlement and beyond. His reputation as a printer spread, and he was turning a tidy sum for himself, most of which he shared with those less fortunate. I wanted him to stay in Elgin, to keep watch on my home and property the times I was away, but he nearly always insisted upon coming along with me. Lucius and Tasby were not well-versed in reading and writing, so I needed Henry—and he knew it. Through the years, his skills had often removed us from harm's way, and for that I was truly grateful. Still, he was a fragile soul, and I worried about him constantly.

Lucius finally walked over and said, "Found these two idiots playin' cards off in the woods. Playin' cards! Weren't watchin' the trail a whit. Sittin' so close together I coulda killed both with one shot."

Tasby and Henry just shrugged their shoulders. I groaned, then said, "You know better. One of you must stand guard at all times. If this happens again, and you somehow manage not to get yourselves killed, I swear I'm going to let Lucius shoot you—and we'll find others to take your place. And don't you think I'm kiddin' either."

"Oh, I b'lieve you. Truly I do," Tasby replied. "But wouldn't had to play cards if you'd been more on time. That shoulder slow you down, did it?"

I glared at him and said, "Never you mind. Just mark my words. Don't do it again."

I called Toby over to mind their horses. As he led the horses away, I asked Lucius, Tasby, and Henry to follow me over by the brush because I had something to tell them I didn't want our passengers to hear just yet

"I'd say we've been on the high side of good fortune so far. Looks like everyone from West Liberty has given up on us, and the slavers Lucius and I came across, even if they find the one of theirs we sent to his reward, won't likely follow. No, I'd say this is about as clean as we can be for now."

I lowered my voice. "I know it'll be a first this far north, but I'm going to suggest we split up again."

That immediately caught their attention, and all three looked up, waiting for my next words. "We can make light of it all we want, but Tasby's leg needs care, and I'm some better but still carrying a fever. You know we can't go to a doctor in any of the towns up ahead. It would be too risky. But, we're not all that far away from Hanover, so Tasby and I need to get ourselves there fast as we can so Dr. Robertson can tend to us."

"And what about them?" Lucius asked, pointing toward our passengers. "What do we do with 'em?"

"You and Henry are going to take 'em to Columbus—to the Keltons. They'll remember you. And they'll provision you and help make the arrangements to get you and our passengers to the next depot at Mansfield. From there, this time of year it should be an easy ride to Ashtabula—and across to Canada. We'll meet you back at Elgin Settlement when we can."

"But, John..." Lucius said, his voice questioning. "I've never...."

"You're ready for this," I said, reaching over and placing my hand on his shoulder. "You were born to this work. You don't need me. And besides, it'll be good for you—good experience. I won't always be around, you know."

Lucius was still not convinced, so I continued, "We'd just slow you down and likely get everyone caught. Or, we'd just up and die along the trail. This way, Lord willing, we can get our wounds taken care of and get back to you soon as we're able."

"I don't know," he hesitated. "We always work together. You think I can do this?"

"Well, I ain't so sure 'bout you," Tasby needled him. "Like as not you get everyone killed off, and we won't get a cent out of this."

Henry, to this point quiet as ever, joined, pretending to shiver, "I don't know, either. Don't know if I want to move on with him. The way he looks at me sometimes I'm feared he's just waitin' for a chance to sell me off again."

"Good," I said. "Then maybe that fear will keep you away from those cards—and keep your eyes and ears on the trail for a change."

They all chuckled, including Tasby. Taking advantage of the moment, I turned to Lucius. "You know I don't like to get close to others, and I seldom offer words of praise—especially to you three—but I'm going to say this anyway. I couldn't be more proud of you if you were my own kin, my own brother. I know you can do this. I have no doubt. None at all."

Lucius and Henry finally seemed resigned to the charge I'd given them, so I pointed toward our passengers. "I suppose I should say a few words to them about this. Then get ready to move. Ought to be safe enough for you from here to Columbus if you can get across the Scioto River and use the water to shield yourselves from the east. If there are any slavers in the area, they'll keep to the east of the river this time of season. And don't worry about fording the river. Our passengers made it across the Ohio, so I judge they won't have any problems with the Scioto. While you're movin' north, Tasby and I will head straight for Hanover. We can travel in broad daylight, so it won't take us long."

Pausing one last time, I added, "Well, give me a few minutes with them, and then let's get about it. Time's wastin'."

Our passengers were standing and waiting for me as if they already knew a change of plans was in the wind. They were still very frightened, but I felt it best to be direct with them and not mince any words.

"You're all going with Lucius and Henry to the next depot. Lucy has done a fine job of keeping me in the saddle, but it won't be long before I need more than a poultice to keep upright. And Tasby over there has a wound that a doctor should look at. We know one—a good one—who helps men like us. We're soon off to see him. But, I don't want you to worry."

As I looked at this group, I could tell they needed as much convincing as the last one. "Lucius is a much better woodsman than me. He knows the land as good as anyone we could conjure.

That's the truth. He'll get you along safe, so don't you have a worry. Narry a one. I've also a favor to ask. Please keep close to Henry and help keep him safe. He's the most important of all of us. The next time you camp, he's going to ask your names. Know what he's going to do with 'em? He's going to write them to papers that will show you have your freedom. Don't lose those papers. They might mean the difference between life and death someday."

Seeing their stunned faces, I felt I needed to say more. "It's been an honor to travel with you. I won't forget you."

Lucy stepped forward and asked, "Will we see you 'gain, Suh?"

"I think it likely. After all, I know where y'all are headed, and I'm always there by and by. I'll look for you. I promise I will."

One at a time, each moved forward and nodded to me without words.

Toby clasped my hand. "The Lord be with you, Suh. And keep you from harm."

"Thank you—all of you," I said, turning, and quickly walking away. I didn't look back.

I never could.

....

Not quite an hour after we separated from the others, Tasby started in, as he always did when we were alone:

"John."

"Yes, Tasby."

"Why you still doin' this? I seen you bound, hog-tied, beat with a knotted club, whipped, and shot more times than I can conjure back up. You used most of the nine lives. And you ain't no holy man, neither. Why you still doin' this?"

"Why, for the money, of course."

"Could make a lot more robbin' banks. I seen that money we left back there to West Liberty. And it'd be lot safer."

"But then I wouldn't have the pleasure of your company, would I?"

"My company ain't worth spit. You tell me—truth now—why you here?"

"How many times I have to say it? For the money."

"You a bad liar, John. Your share most times give to those we take north, to put 'em to a new start. Your pockets then empty. Sometimes I think you just crazy."

"I know many who agree with you," I said. "But the money is important to me. Think what it buys. Think how we pay for our horses, our food, the stores we need for each trip. Couldn't do what we do without that money. And, while I'm thinking about it, I want to ask you something. What happens to your share? How is it you're always broke?"

He didn't respond. I already knew the answer, and I suspected he knew that. Tasby kept just enough of his share from each expedition for the barest of necessities. The rest he gave to the new church at Elgin Settlement—to help care for those who arrived with nothing but their newly-gained freedom.

"So don't you talk to me about money. It goes through your hands like spring water through a sieve. If you ever had in your pockets two coins to rub together, I'd faint dead away. How's that so?"

Tasby didn't like talking about himself, so I knew such a question would close his mouth for at least a few miles. As we rode along in silence, I began soaking in the beauty around us. Nowhere other than in this part of Ohio had I ever seen so many pear trees blossoming in late spring. Their white and pink petals were gently spinning to the ground as we made our way up the trail. Off to our right, a stand of cottonwood trees added their snow-white seeds to the breeze swirling around us. Farther off in the distance, I caught sight of a doe darting into the first of the lilac bushes to show bloom. As always, however, these moments of peace didn't last, especially when Tasby was close at hand. I was near to falling asleep in the saddle when Tasby spoke up again.

"John."

"Yes, Tasby."

"I'm scared of that Dr. Robertson. I think he just as soon chop off my leg as look at it. I s'pose he make me one of his—what they call 'em?—'speriments? He ain't quit cuttin' up bodies, you know. Just might take your arm, too. You watch! We look powerful odd, me with one leg and you just one arm. What good we be then?"

I knew there was more than a touch of truth in Tasby's worries. Dr. Robertson once told me a cousin of his was schooled three times as much to become a pastor as Robertson was to become a healer. For him, the inequity in education was appalling and mightily misguided. Granted, for most people the soul likely takes more care and shepherding than their earthly bodies. Still, without the skills of healing, many of those same souls would prematurely end up in heaven—or elsewhere. Believing this way, I wasn't bothered by the stories surrounding Dr. Robertson. According to many of the locals in Hanover, he had long been suspected of digging up the remains of the freshly buried, taking them to secret locations, and cutting into the bodies to study them before taking the deceased back to the cemetery. One evening, after several glasses of brandy, I found the courage—or foolishness—to ask him about the stories. He laughed—but didn't deny them. I didn't press the matter any further, but I left his parlor that evening fairly certain I didn't want to die anywhere near Hanover just in case.

But no matter how he schooled himself in the art of medicine, he was still a man of vital importance to the Underground Railroad. Only a few of us in the cause knew of this, but his home had been built so that on the second floor a room existed that appeared visible from the lane below, complete with window and curtains,—but could not be found from within the house. A false wall in an upper room hid this secret location so it was impossible to detect by those entering that part of the home. The only access was through a secret entrance behind the bookcases. This room was where many runaways had been housed until such time they could be sent along the next part of their journey. Many also believed it was where he brought bodies for study. I suspected the same, but that wasn't what concerned me the most about Dr. Robertson. He was already leading a secret life in helping so many to their freedom. If the other stories were true and he were caught, the cause would lose a man so important to our efforts. So, selfishly, I was concerned about Dr. Robertson keeping all his secrets, no matter what they actually were.

Turning to Tasby, I said, "Whatever Dr. Robertson is, he's still the best healer I've known, and we need him—both of us. That leg of yours isn't gettin' any better, and my shoulder feels like a hot iron's been touched to it. Let's not worry about the good doctor. We need to worry about getting to his home—and fast. So, how 'bout you shut up for a while and get that nag of yours at least halfway to a gallop. Think you can keep up with me?"

He did shut up, but as I knew would be the case, the silence didn't last long. Not even half of an hour later he was at it again. This time he brought up the one subject I was hoping he'd avoid—but knew he'd land upon sooner or later.

"John."

"Yes, Tasby."

"She gonna be madder than a wet hornet, you know. You best sleep with one eye open—or she like as not stab you when you sleep. Wouldn't blame her. You lie to her—again."

Drawing out my words, I said, "I did not lie. I never said I'd marry her."

"Not what she say," Tasby shot back. "She say you do everything 'cept get on one knee. That you near on to beg her."

"Must have been in her dreams," I replied. "I certainly recall no such scene."

Tasby was referring to Catherine Rhodes, known as "Cat" to her closest of friends and acquaintances. Cat was the inkeeper of the Spread Eagle Tavern in Hanover. Her uncle, William Rhodes, had built the Spread Eagle in 1837 during the heyday of shipping along the Sandy and Beaver Canal, a waterway constructed to help farmers and businessmen move goods along to the major markets of the region. The Spread Eagle soon came to be known far and wide as the best choice for a meal, a drink, and a comfortable sleep for those traveling through. Its brisk patronage masked the fact it was one of the most important depots in northeastern Ohio.

Cat's aunt, Dorothy Rhodes, had served as innkeeper until she was lost in a cholera outbreak four years before. Her uncle, mired in his grief, turned away from his duties at the Spread Eagle, and for a time it fell to disarray. Cat, out of family obligation and pride, took charge and soon had all returned to its former state. Her uncle, finally able to live with his loss, was so grateful for her actions he kept her on at her work, work he had discovered she was more than well suited for.

Cat was nearing the age of thirty, and she'd yet to marry, a fact she reminded me of at every opportunity. In her, I saw everything I held beautiful in a woman. She was tall and well-proportioned. Her eyes were light hazel, and her auburn hair, a mass of curls cascading half way down her back, swished and swayed as she walked. Her lips and smile were captivating and always drew me in close. However, for most men, her beauty faded the moment she opened her mouth. She was never shy about sharing her views on any subject brought forth in the tavern. And with great precision and accuracy, she could, and often did, use all the words the canal workers carried in with them.

She was also good with a knife, a skill that caused many a burly man to shrink away like a spider on a spit. Knife throwing matches between drunken hunters and trappers were frequent occurrences at the tavern. The sight of a woman throwing a knife most often brought laughter and teasing from the men. Cat learned she could lessen the tensions, help keep the peace, and preserve the furnishings by joining in during the matches. Along the way, and as her skill improved, the laughter and teasing stopped. Her skill with a knife didn't bother me, but it did most men. For me, she was a woman strong and without pretense.

Others thought her overbearing and loud—and dangerous. Why I was so attracted to her I couldn't quite put to words, but I did know this much: she had my heart, even though I dared not reveal it to her.

Tasby interrupted my thoughts and said, "You strung her 'long for years now. If you don't marry her soon, wouldn't want to be in your boots."

"I can't marry her—at least not now. There's just too much risk to it. What kind of life could I give her?"

"She don't care. All she want is you." He laughed. "I want to be there when she see you this time. Might just chase you with a axe!"

"She might at that," I said, matter of factly. "She just might."

"Will sure be fun to see," Tasby laughed again.

"Shut up and ride," I said, kicking my horse into a cantor. "That's enough of you."

Sadly, it wasn't.

After two full days and nights of Tasby's observations on everything from who had the more serious wound—he allowed he did, of course—to what he saw as my faults as a human being—too numerous to recount—an idea occurred to me: if Dr. Robertson's treatment didn't kill him, I most certainly would.

The rest of the journey to Hanover couldn't come fast enough.

....

Chapter 8

Licking Our Wounds

Hanover, Ohio

JUST AT SUNUP, WE FOUND ourselves at the rear door of the summer kitchen of the Spread Eagle Tavern. Through the open window to our right I heard a distinctive, commanding voice call out, "Go fetch a pail of eggs. Got hungry men comin'. And if you two drop any this time, I swear I'll make you eat 'em raw. And don't you tarry. I want you back here before I get this skillet hot or I'll roast your ears with it. Now get gone!"

It was Cat.

In the blink of an eye, Cat's helpers, two young girls wide-eyed and full to purpose, swung open the door and darted past us.

Tasby whispered to me, "She already full of fire. I'm not rappin' on that door. She your woman—not mine."

"Move off to the side," I said, playfully shoving him. "I'll do it."

When I turned around, she was standing in the doorway right before us.

"I thought I heard some men," she said, flatly, staring right at us. "Guess I was wrong, though. All I see are a couple of jackasses." With that, she quickly swung shut the door.

"Bet she goin' to get the axe," Tasby said, his eyes widening. "Don't know 'bout you, but I runnin' off."

I grabbed his arm and held firm. "I'll try again—jackass," I said. "She'll let us in."

"You take a wager on it?" he asked.

As I reached for the handle, the door opened again.

"How bad is it this time?" Cat asked, crossing her arms. "Posse close behind? You wounded? Out of money again? Starved out? Come now—loosen those tongues. I don't have all day."

Before I could respond, Tasby spoke right up. "He come to marry you!"

The door was instantly slammed shut again, the concussion of which caused puffs of dust and dirt to swirl around our heads.

"You truly are a jackass," I said, stunned. "How could you possibly say something like that at a time like this? You lose your mind completely?"

"Just tryin' to help is all. Thought that get us inside for sure."

"Well, stop trying to help. You just keep quiet and let me think of something."

The door again swung open. "Well, you two comin' in? Might as well. Fannin' this door so, I've already let in enough flies to fill a room. From your looks and smell, they'll likely light on you—and stay off the food. At least you'll be good enough for that. But catchin' flies is all you look good for."

With a look of sheer disgust, she added, "You comin'?"

While stepping inside, I said, "Thanks, Cat. I...."

"I know," she interrupted. "You're sorry. You feel bad. You feel guilty. You feel.... But I can tell you this. You and me are done. We're over. I want nothin' to do with you. Not now—not ever again."

After seeing how stiffly I was holding my arm and Tasby's obvious limp, she shook her head and said, "But I'm not going to let you die here. That'd be bad for trade. Don't think anyone else is up and movin' yet, so we better get you to Dr. Robertson. He better look to those wounds."

I started to thank her, but she stopped me. "Don't you talk to me," she said, her voice firm. "I don't want to hear anything you could say. Not one peep, you hear me? And where's your coat?

Never seen you without one before. You look 'bout naked as a jaybird."

Out of the corner of my eye, I saw her turn toward Tasby and wink. He grinned and started to speak, but the look she gave him I guessed could have frozen stone.

In the cellar of the Spread Eagle, there was a tunnel used for quick exits and at times secret entry. Out of habit I started for the steps to the cellar, but Cat corralled me and said, "Now just where do you think you're headed? If you're not being chased, no need for that. It's early enough we can just walk over, but I better go first to make sure he's there—and that he's not tending to someone already. Then I'll come back for you, but for the life of me I don't know why I should."

She narrowed her eyes and looked me up and down. "And I suppose you're starved, right? Here—gnaw on this while I'm gone."

From the sideboard she picked up a plate of hot biscuits and a small bowl of honey, then set them on the table before us.

"Well, go ahead—eat!" she commanded. "And sit down before you fall down. You look sick as dogs."

The words weren't out of her mouth before Tasby dug in with both hands.

"You're welcome!" she shouted at him while shaking her head. "Wouldn't stop eating for his own burial. What a sight! Does he have any manners at all?"

"None that I've ever noticed," I replied. "So, I'll thank you for the both of us. Thank you, Cat, I...."

"You better stick a hand in that plate, or you'll have nothing but crumbs. Look at that man—never seen anything like it. I've seen hogs eat slower than that."

Tasby, who had stopped using his knife to spread the honey on his biscuits was now instead simply dipping them between bites. He smiled at both of us but didn't slow his movements one bit.

"Well, you goin' to eat anything?" she asked. Before I could reply, she turned and was on her way out the door.

The biscuits were superb, just what my aching stomach needed. A large coffee pot was sitting on an edge table, so I reached over to see if it was hot. It was, so I poured us some.

"Here," I said, handing a cup to Tasby. "Wash 'em down with this before you choke to death."

Without looking up he grabbed the cup, gulped half of its contents, and immediately reached for another biscuit.

It wasn't long before Cat returned. The moment she entered the door she said, "Get up. He's ready for you. Street's still empty, so we need to be off right now. I don't want nobody to spy you with all that blood on those rags you're wearin'. Think you can make it—or do you want me to carry you?" she asked, sarcastically.

"You can carry me," Tasby said, smiling and grabbing his leg.

"I ought to carry you to the cemetery instead. It's where you both are likely to end up soon enough anyway. Now get up!"

"Thanks for the encouragement," I said, frowning. "You're all heart."

"What I am," she replied, "is of half a mind to shoot you right now for the reward money, so you better follow me and keep your mouths shut."

"Yes, Ma'am," I said, bowing slightly toward her. "Anything you say."

Then, turning to Tasby, I said, "Put the last of those biscuits in your pocket—'cause I don't think she'll let us back here any time soon."

Cat glared at me, "Get movin'! And don't you die in the street on the way. Got too much to do today to stand around and make up a story about what you were doin' here."

"Yes, you're all heart," I repeated. "No doubt about it."

The look she gave me told me to close my mouth and follow silently. I motioned for Tasby to do the same.

When we reached Dr. Robertson's door, Cat didn't bother to knock. Instead, she opened it and urged us inside. Dr. Robertson, who was sitting at a small desk and leafing through one of his medical books, immediately stood up and walked toward me, extending his hand.

"John," he said, "so good to see you again. What has it been—four, five months?"

"Seems longer," I said, firmly shaking his hand. "Much longer."

Cat interrupted us and said, "I've work to do. Do your worst, Doc. I mean worst—that's what they both deserve."

Before either of us could reply, she was gone.

"Seems she isn't so happy with you this morning," he said, lowering his glasses. "I take it you still haven't proposed?"

"You, too?" I asked, laughing. "Don't I get any say in the matter?"

"Do men ever have a say in matters of the heart?" he asked, looking past me at Tasby, who was rubbing his leg. "We can debate the point later over some hot rum, but I believe I better start with the examinations. Follow me," he said, pointing to a door toward the rear of the room.

Dr. Robertson was a tall, stocky man just past the age of fifty with wavy hair that had turned almost full to white, making him appear much older. He walked with a slight limp, the result of a mule kicking him in the knee when he was a small boy.

Shortly after leaving his family homestead just south of Cincinnati, he had studied medicine with Dr. John Potter, a fine doctor in New Lisbon. Working alongside Dr. Potter, he soaked in the knowledge and skills of the profession for two years before striking out on his own, settling first in Salem, Ohio. However, it wasn't quite a year after that he was asked by the town council, for reasons still shrouded in mystery, to move on.

There were plenty of rumors that followed him when he first came to Hanover, but the townspeople chose not to investigate any of them because Dr. Robertson appeared the same week the town doctor of over forty years passed away. Doctors in this part of the state were scarce as hens' teeth, so all were grateful to gain another healer so quickly, no matter the circumstances that led him to Hanover. Whatever his past, it didn't bother me. With my own background, I couldn't throw any stones. In some ways, the fact we both harbored secrets formed a bond between us. And, above all, through the years and his treatments of my many wounds, I had learned I could trust him with my life. In return, I had told him on more than one occasion that my own special skills with arms would be at his disposal should anything in his past call upon need for them.

However, as close as we'd become, he was still hesitant to share even a sliver of his past with me, and I never pressed him. At the same time, he never asked me the specific circumstances behind the chunks of lead he removed from my body or the wounds that required a good sewing. As odd as it had seemed at first, I grew to enjoy this friendship of silence. On occasions when we did meet for drink and a meal, the talk most often turned to the local and regional happenings described in the town newspaper, which was welcome diversion for us both. Neither of us could afford to get too close to others, so friendships were few and far between. In many ways, therefore, we needed each other, needed the time together to escape the darkness in our lives—if only for a few fleeting moments.

"I better look to you first," he said, taking Tasby by the arm and urging him to stretch out on an examining table. He eased Tasby's trousers to his knees, allowing for a full view of the wound.

"I've seen better," he said, reaching into a tray of instruments and picking up a long, silver probe and a scalpel. He placed them on the table right next to Tasby's leg.

"What you goin' to do with them?" Tasby asked, swiftly sitting himself upright. "Ain't cuttin' my leg off, are you?"

Dr. Robertson frowned and said, sternly, "You get back down on that table. Cutting off your leg is the last thing I'm thinking about, but if we don't get rid of the poison in there...."

After examining Tasby's leg, he turned to me and said, "It's plain what I need to do with him. Let me look at that shoulder now."

As soon as I removed my shirt and he looked at the poultice, he said, "You do this?"

"No," I replied. "A friend did it. Someone I met along the way."

He smiled and said, "Well, that friend of yours probably saved your life. I've seen this kind of wound before. You've still got some bullet left in there. It's probably a fairly good fragment. I'm going to have to take it out, but I think you'll live."

He shook his head. "If I recall correctly, this'll be the fourth I've removed from you, right? I'm going to start saving the pieces and make a necklace."

Dr. Robertson walked to a cabinet and withdrew a small bottle and two glasses. He pulled the cork from the bottle and poured a small amount of liquid into each glass. From where I was sitting I detected the faint odor of cinnamon.

"Here, drink this," he said, handing each of us a glass.

"What is it?" Tasby asked, his voice ripe with suspicion.

"Laudanum. It'll make you sleep and help ease the pain."

"I'd rather have whiskey," Tasby replied. "You got some?"

"I'm sure you would," Dr. Robertson shot back. "But you'll take the laudanum and like it. Drink it down. Now."

He walked to another cabinet and drew down a large blue bottle, an oblong glass bowl, and a small stack of what appeared to be pieces of cloth.

Sensing my curiosity, he volunteered, "What I need to do to both of you will have some pain. So, in addition to the laudanum, I'm going to administer this to both of you. It's called ether. Don't be frightened of it. This is actually very simple and safe. I'll put a piece of cloth in this bowl and pour some ether to it. Then I'll put the bowl over your nose and have you breathe deeply. You'll be asleep almost instantly, and you shouldn't feel anything I'm doing to you. Then, when you wake up, the laudanum will continue to keep a goodly amount of the pain at bay."

We both looked at him skeptically. "I've only made use of it a few times, so I'll be truthful and tell you I'm still learning. However, what I've seen so far I like very much. And besides, if I don't use it, I'll have to hit you over the head with a log and render you senseless so you don't scream and squirm around while I work. Which would you rather have?"

"I'd rather have whiskey," Tasby said, "Won't feel nothin' then!"

Dr. Robertson didn't reply. Instead, he finished his preparations and placed the bowl over Tasby's nose. Tasby started to sit up, but his eyes rolled back and his body went limp almost immediately.

"That'll do," Dr. Robertson said. Then he turned to me. "No need for you to watch this, so I'm going to have you get on that other table and see if you can get to sleep. The laudanum should be working any time now. Close your eyes and rest. I'll get to you soon as I can."

Out of the corner of my eye, I watched him pour alcohol on Tasby's thigh. The ether must have been working its magic because Tasby didn't move a muscle. Dr. Robertson then picked up a thin scalpel.

I was growing very sleepy, so I decided to close my eyes just for a minute....

....

When I woke up, Dr. Robertson was placing a large bandage across my shoulder.

"Aren't you abolitionists supposed to be men of peace?" he asked, shaking his head. "If you get much more of this peace, you aren't going to be around long."

"Abolitionist?" I replied. "I'm a businessman, plain and simple. That's all."

"What you are is lucky to be alive," he said, tightening the bandage with one last tug. "Here, put your eyes on this."

He picked up a small dish and placed it on my chest. Resting in the center of it were two large shards of lead.

"Almost missed the second one. Was just behind the muscle. Those make either five or six I've dug out of you. I've lost track. Maybe I can give that necklace to Cat as a wedding present."

"You aren't very funny," I replied. "And when did you pull these out of me? I don't remember a thing."

"Ether," he replied. "That's why you don't remember, and I'm glad of it. It's going to change the world of medicine, you mark my words."

Then he asked, "How's the arm now?"

"I ache pretty good," I replied, "but not near as bad as before."

"Good sign. That means I've done my job proper. It also appears what you're always saying likely is true—that you're too mean to die."

I smiled and asked, "How's Tasby?"

"He should be dead, but I'll be hanged if I know why he's not. I drew out the poison and did the best I could. There's so much we just don't know about why or how the body heals. We learn more all the time, but for now, we just do the best we can— and then pray."

He paused and added, "He's strong. I'll need to keep him at rest for another two days or so, but I think he could ride in three if he had to."

"Thank you for everything—again," I said. "My visits seem to be getting more and more regular."

"Do me a favor and don't make them too regular. You won't be around long if this continues."

Thanking him reminded me I had brought something for him. "Doc, would you mind finding that saddlebag Cat was carrying when she helped me in here? There's something in it you should see."

"It's still out on a chair. I'll go take a look."

When he returned, I started to sit up, but my shoulder immediately reminded me I best keep on my back. I said. "Untie the flap and fish out the box in there."

When he did, I asked him to open it. A look of surprise spread across his face. The day before the bank robbery in West Liberty, I had been in the general store when a new set of surgical instruments arrived for the town's doctor. The proprietor was quite busy that day, so I casually mentioned I was on my way to the doctor's office—and would be honored to deliver the box. I just didn't mention to which doctor I'd be delivering it....

"For me?" he asked, not looking my direction.

"For you. Just a small way of thanks is all. Thought you might find them useful."

"I don't know what to say," he said, his voice rising. "They're... they're beautiful."

"Maybe it's a selfish gift on my part. Maybe those will save this sorry life someday."

He took the instruments out one at a time, studied each carefully, and placed them in a row on the table in front of him. Finally, he said, "Thank you, John. I've read about these new scalpels. Wherever in the world did you find them?"

"Let's just say I liberated 'em and leave it at that. Knew they'd go to a good cause."

"And they shall," he said.

After carefully placing the instruments back in the box, he inspected my bandage again. As he did, he cleared his throat, lowered his voice, and asked, his tone serious as I'd heard him in a long time, "I don't know if you've noticed, but Cat has a bad cough. Had it for quite some time now, and I'm growing concerned. She'd be much better off if she'd move on west, and I've tried a good dozen times to make her believe it so. However, for some reason she would like to stay here."

He looked me right in the eyes.

"You're beating 'round the bush, Doc," I said. "Yes, I can imagine why, but that's a bad reason for her to suffer her health. If it's best she goes west, then she should go west."

"If you care for her, and I know you do more than you'll ever admit, you might want to see if you can do something to light a fire under her. The sooner, the better."

The look on his face told me I needed to change the subject, so I asked, "And what about you? You movin'—or stayin'? Might you be headed to the west?"

"Here I'm the best doctor around—the only doctor around. I'm needed, and that's enough for me for now."

I chose my next words carefully. "But, is it safe for you here? I know a little about movin' on and covering up the past. One more change of scene for you might not be such a terrible idea."

He shook his head and said, "I assume that's your polite way of referring to the stories that seem to be making the rounds. Oh, I know about them—that I spend a little too much time up at the cemetery. You believe those stories?"

"I might be the only person who hopes they are true. I understand how difficult it can be to do something you feel is right, especially when those around you aren't sure of your motives. I've always believed as long as a man's heart is good, his actions shouldn't be faulted. Your heart's good. That's all I need to know."

He nodded but didn't reply. Next, he filled a glass with water, added some powder from a small envelope, and handed it to me. "Drink this. It'll make you sleep again. When you wake, you should be ready to get up and move around."

As I swallowed his concoction, Dr. Robertson pulled a chair next to the table, sat down, and asked, this time his voice even more serious, "And you, my friend. You thought of engaging in a new line of work?"

"I have," I replied. "My father taught me a great deal about commerce, and I've been thinking the time might be close for me to get to that new Kansas Territory."

"Kansas Territory? Why there?" he asked, leaning forward.

"Because I think a shrewd man could do well for himself supplying stores and provisions for those moving farther west. I've been told there aren't many outposts along the main trails out there."

"You—a shopkeeper?" he interrupted, laughing.

"Yes, a shopkeeper. One who just might be able to help along a good many souls leaving the south for a new beginning. Who knows? Some of 'em might just need a place to stay while they rest up or make themselves scarce. I might be able to teach them a skill or two—maybe even to read and write some—before they continue on."

"I understand now," he said. "Some of those people going through wouldn't be runaways, now would they?"

"Maybe," I said. "You never know." Beginning to feel the effects of the drink, my eyes started to grow heavy.

I'd lay money on it," he replied.

"They need doctors there, too. Might be a fine place for a healer to find new patients."

"It might be at that," he said. "First, though, I want you back to sleep. It'll be the best thing for you. So, close those eyes—and think of Kansas Territory while I go look in again on Tasby."

He stopped at the door. "Thank you for the instruments. I...."

"You're keeping me awake," I said, raising my voice. "How's a man supposed to get any rest around here?"

Dr. Robertson just shook his head, turned, and left the room.

....

Chapter 9

"Wanted—Dead or Alive"

THE NEXT MORNING, JUST AFTER first light, I was already wide awake when Cat opened the door and walked in carrying a small tray. I was standing to the right of the curtains at the side window, so she didn't see me right away.

"Good morning!" I said, nearly frightening her out of her skin. She jumped back, and I heard dishes clinking against each other as she steadied the tray.

"Good morning yourself!" she shot back while placing the tray roughly on the table closest to me. "Ham and eggs—and more biscuits. Eat! Doc says you need it to get back your strength."

Then, moving to her and trying to draw her close, I said, quietly, "Cat, I feel some dizzy. Could you please help me to the chair?"

"You all right?" she asked, concerned, stepping forward to inspect the sling holding my left arm.

"I am now," I said, putting my other arm around her and kissing her fully on the lips. She tried backing away, but I tightened my grip, pulling her even closer.

When she finally pulled back, she said, "And here I was feelin' sorry for you. Thought you were truly on your sickbed. Should have known better. You're a terrible person, John Fairfield."

"But you've known that for a long time," I protested. "What's different now?"

She moved back close to me and said, "What's different is I'm tired of you breakin' my heart. You come and go like the wind. I never know where you are—or who you're with. You're a ghost. Nothin' more."

"We've talked about this before," I reminded her. "I have to be a ghost. Deep down, you know that. If I ever get caught, you know what'll happen."

She bit her lower lip and looked as if tears were close. This time I gently pulled her close and hugged her. She, in turn, wrapped her arms around me and put her head to my shoulder.

"Look, Doc said if I was up to it, I was to take a good walk this morning. Why don't you come with me? We'll go down by the canal—where we used to go. We'll talk more about this."

She eased back from me and said, "If you want to talk, you must still have powerful fever or be right at the edge of dyin'. Got to be one of the two."

"I'm fine," I said. "Just a little tired is all, but the walk'll take care of that. Will you join me?"

"Eat your breakfast first, and I'll think about it. I've got to get back to the Spread Eagle and get the others to their work. I might be back. Then again, I might not. Don't get your hopes up."

"I'll be right here waiting for you," I replied. "And thank you for the breakfast. I am ready to eat."

Cat looked as if she wanted to say something else, but she didn't. Instead, she turned, and without looking back, walked briskly from the room.

....

The Sandy & Beaver Canal, just a few years before the favored route for transporting goods and crops across northern Ohio, was fast becoming little more than a figment of memory. Once the railroad had come through, the same shipments made their way to destination days ahead of what it had taken the rafts and small boats that once dotted the canal. The town of Hanover, the hub of the canal activity during its heyday, had initially grown to a population above two thousand. Now, however, well over half of those, those who had made their living working at the docks and on the water, had moved on, and more and more were leaving every month. If it weren't for the Spread Eagle Tavern and the fact the many roads and trails leading to and from Hanover were the best in the region for those traveling by wagon, the whole area would likely have already dried up and blown away.

"Hard to believe it's the same place," Cat said as we carefully walked arm in arm along the well-worn path just above the canal. "Look at the vines and scrub growing up everywhere. All this was once cleared all the way down to water's edge. And do you smell that? Canal's gettin' rank. The water just doesn't get moved anymore."

"I'm surprised how much has changed in just the past half year," I said, shaking my head. "If I close my eyes, I can still see and hear the activity that was always right across there at the loading docks. There isn't a soul there now, and it's already well into the morning. Year ago at this time there would have been boats lined all the way up around the bend waiting turn for loading. Now there are none. But, I guess nothin' stays the same. That's just the order of life."

I looked again at the deserted docks. "But there is an advantage for me in all this. The canal could have other uses now, those more to my purpose."

"How do you mean?" Cat asked, surprised.

"Think you can find me a boat captain? I'd like to visit with one."

"I know one or two, but why ever so?" she asked, dropping my hand and stepping back. "What do you have in mind?"

"I thought of this on the journey here," I replied. "There are barely enough boats on the water any more to make a ripple. Everything's growing back along the banks, and the tunnels through the mountains to the east are still there. If a man wanted to move special cargo through here and not be discovered, the canal would be the way to do it now. The travel might be slow, but it would also be hidden from view—and there'd be no tracks left behind for anyone to follow."

"You're serious?" Cat said, disbelief filling her voice. "By boat?"

"Yes, by boat. By cover of night, no one would be the wiser. And, the passengers could get a good rest if they didn't have to worry about falling out of a saddle. Time in the boat would get them ready for the last and most dangerous leg of the journey north. What do you think of the idea?"

"I think it's just one more risk—one more way you are going to end up at the end of a rope. Why are you still doing this? Tell me truthful."

"For the money," I quickly replied. "What else?"

"I know that's not true," she said, "Not a lick. But I'm not sure the risks you're takin' are worth your life." She reached into a pocket at the side of her dress, drew out a piece of thick paper, unfolded it, and handed it to me. "I couldn't figure when I was goin' to share this with you, but I expect this is good a time as any. This is what you best be thinking about now—not how to boat some canal. You've been a wanted man as long as I've known you, but now there's a face to go with the bounty."

It was a wanted poster—and I was the one wanted.

"How'd you come by this?" I asked while scanning its contents.

"A trapper brought it in. Had just come from Tennessee and said they were tacked up in towns all his journey north."

As I studied the poster, she went on, "That drawin' doesn't appear like you at all, thanks to goodness. But they got names for you now. Look to the bottom."

Under the crude illustration, which made me look a good many years older and quite stout, several names were listed: Fairborn, Fairchild, Freemont, Johnson, and Fredericks. The first three I had used in the past; the last two I had not. Smaller script below the names stated I had been seen in Kentucky, Tennessee, Mississippi, and Georgia—and possibly even Alabama. I had conducted "expeditions" in them all.

"And did you note this?" Cat said, pointing several inches

above the image. There, in large, bold type, were the words "Wanted—Dead or Alive" followed by the reward sum of $2,500.

"I'm flattered," I said. "I'd halfway think about turning myself in for that pot of gold."

"This isn't funny," she said, flicking the paper with her finger. "Every piece of trail scum from here to 'Bama will now be lookin' for you. You know that, right?"

I didn't reply. Instead, I said, more to myself than to her, "Why such a big reward?"

No sooner had the words come from my lips than I noted the reason. At the very bottom edge of the poster was the name and location of the printer responsible for the poster: "Thompson—Jackson, Tennessee." Just over a year before, I had been assigned the deliverance of seven slaves from the plantation of Frederick Allanton—of Jackson, Tennessee. While there, under the guise of procurer of land for the railroad, I had also secured the sum of $3,000 from Mr. Allanton, money that I promised would be invested in the railroad expansion—bringing him a sizable return on his investment. He was a proud man, and I almost felt guilty about taking his money. Still, he was a slaveowner wholly devoted to fostering the institution, so I didn't lose any sleep over taking away both his slaves and his cash. As the poster in my hands originated in Jackson, I believed his damaged pride was now likely responsible for the reward. After what I had done, I couldn't say as I blamed him.

"Well," Cat said, "now do you understand why I've been in such a worry? Add to this the trains coming along from every which direction and the new telegraphs, and I've no doubt you're goin' to get caught—soon."

She stared at me intently. "Every time now a stranger comes by, I get worried he's either after you or is bringin' me news of your death. It doesn't help that I keep hearing stories about you and how you've barely dodged a noose. Just the other day I over-heard some men talking about this abolitionist who powdered up the faces of some light-skinned slaves, dressed them fit for a ball, passed 'em off as white, and got 'em aboard a train out to the east just ahead of a posse with fire in their eyes. I knew right away it was you, so don't you go denying it. I don't know how much longer I can stand this. You're in too much danger now. I'd like to believe otherwise, but I can't. John, it's time for you to let go—to let someone else pick up the work."

"You're probably right," I replied. "But there's so much more to do. So much...."

Cat threw her hands up in the air, exasperated. "You'll be no good at all to the cause if you're dead! Time you think of other ways to help."

I considered my words carefully, not wanting to share too much for fear of revealing something that would place Cat even more in harm's way. "I'll admit I've had a notion or two in that area. I'll tell you some, but this has to stay between just the two of us."

For the next quarter hour I explained what I'd shared with Dr. Robertson about my thoughts of moving to the new Kansas Territory and helping the cause as best I could from there. I even suggested, if I had the right helper, I'd provide aid to those forced to a quick journey to the west. When I had shared as much as I dared, I added, "Know anyone who might want to join me? Know anyone who might be able to leave all this behind?"

Cat stood up straight. "You asking me to marry you? That what you mean?"

"Not now. Not yet—and it's time I be honest with you on this. You've a right to know. I'm not free to ask such a thing of anyone until I shed myself of someone blind-raged for my capture. His name's Taggart. Wilson Taggart. Know the name?"

"I do. I've heard. Slave catcher—and cold killer, from what I gather. Not a man to cross. Out of Tennessee mostly. What's he to do with you?"

"He's my shadow—for now. I didn't think I should tell you before, but now I'm of a mind to. I'd have to say he's in with the top of the reasons I'm still pressin' on. I'm not particularly carrying worries about anyone else I've wronged in the past, but this Taggart isn't likely to let go the chase. You see, I hurt him once, and he can't forget. Until he's gone, I have little choice but to stay the course. As strange as it sounds, he's now keeping me at my work just as much as the cause itself because I'm going to have to find him before he gets to me. But don't you worry. I'll be fine."

"Anything I can do to help?" She asked, moving toward me.

"Maybe. Possibly. I don't like the thought of drawing you in, but I may need to ask a favor or two eventually. It would be more danger than I'd ever like you to harbor, but shaking loose of him won't be an easy task."

"I'll do whatever you ask. You know that, yes?"

"I do—and it means more to me than I can say."

I drew her to me again, kissing her softly, gently, finally looking deep into her eyes, hoping she'd feel what was inside my heart. Possibly, she did—that is until the small revolver I had tucked inside my sling slipped out and fell to the ground, just missing her foot.

She backed away, crossed her arms and said, dryly, "Don't you ever go anywhere without one of those? What—you feel bare without one?"

"Maybe you better take a look at the poster again," I said. "Would you go unarmed if you were me? I'd rather not be this way, but I don't see as I have much choice to the matter."

I pointed to my left boot. "I've one there, too. Always there—just in case." Shrugging my shoulders, I said, "I'm sorry, but this is another reason I can put to those keeping us apart. Still too much danger about us right now."

She picked up the revolver, and I tucked it back inside the sling. "Let's go," she said, shaking her head. Then, taking my other arm, she started leading me back up the path. We hadn't gone twenty feet when she turned to me and asked, "Tell me—please. What's to happen next?"

"I hate to leave so soon," I said, lowering my voice, "but if

Tasby's able, we'll be off tomorrow by first light. I have to get back to Elgin and have at least one, possibly two, more trips to make soon as I can. At the same time, I've got some thought to give to Taggart so we'll never have to be concerned with looking over our shoulders."

Cat, who had been staring at the ground as we walked, finally spoke up. "Just don't you break this heart again," she said, tears welling in her eyes. "Couldn't take it...."

"I won't," I replied, drawing her close. "If it's at all in my power, I promise you that."

Cat stepped back, looked directly into my eyes, and said, her voice trembling, "I think I finally believe you, but now I'm more worried than ever. I just don't know...."

"Let's get back," I said. "We both have much to do."

"Will you supper with me tonight?" she asked as we moved along the path. "If you're leaving out in the morning, best have a good meal first."

"I'd be honored," I replied. "You call the time. I'll be there."

"Let's say just past eight. I'll have your favorite stew hot and ready."

"Eight it is," I said. "Until then, I want you to remember this."

I took her in my arms and kissed her with an intensity known by those joined at heart. When we finally stepped back from each other, I nodded.

She did the same.

Our hearts were, at long last, beating together.

We held hands, but didn't speak, all the way back to the Spread Eagle.

....

Chapter 10

"Ain't No Harm to Kill the Devil"

CAT ARRANGED FOR US TO supper in a small, private room down the narrow hallway from the bar and main dining area. Millie, a widow woman of considerable girth hired the previous winter to help run the tavern, would keep the trade going while Cat ducked out for a meal with me.

I arrived just before eight, and Cat immediately whisked me into the room and commanded, while pointing to a table in the corner, "Sit! There! I've one more order for Millie, and then I'll be back with our food."

It had been a good six months or better since I enjoyed the comfort of a quiet meal, so I was beyond overwhelmed when I saw to what lengths she had gone to make the meal so special for me. When she returned, she carried a tray holding a steaming bowl of venison stew, my favorite. She also brought a basket of cornbread and a pitcher of cool milk. I didn't say much while I ate, but I guessed the look of pleasure on my face likely spoke volumes of what I was thinking. At one point, I looked up and noted Cat just picking at her food and staring off to the fireplace across from us.

I put my fork to the table and asked, "Where are you, Cat? Looks to me as if you're miles off."

Her hair shone bright in the firelight as she leaned forward and said, "There was a time these meals weren't so long in comin'. I... just miss you is all. I wish...."

She didn't finish her thought. I had a fair notion of what she would have said, and I felt the same, but I also knew it wouldn't be fair, or right, to bring her closer to even more danger. Just a simple act, like sharing a meal together, was dangerous enough because of the bounty that followed me everywhere. And now there was the poster. I didn't know what I could say, and it appeared to me that Cat, while she wasn't happy about it, under-stood—at least somewhat. We were two people of like heart—but kept to distance by circumstance.

I took her hand, squeezed it, and said, "I don't know how it's going to happen. But I do want you to know this. If I didn't feel in my heart there was a place for us, someday, I would never come here."

Her eyes grew wet and she started to speak, but I cut her off. "I've told you what I need to do, and I'll do it—somehow. Then, maybe, at long last, I'll move along to the new Kansas Territory. Don't know if I have the smarts to run an outpost, but maybe I'll have some help. Likely the best help would be someone who, say, had kept a tavern and inn going. Maybe I'll find someone like that if I'm fair to lucky."

She leaned forward and said, "If you don't kiss me right now—and I mean right now—you'll never get a morsel of food here again. Ever."

"Well, you do have mighty fine antelope stew," I said, smil-ing. "I guess it'd be worth a kiss to know I might have some of that again next time through."

"You shut up!" she said.

The moment our lips touched I felt it, a bond I knew would never fade. I closed my eyes and drew her to me, holding her close.

When we finally drew back to catch our breath, Cat's cheeks were flushed. She was so pretty, so full to joy as she looked to me, I wanted to remember the moment forever.

Our lips had just barely touched again when we heard a loud crash, followed by thunderous shouts, coming from the direc-tion of the bar.

"What in Heaven's name!" Cat said, jumping to her feet. "I better go look."

"I'll come with you," I said, moving my chair out of the way. "Doesn't sound good, does it?"

"Sounds like most nights," she said, drolly. Then, she lowered her voice. "Don't you go doin' anything foolish—you understand? I'm used to this. I'll take care of it."

I nodded—and followed her down the hall. Just as we were to enter the bar, a bottle crashed to the wall in front of us, shards of glass raining at our feet.

As soon as Cat stepped into the room she shouted, "Stop it! Stop it!" Then, walking quickly behind the bar, she drew out a rifle, aimed it over the heads of those fighting, cocked the hammer, and pulled the trigger. A mighty blast followed, and smoke and spent gunpowder showered everyone in the center of the room.

All motion stopped, and all eyes moved to Cat. "That was a dry shot—no lead—but this one's ready," she said, holding up a pistol she had drawn from behind the bar. "I've six shots in this—and another six here," she said, reaching down with her other hand and raising yet another pistol.

Looking over the stunned faces, she warned, "I'm not the best shot in these parts, but I'm typical to hit what I aim at."

Cat then used the guns to point at the men standing around the room. "Bet I could drop twelve of you before that ugly man in the corner could put down that glass. Want to take a wager?"

"And you two will be first," she said, cocking both pistols and pointing them at two men still holding tight grip on each other. "Well?" she asked when no one moved. "Do I shoot you down like dogs—or would y'all rather come to the bar and have one on the house?"

"The man she had called ugly, a burly trapper wearing a beaver hat, held out his glass and said, "Don't know about others, but don't care to have lead with my drink. I'm comin' to the bar."

His words eased the tension, and most laughed quietly and moved with him toward the bar. However, the two holding tight to each other kept the same looks in their eyes. Cat walked from behind the bar and slowly and deliberately eased between them until they separated.

"That's better," she said, urging both to step even farther from each other. "Whatever this is about, I don't want it settled in here."

She then motioned for me to join her. "Here," she said to me, "Help this gentleman to the door and see he gets on his way. He can come back another night when he's of a peaceful mind."

Turning to the other, she said, "You come to the bar. I'll have words with you."

I reached to grab the arm of the man I was to escort to the door, but he jerked away. His clothes were tattered, and he smelled as if he hadn't seen any water in weeks. He had a pistol and a long-blade knife tucked in his belt. I kept my eyes to those as he slowly backed his way to the door where he stopped, sneered at Cat, and moved outside.

"Join us at the bar," she said to me while urging the other man forward. "I want you two to meet."

The man Cat held in her grasp I placed to be near sixty. His sparse hair was edged with silver. He was well-dressed, and his manner seemed gentle enough when he bowed slightly to Cat and said, "Very sorry, Cat. Just couldn't help myself. I'll pay for damages we caused."

"We'll talk about that later, Captain Murdock," she said, picking up a towel from the bar and blotting a steady stream of blood oozing from just above his eyebrow. "What I want to know is what started this? Not like you at all."

He winced as she continued at his forehead, then replied, "You take a look outside and tell me he didn't deserve that busted lip I gave him."

"What's out there?" I asked, finally getting into the conversation.

"He's a slaver. Has a runaway chained to a old Conastoga. Poor creature's been beaten so bad I thought he was dead. Didn't move when I prodded him. Finally saw his chest move up and down, so I guess he still has one or two breaths left. Pitiful. No—shameful. Wouldn't treat a rabid dog that mean. Slaver was braggin' how he was cartin' him back to Richmond. Five hundred dollars reward...alive. Two hundred if dead. Said he didn't much care which, and I believe that's so."

He winced again as Cat continued her doctoring. "While he was spillin' his mouth, I went out to see for myself. Poor creature's about dead. He'll never make it ten miles toward Richmond, so I come back in and asked what kind of man treats another like as that. Next thing I knew, he was on me. Sorry, Cat, but I took pleasure in givin' him a spoon of his own medicine."

"I'm not saying what you did was wrong," Cat replied. "But why can't the sluggin' ever go outside? Just look at this place! Three chairs busted this time."

"I'll make good on it," he said. "Swear I will."

"I hate slavers myself," she replied, looking first at me, then back at Captain Murdock. "So I'll pay half damages myself. Now you get shed of here. And I mean right now. He might come back, and I can't afford any more fightin' tonight."

"He won't be comin' back. Heard him say he was to camp by the first canal tunnel toward Leetonia. Said he'd put on a show for anyone who'd come with whiskey. Was loud about how he'd take a strip of skin off the back of a runaway without blood showin'. I've half a mind to go there and make a good skinnin' on him!"

I'd kept myself quiet to this point, but I could hold my tongue no longer. "Fugitive Law says he can do it if he's of a mind. Doesn't make it right, but makes it so. And you've been seen here with him already, so if anything happens to him and you aren't here, the law would be on you. No, you have to let this one run on. Sorry, but you appear more important than any slaver. You stay right close to here tonight. I know you don't want to, but it's for your own good."

"He's right," Cat said, tightening a bandage around his head. "And hold still!"

"I ain't no coward," the captain bristled. "I could do it."

"I believe you," I said. "I also believe you need to take care of that cut. What do you think, Cat? The bandage enough—or over to see Doctor Robertson?"

Before she could respond, he said, "Young man, I was stitchin' wounds 'board ship before you was born. Just get me a lamp, needle, thread—and a good draw of whiskey. Then stand back, and I'll show how this is done."

"I'd be honored to see you at work," I said, "but I've a commitment to meet a friend. Cat, why don't you take the good captain to the back meeting room and get him situated there. I have to be off, but I'll come back later in the evening."

Cat gave me a look that said she didn't believe a word I was saying, but to her credit she kept still. Finally, she said, "You watch yourself. That arm's not all healed up yet."

"I will," I replied. "Be back soon."

"Young man, what's your name?" the captain called after me as I headed out the door. "Never got to introduce...."

I didn't turn around. The less of me he knew, the better off I'd be. And, besides, I was in a hurry. I had a friend I was looking forward to meeting....

....

Heavy clouds hid the moon and stars, so it was difficult for me to make my way along the banks of the Sandy & Beaver Canal. The once smooth and wide path had become quite narrow and full of ruts for lack of use since the railroad's arrival. I knew one misstep could mean a twisted ankle or a fall to the water below, so my movements were careful. The path, once full of activity even at night, was now deserted and used mostly by those with less than pure intent.

I had just turned a bend in the path and could no longer see the lights of Hanover when I heard the squeaking of wagon wheels ahead. I quickened my pace, trying to close the distance without being discovered. I followed, matching my footsteps best as I could with the regular squeak-squawk of the wheels. When the sounds stopped, I suspected he had found place to set up camp. As quietly as I could, I moved ahead until I could make out the back of the wagon. A figure then moved several feet away, struck a match, and lit a lamp. It was the slaver, staggering to and fro, obviously still held firm by the whiskey he'd consumed. The faintest outline of the canal tunnel was just beyond.

I inched forward, being careful not to make a sound, and watched as he set down the lamp and spread a bedroll between two large oaks. He appeared too much into his liquor to lean down and smooth his blankets, so he instead kicked at the corners. He then went back to the wagon and, holding the lantern in one hand, took hold of a bucket with the other and staggered down the bank toward the water. This was the chance I'd been waiting for. I walked quietly behind the oak to the left of the bedroll, drew my pistol from the sling, and steadied myself for his return. At that moment, however, a thought came to me, one I should have considered earlier. The sound of a gunshot this close to the water and the cavernous tunnel just ahead on a night as cloudy as this would likely carry all the way back to Hanover. I stashed the pistol back inside the sling and, as I knew I didn't have long before his return, started searching the ground around me. I finally came across a section of branch near to two feet long and about as round as my forearm. It would have to do.

The slaver was muttering something to himself as I saw his head appear back above the bank. Water sloshed out both sides of the bucket as he made his way slowly and directly toward me. He stopped once about half way to my hiding spot, putting lantern and bucket to the ground, and taking a long drink from a bottle of whiskey tucked in a pocket at the front of his shirt. When he was sated, he continued forward, staggering mightily. He was right at the edge of the bedroll when he bent down and eased the bucket to the ground.

I lunged out and drew the branch down hard as I could to the back of his head. He didn't fall right away. Instead, I heard a gurgling sound as he started to rise, then fell sideways, the glass of the lantern and the whiskey bottle shattering under his weight. Oil and whiskey must have soaked across his shirt because the fire from the lamp instantly followed. Before I could turn him to his back, he was engulfed in flames.

Grabbing his boots, I dragged him quickly as I could toward the canal as the stench of burnt flesh followed. He came to consciousness and started screaming just as I flung him into the water. Instantly, the fire was gone—but so was he. I expected him to float, but the drop-off below must have been steeper and the current much faster than I thought for water so still at the surface. I started wading in, searching for him with my feet, but nearly fell to the deep water myself.

I stood for a moment waist-deep in the canal, looking into the blackness of the water. I tried to feel sorry for him. I couldn't. He was a slaver, no better than the Devil himself. I trudged slowly back up the bank. At the top, I turned one last time, and looked downstream to make sure his body hadn't come back to the surface. Seeing nothing, I started for the wagon.

As I lowered the wagon's gate, I saw the runaway huddled in the far left corner. He cowered when he saw me.

"I'm not going to hurt you," I said, slowly. "I'm here to take you away—from this. Please, trust me."

The chains at his wrists and ankles jangled as he continued to draw back even more tightly to the corner.

"Can't do nothin' about those now," I said, pointing to the shackles. "We'll take care of those later. Crawl over to me, and I'll help you down."

He didn't move, despite my gently urgings—not an inch.

"He's gone," I said, trying another direction. "He'll never hurt you again. I'm going to get you away, but we have to leave right now."

My shoulder still ached, but I managed to climb in the back of the wagon and stood there, motioning him to come toward me. I didn't know if he'd seen what had happened to his captor, so I said, again calmly, "He's dead, so I'm pushing this in the canal.

You can stay here and sink with it, or you can come with me back to Hanover. You best make up your mind—and but quick."

I then pretended to ignore him as I rifled through the contents of the wagon. There was nothing of value, but I did find a shirt and trousers.

"Here," I said, tossing them over to him. "Won't fit over the chains now, but you'll have use for them soon enough."

Then, just behind the seat, I came across a small bundle of papers. On top was a poster that read:

Reward

Ran away from the subscriber, living in Richmond, a negro man, named Finch, about twenty-five years old, quite black and near to six feet and better high. Is intelligent and speaks softly. Yellowish scar about the centre of the left side cheek. Any notice from persons having seen such a negro, communicated through the post-office at Richmond, will be thankfully received by subscriber.

After reading it, I folded it carefully and placed it under the pistol inside my sling. If I were caught with him later, I could always protect myself by saying I was returning him for the reward, a fact the poster would prove.

"Finch your name?" I asked, finally looking back to him.

His voice cracking, he answered "Yes, Suh. That me."

"Well then, Finch. I can tell you've seen bad times with that slaver, but if you've now the energy, we need to unhitch those horses and roll the wagon over the bank. You up to helping me?"

He nodded and finally moved toward me. "Good. Let me help you down, and we'll get at it."

Once out of the wagon, I noted he was dragging his right leg slightly. He was also not much more than a bag of bones.

"I'll get you food in Hanover," I said. "When's the last time you ate something?"

He shrugged his shoulders and moved slowly toward the horses.

"Go ahead and unhitch 'em," I said, handing him the knife I had tucked in my trousers. "Cut the reins apart so we can each ride one of those nags back to town. Can you ride?"

He again nodded, staring intently at the knife he held in his hands.

"I told you I was going to help you, and that's for true. I'll explain more on the way back. Now get busy. I've got a few things to do myself."

I walked over, picked up the bedroll and what was left of the lantern, and threw them into the back of the wagon. I then scoured the immediate area as best I could to make sure no other signs were left about. I finally picked up a few dead branches and swept the path I had taken to drag the slaver to the canal. When I was finished, Finch had already moved the horses away from the wagon and was standing quietly, as if waiting further orders.

"Tie 'em to that tree," I said, pointing off to his left. "Then come help me with the wagon. Let's raise the tongue up first so it don't catch anything."

It took all the strength we could call forth, but we finally eased the wagon to the edge of the bank. "Now push as if the Devil himself is at your heels. We need to make sure it rolls beyond the ledge so it sinks. Put your back into it—now!"

As soon as the front wheels were over the edge of the bank, we let go. The wagon was moving rapidly when it crashed to the water. At first it seemed to stop firm, but then the water rushed back and pulled it forward. The front end quickly disappeared from view and, in a matter of seconds, all that remained was a thin line of ripples and bubbles.

"Time we're off," I said, turning to Finch. "Let me help you on your horse. You'll have to ride side-saddle 'till we get you away from those chains."

My shoulder throbbed again as I hoisted him up. However, at that moment, looking at the scars on Finch's back and legs, I decided I had nothing to complain about. Nothing at all.

"What happened to him?" Finch asked as we watched the last of the bubbles float downstream.

"Went for a swim," I said, pointing to the canal. "His last."

Finch just looked at me with wide eyes.

....

"Wake up—wake up," I said, gently pulling at Tasby's shoulder. "Got someone here to share the rug next to you. Name's Finch. He'll be movin' on with us in the morning."

Tasby rubbed his eyes, then looked down as he heard the chains rattling at Finch's ankles.

"Where'd you find him?" he asked, sitting up.

"Never you mind," I replied. "Just thought I'd get someone new to listen to your stories. Had to chain him when he found out he'd be traveling with you. Only way to keep him here."

"You what?" Tasby asked, swinging a leg from the bed.

I pushed him back down and said, "Just give him one of your blankets—and go back to sleep. I'm going to say goodbye to Cat and bring back food for Finch. I won't be long. Sunup will be on us before we know it, so we best rest all we can."

I then asked Finch to ease himself to the rug and covered him with one of Tasby's blankets.

"I'll be back soon. We'll have those chains off tomorrow. For now, you just sleep."

His eyes were closed before I left the room.

....

Chapter 11

The Vow

Chattanooga, Tennessee

WILSON TAGGART WAS PLAYING POKER at the farthest table from the front door in the gaming room of the Bristol Hotel when Warren walked in. Warren strolled to the bar, removed his hat, and placed it upside down next to a stack of glasses; this was the sign he hadn't been followed and it was safe to talk.

As soon as Taggart won the hand, he slapped the deck to the table and announced, "I'm off for eats. Any objections?"

He had been playing cards with the same five men each evening for the past week. In that time, there had been no objections of any type to his good fortune. The others knew of Taggart and his reputation as a bad loser, so even though they were better card players, they still allowed him to end each evening with winnings. Although they were growing weary of their donations to his disposition, none dared miss a game for fear he'd come looking for him. They didn't know when he was leaving town, but for all of them the time couldn't come soon enough.

"Good," Taggart said when no one spoke up. "Same time tomorrow night. I expect you all here." His last words were spoken deliberately. Their meaning wasn't lost on the others, all of whom just nodded and smiled weakly.

Taggard scooped up the money before him and motioned for Warren to follow him into the dining area. When they were seated, Taggart didn't waste any time. "Well, talk. I'm waitin'.

What news do you have? Tell me everything's in place."

Warren bent slightly forward and said, almost in a whisper, "I did all you told me. We've men now near Maysville and Columbus and as far east as Richmond and as far west as St. Louis. All have orders to send word here if they come on to somethin'."

"They better," Taggart growled. "If he gets through any of 'em, I want you to make 'em wish he hadn't. I'm tired of this."

He called the waiter over and ordered, "Steak and potatoes for both of us—and a bottle. And I don't want to be kept waiting. Get my meaning?"

The waiter did and immediately rushed back to the kitchen.

"And what of Mr. Boyle?" Taggart asked. "How does he fare these days?"

"Liked the idea of you payin' his gamblin' debts. Wasn't as joyed 'bout goin' to Canada, though."

"You make him understand?" Taggart asked, moving his chair closer to the table.

"I did."

"How?"

"Small fire in his barn got his attention, but when we took his brats for a ride, he caved in but good. Said he'd do anything if we'd leave his family alone."

"When does he leave?"

"Already on the way. Told him you'd pay his debts, forgive what he owes to you, and even put a few dollars in his pocket for his troubles."

"His troubles are just startin'," Taggart sneered. "And how 'bout that pretty wife of his? See her?"

"Beauty as ever," Warren replied, making sure not to show too much enthusiasm. Taggart had already claimed her for his own purposes, so he knew better than to provide any details other than exactly what he was asked about her.

"How soon will he be to Elston, or Elgin, or whatever that pigsty of a place is called? What do you figure?"

"'Bout a week. Has to get a ship across Erie. It'll take some time, but he'll move like a fire under him. Know why?"

When Taggart didn't reply, he continued, "'Cause I told him you'd be looking in on his wife while he was away."

"How'd he take to that?" Wilson asked.

"Ever seen a man what took a step into brush and heard a rattler close by? He looked the same, only more so. He won't waste a minute if he can help it."

The waiter brought their food and placed it on the table. "Anything else, Sir?" he asked.

Without looking up, Taggart asked, "Where's that bottle? Don't see it. Do you?"

The waiter, a horrified look on his face, backed away and replied, "Right away, Sir. Very sorry."

As he watched the waiter scurry away, Warren said, "Plain to see those around here know who's not to be trifled with. Never takes you long, does it?"

Taggart just glared at him and said, "Eat your steak and tell me more. Everything."

Warren had just taken his first bite when he put his fork back to the table and reached into his trouser pocket. While chewing loudly, he said, "Picked this up over to Knoxville. Pulled it from a tree just along the trail. Saw quite a few back this way."

He unfolded the poster. "It's him. Saw him only the once, but I'm fairly certain of the likeness. And now he's for 'Dead or Alive.'"

Taggart snatched the poster from his hands and read through the description and list of locations. "Don't like this. Not one bit," he finally said, flinging the poster to the table. "Don't want nobody findin' him but me. He's all mine. All mine. Get word to all the men. Have 'em tear down every one of these they see. Don't want nobody else gettin' any ideas."

Taggart continued to stare at the poster as he cut into his steak. After a few minutes, he snorted, "Got more work for you. You'll leave in the morning."

Warren looked up and replied, "Boss, I been in the saddle

near to two weeks. Thought I'd take some rest here. You said...."

"You'll rest when you're dead. That'll be enough for all us. Meantime, three runaways got off yesterday from the next county over. Look to be headed straight up along the river. Good bounty on 'em. Jake and Kendrick are camped just outside town, and they're waitin' for you. I want you three to get them runaways. Get 'em back here. No use lettin' good money float off while we're waitin'."

"You comin' with us?" Warren asked.

"I'm stayin' right here," Taggart replied, his voice even, calm. "Any objections?"

Warren knew to change the subject right away, so he pointed back to the poster and said, "Think we've done all we can for now, lest there be somethin' else you want."

Taggart put the last piece of steak in his mouth, and replied, "What I want is this."

He then drew a long-blade knife from a sheath at his belt and slammed it squarely in the middle of the image on the poster, its tip sinking deep into the table. Then, with little more emotion than if he'd just been brushing a scrap of bread from the table, he leaned back in his chair and said, "Tell me more about Boyle's woman. How'd she look?"

Warren, having through time grown used to Taggart's manner, barely paid notice to the knife as he replied, "Looked like she needs a man, not that milksop she calls a husband."

"Good," Taggart replied, pouring both of them another glass of whiskey. "I know just the man."

Warren tilted his glass toward him and nodded. Choosing his words carefully, he changing the subject again. "Jake's as good a trapper as I've known. We'll get them runaways. Don't you worry none. And what's next for you while we're off?"

"Me?" Taggart said, removing his knife from the table and pointing it toward Warren. "Why, I'm going to be right here. I'm going to wait—and take rest—and see if I can catch me a fly."

Warren chugged the last of his whiskey, set the glass back to the table, and said, "I believe you will."

"Oh, you can count on it," Taggart said, slamming the knife into the poster. "I swear to God I'll catch this fly."

....

Chapter 12

Mother Hubbard's Cupboard

Ashtabula, Ohio

MUCH TO MY RELIEF, THE journey from Hanover to
Ashtabula was relatively uneventful. The only real difficulty we
faced was devising new manners of keeping Finch in the saddle. I
hadn't noticed when first delivering him from the slaver, but he'd
been beaten so severely his back had started to fester in several
areas. Every movement for him was a tight step toward agony. I
applied the hog lard I used to keep bullets from rolling out of the
chambers of my pistols liberally to his wounds, but even that did
little to help. We made our stops to rest the horses longer than
we should have so that he could escape as much as possible the
swaying in the saddle. That, too, offered minimal relief. I finally
tried humor, as grim as it was, to make him understand we knew
of his suffering—but still had to push forward. After one of our
shorter stops to water and feed the horses, I said, dryly, "Know
you'll hate to lose all the pain that's keeping you alert, but once
we get where we're going, we've a doctor who'll take it all away.
Think you could forgive us for that?"

I still had little information about him, but the way he nodded and smiled in response told me everything I needed to know:
he was not about to let any amount of pain, no matter the sever-
ity, keep him from free soil.

We pushed on, first stopping briefly at Leetonia, the eastern-
most port of the Sandy & Beaver Canal, then veered due north

toward Ashtabula, where we were to board ship for Canada. The ride was hard because there were precious few trails through the dense forests and rolling hills of northeastern Ohio. Still, I made no complaint because this also meant we were unlikely to come across other travelers along the route.

Once we were just shy of Ashtabula, I told Tasby and Finch to rest themselves a spell while I rode ahead to make sure it was safe for us to call upon the home of William and Catherine Hubbard. William and Catherine were hosts of the Underground Railroad depot known by those in the cause as the "Great Emporium," and "Mother Hubbard's Cupboard." They were among the most active of those harboring runaways, and many argued the Hubbards had the most dangerous of all duties. Because their home was the last stop before those seeking freedom boarded ship for Canada, it was regularly kept under surveillance.

The code name "Mother Hubbard's Cupboard" was more than appropriate for their home because they had built false walls in the hallway between the main parlor and the rear kitchen area. Accessed by a secret panel, this large area, this "cupboard" inside these walls, regularly provided safe haven to those on the run.

Once I had determined Ashtabula was safe to enter, and after returning to collect Tasby and Finch, we made our way quickly as we could to the Hubbard home, located at the top of the hill ovrelooking the nearly constant swarm of activityat Ashtabula Harbor, the main shipping port of the region.

I had Tasby and Finch remain with the horses while I walked up their broad front porch and knocked to the door.

"John!" Catherine called out, swinging open the door and hugging me so tightly my breath caught. William edged around her and shook my hand firmly while asking with a smile, "Why aren't you dead yet?"

"Well, they did try again," I said, raising my left arm and wincing. "But, our good friend, Doc, managed to keep the Grim Reaper at bay one more time."

Catherine stepped back, wagged a finger at me, and said, "Sir, if you don't slow yourself down some, I expect the old Reaper will soon enough catch hold of you, and I don't want be there to say 'told you so!' again."

"Actually," William interrupted, "we were already fearing the worst. Heard your man Lucius and a pretty sizable party came through last week. We didn't see them, but I know for a fact they made away just fine. Went straight to the harbor this time, and it's a good thing, too."

Catherine glanced sharply his direction as he continued, "When we found out you weren't with them, well, our worries began. Thought maybe you'd finally...." He stopped and looked directly at me. "When *are* you going to slow down? Best be soon if you ask me."

"You're right," I said, shrugging my shoulders. "But I'm not ready to stop yet. And what about you two? Why haven't you locked your doors and headed west? Seems you're 'bout as in demand with the law as I am these days."

They looked at each other. Then Catherine turned to me and said, "Let's get inside."

William agreed. "Better not talk about this out in the air. Get yourself in here, my friend. I want to hear all about your adventures of late. But first, you'll have to excuse me for a moment or two. I've a man out back I'm sending with a message down to the harbor. Need to see to him."

"I understand," I said. "Go 'bout your business. That is, go if you dare leave me alone with this beautiful woman."

I leaned forward and kissed Catherine on the cheek. She blushed crimson.

"That'll be enough of that," he said, squinting and pushing out his chin. "Might have to shoot you myself before the night's through."

"You might at that," I said, laughing and stepping back from Catherine.

Catherine moved directly between us and said, "You two! I

swear you're worse than little boys when you're together. What am I to do with you?"

"I'll be good," I said. "I promise. Well, I'll be good at least until he's out of sight."

She playfully slapped at my arm and said, "Where you go, trouble naturally follows, but I guess I better let you in—though against my better judgment. But before I do, where's your coat? You never go anywhere without it, even on the hottest of days."

"Just got ruined is all. I'll get another when I get home. I imagine I do look somewhat unfinished without it."

"That's putting it mildly," she said, eyeing me from head to toe. "Well, get going—before I take a switch to you."

I jumped forward and reached for the door. From behind me I heard Tasby loudly clearing his throat.

"Hey, what about me?" Tasby finally asked, pouting. Catherine adored Tasby, but she was also fond of teasing him—at times unmercifully. "Well," she said, "I guess you can take your friend and go across to the barn. There's a fresh trough of water there, and you can sit yourselves in it and wash away some of that trail grime. I swear I could smell you before you came into view."

Tasby's mouth fell open, and just as he was set to reply, Catherine interrupted, "Oh, I guess I can put up with your stench, at least for a short spell. Get yourself over here!"

Tasby was out of his saddle in an instant and ran up the steps, swept her up in his arms, and twirled her round and round.

"You stop that!" she said, laughing and finally stepping back from him. "If I get any more dizzy, I won't be able to finish the chicken and dumplings I got heating up. Think you could stomach a bite of that?"

"You just lead me to the table," he shot back, rubbing his hands together. "Your cookin' the best in the whole country. How soon we eat?"

"No need for false compliments—though I appreciate them," she replied. "You'll be fed anyway. Get over to the well and draw you up a bucket so you can splash yourself some. I wasn't bending the truth when I said the trail grime had a grip on you. And don't you break anything this time! Last you were in my home, you dropped a plate and a cup if I recall."

"I'm goin'," he said, running toward the well. "You just get that table ready. Won't use nothin' but my fingers this time so won't break anything."

Catherine just looked at me and rolled her eyes.

"I know," I said. "He's definitely one of a kind."

When she stopped laughing, she pointed to Finch and asked, "What about him? Safe to bring him in?"

"Don't think we better," I replied, lowering my voice. "Picked him up down to Hanover. I doubt anyone else is looking for him, but he's got fresh stripes on his back, and that'd mark him if we got unexpected visitors. No, I think the barn's the place for him tonight. I'll take him over and get him settled."

As I headed toward Finch and the horses, I stopped. "Were you serious about chicken and dumplings—or just teasing Tasby?"

"They'll be ready by the time you're at the table," she said, turning and heading back inside. "You hungry?"

"I am," I replied. "For your food—and your company. Never know which is the better of the two."

"You're a flatterer," she said, smiling. "Worse than Tasby. I swear you two could lie yourselves into Heaven itself."

"If you truly have chicken and dumplings, I'll already be in heaven," I said, bowing slightly and removing my hat with a flourish.

Catherine shook her head again and pointed toward the barn before closing the door behind her.

"Sorry," I said to Finch as I grabbed the reins and led the horses toward the barn. "Hope you understand. I'll bring you some of her cookin' soon as I can."

"I be grateful," he said, his eyes rhythmically narrowing in pain each time his horse took a step.

"I know that for a fact," I replied.

....

As soon as we were all seated around the table and William had shared a blessing, Tasby dug into his food like a man who hadn't eaten a morsel in weeks. He hadn't been kidding about using his fingers, so Catherine had to scold him and remind him he wasn't eating in a barn. With that admonition, he slowed down, picked up his fork, and then went at it again.

There was much I wanted to share with them, but the chicken was so juicy and tender my mouth wasn't empty long between bites. Every time I intended to slow myself so I could speak, Catherine pushed another bowl toward me and urged me to add more to my plate. Selfishly, I pushed all guilt aside and was entirely content with stuffing myself.

As my knife and fork danced, I noted again the striking features of both of my hosts. I guessed Catherine to be toward the middle of her fifties, but she still possessed the beauty of youth in both her face and spirit. She was tall and quite slender of build. Her once dark brown hair was fulling to gray, which complimented her soft blue eyes. William was quite a handsome man by all measures. He was approaching the shady side of his sixties, but he held himself as one in his twenties typically would. He had a full head of dark, wavy hair, parted at the left. As stately as he appeared, we teased him often as we could about his middle, which appeared thicker with each of my visits. Still, he couldn't be faulted much, not being married to one of the best cooks I'd ever known.

"Good to see men eat like they enjoy it," Catherine finally said. "But that Tasby—looks as if he might gnaw into my new tablecloth if I don't keep watch to him."

"I've seen him chew rawhide when he's even half hungry," I said, picking up a glass of cool milk. "So, I'd watch him like a hawk if I were you."

Tasby smiled, but the conversation didn't slow him in the slightest. If anything, he took our words as a challenge and picked up his pace.

Catherine and I were still laughing when I looked over at

William, who had placed his fork back to the table and lowered his head.

"What is it, Will?" I asked, reaching over and placing my hand over his. "Your eyes have been dark since we got here."

He looked at Catherine, then back at me, before saying, "I don't suppose I should put sugar to any of this. You've been a dear friend long enough I want you to know."

"Know what?" I asked, growing more worried as I studied his face. "Tell me."

He pushed his plate, barely touched, toward the middle of the table, leaned back in his chair, and began, "We arrived back home just two weeks ago. This time I wasn't sure we'd make it back at all."

Catherine moved her chair closer and put her hand to his shoulder as he continued. "The law took us to Columbus courthouse again. The sheriffs in Grove City and Mansfield had warrants drawn on us because they said they had proof we'd been helping the runaways again—said we'd be locked to prison for what we were doing."

He paused and took a long sip of his milk. "Funny thing is, we didn't do what the warrant said. Could have understood if they'd actually caught us with a hand in the bucket—and we all know it wouldn't have been difficult to pull out something we'd actually done—but how's that for irony, after all these years, that we get hauled to court for something we weren't part of?"

His voice cracked, and he looked back down to the table. Catherine patted him on the shoulder and said, "Will's right, but anger is more to the truth of the matter. Those lame-brained sheriffs were still steaming over times they rummaged through our home trying to find runaways we had hidden right under their noses. They were just out for revenge of some sort."

Here she pointed down the hall toward the "cupboard," then continued, "They're mean men who have nothing better to do than thrive on the misery of others. Still so many like them out there. So many it makes my stomach ill."

"So what happened?" I asked. Even Tasby stopped eating and looked up from his plate.

William, composed again, spoke. "They claimed we had violated near to all of the points of the Fugitive Slave Act—and even most of the Black Laws of Ohio, especially the areas involving 'aid and comfort' to those legally in bondage. They kept into our faces the whole time we were there about some witness they were going to produce who would tie the noose around our necks. Said this witness saw us put two runaways on a ship first day of last month, which we didn't do. They were trying to scare us to confessing—and said our punishment would be considerably less, especially for Catherine, if we'd acknowledge our guilt."

He picked up his fork, picked at his food again, and said, "I wouldn't have confessed to them about seeing the sun come up in the morning, let alone own up to something I didn't do. So, we kept mum and professed our innocence at every turn. The judge ran out of patience near the end of the second day and finally insisted the sheriffs bring forth the witness they kept yammering about. As it turned out, they were running nothing but a bluff, and a bad one at that. They had a runaway they'd beaten half to death they wanted to speak before the judge. Said he also saw our actions. Likely they offered him something if he'd swear out on us. When they finally paraded him in, I didn't know him from Adam. The judge took one look at that poor creature and reminded the sheriffs that no black man could give legal testimony in a court of law. That was it. There wasn't anything else the sheriffs had up their sleeves."

Catherine interrupted, "Oh, they tried to have him heard, but the judge threw it all back in their faces. He gave them the what-for, dismissed all claims toward us, and cleared the courtroom quick as he could."

William cut in, "But not before asking us to wait so he could talk with us after all others had gone. He seemed a kind man, one who is most likely sympathetic to the cause, but he didn't hold back any words when we were finally alone. Said he'd heard about our work with the Underground Railroad—that we weren't exactly one of the 'best kept secrets' in this part of the land. Said if we were brought before him in the future with any type of real proof, he'd have no choice but to draw the law down on us to the full extent—that all we have would be seized and we'd both be chained tighter than the runaways some thought we were aiding. His eyes may have been full of sympathy, but it was also clear he was going to hold fast to the law to the end. I can respect that. I just don't agree with it."

"And what will you now do?" I asked, suddenly feeling very guilty I had asked shelter for Finch at a time when scrutiny was tightening around my dear friends.

"What do you think we'll do?" Catherine said, smiling and rubbing William's shoulder. "We'll just find another way to help. Principles don't get sacrificed because of worry over losing something like this house or the few trinkets we own."

She pointed out the side window before continuing, "We have warehouses all along the docks at the harbor. Wouldn't take a carpenter long to put a few cupboards in there. I think it would actually be better to make use of the warehouses because we could get passengers aboard ship in a breath. Would be safer for all of us, don't you think?"

"What I think," I said, "is you should give this a lot more thought. I don't ever want to hear you've been put behind bars. The cause does need you, but you've so much more to give than what you're doing right now. It's what you know, what you can share with others about what you believe, that is most valuable of all. Why don't you move from here—go somewhere where you can help get others into the fight? Why, I'd follow you both to Hades—you know that—and you'd soon have others right there with me. John Brown moved west, to Kansas Territory, and look at what he's doing. You could do the same and without the risks around you now."

"We've thought of it," Catherine said. "But, we still feel we can do the most good right here. Slave catchers are coming farther and farther north these days. I've heard that some have even crossed to Canada to fetch some back. So, if we don't continue on, what will happen to those who count on us? That Fugitive Act is scaring most others half to death, so it isn't likely many would step forward to take our place. No, this is where we belong, even if it means a bad end for both of us."

She squeezed William's hand.

"We're staying right here," he said. "Just have to be smarter, I guess. That man you have to the barn is likely the last to light there. Don't think they'd spy on us again this soon, but they'll be coming pretty quick. We can count on that. Catherine's right— we best look to the warehouses from now on."

I shook my head and said, "You're foolish for staying, but I respect you all the more for doing so. I want you both to know that."

I thought of Finch in the barn. "Last thing I want to do is add to your worries. After night falls I'll go to see Captain Appleby and find out how soon I can get our passenger aboard ship. Hopefully, it'll be tomorrow morning. I'll get him out of here fast as I can. I couldn't live with myself if I ended up causing you...."

I stopped in mid-thought because I saw Catherine glance at William, push back her chair, walk to the sideboard, pick up a folded piece of paper, and return to the table. She unfolded the paper and held it up for me to see. It was the same poster Cat had shown me in Hanover.

"Doesn't look much like me, does it?" I said, taking another bite of dumplings.

"That's all you have to say!" Catherine practically screamed at me. "After what you just said to *us!*"

William joined in. "Picked that up just outside the courthouse in Columbus. They were everywhere. You are the one who should think about moving on. I hope you've considered that."

"I have," I said. "And I probably will. Oh, I'll never give up the cause. That'll never happen. But maybe I've come up with a way I can be of more service than what I'm doing now."

Tasby, who had been focused on nothing but his food to this point, finally spoke, through a mouth full of dumplings and gravy, "He in love with that Cat at Spread Eagle. Takin' her away, I reckon. He got it bad for her, sure enough."

"What's this?" Catherine asked, her voice high, questioning. "You've finally fallen in love? I don't believe it. I hope it's so, but I just don't believe it."

"Am I truly that bad of a catch?" I shot back, smiling at her.

"That's not what I mean, and you know it," she said. "I just thought you'd never be married to anything but the cause. Tell us all about her. Tell me everything."

"You were already taken by that man," I said, pointing to William. "Otherwise it'd be you with my heart."

"Stop it, John Fairfield. You're positively evil," she said, blushing again.

I turned to Tasby, "I ought to choke you. You just keep spoonin' dumplins into that mouth of yours—and keep it shut tight. You hear me?"

He just smiled and took another bite.

Turning back to Catherine, I said, "Much has to happen before I'd give half a thought to keeping a woman in my life. Wouldn't be fair otherwise, and I know it. First on that list is doing something about a slave catcher at my heels. Name's Taggart. He isn't going to stop coming for me, no matter where I go. I know I'll have to settle things with him before long."

William said, "We heard talk of him in Columbus. They say he's as mean as they come. Supposedly killed a wagon full of runaways close to Cincinnati because the river was too high to take them back to Tennessee for the reward. Murdered them all—like he was just swatting flies, and there's one more thing I might as well bring up now. We were going to share this with you before you left us. We also heard he's hiring agents in towns all across the South. Supposed to be looking for someone special. Offering a pretty big bounty from what I gather. Wouldn't know who'd he be looking for, would you?"

Tasby looked up again, but before he could say anything, I said, "I'll take care of Taggart. Don't know how yet, but you can count on it. No slave catcher will ever get the best of me."

"Your bravado is beautiful music," Catherine said, "but, this man is different. It seems he likes killing. You have to promise us you'll keep on the watch at all times from now on. You have to promise me you'll do all you can to keep safe."

"I will," I said, "I know what I'm up against, so don't you go worrying any more. I can take care of myself."

"You better," she said, leaning back in her chair. "And I like how you turned our conversation from this woman in your life to that slave catcher. You think you're so clever, but you're not. I'm not leaving this table—and you aren't either, until we hear all about her. Now put down that fork and start talking—and I mean right this instant."

The tone of her voice told me she was dead-serious, so I knew I was trapped. For the better part of an hour, I shared what I could about Cat—and about my thoughts of heading toward Kansas Territory to help teach and provision runaways moving that direction. Tasby chimed in from time to time, generally doing more harm than good to my narrative, but I never expected he'd do anything other. Catherine was most curious about Cat and asked questions about her past that I couldn't answer. I decided right then and there I had probably always talked with Cat too much about myself and not enough about her wishes and her past. That was a flaw in my character, and I knew it—and vowed to make it right with her when I could. William, on the other hand, was most interested in my ideas for building general stores along the trails heading west from the Territory and even offered to help with the financing of the initial one I'd need. I thanked him—and suggested he and Catherine follow along with me and join the effort.

We also spoke briefly of a dear and mutual friend, Captain Calvin Appleby, master of the *Sultana*, a large, three-masted mer- chant ship that made regular voyages from Ashtabula across Lake

Erie to Port Burwell and Port Stanley in Canada. The below-deck cargo areas of the Sultana had long been safe haven for hundreds of those seeking freedom. Captain Appleby's brother, Gilman, had joined him, not just to help with the commerce, but also to help with the cause. We paused to toast both brothers—an expression of our admiration toward them for the dangers they faced daily. If caught with runaways aboard, their ship would be forfeited and both would be sent to prison. For men of the sea, confinement in a cell would serve as the worst form of punishment, a fact we were all well aware of and which made us appreciate their efforts all the more.

The time flew so fast I hadn't noticed evening was drawing down on us. I knew I should leave to go visit with Captain Applebly. I instructed Tasby to take a plate over to Finch and see to the rest of his needs. Then, first thanking Catherine and William for a most enjoyable evening, I excused myself and started for the harbor.

As I walked down the long and steep hill between their home and the harbor, the lights of the ships anchored below sparkled on the still water close by the docks. It was a beautiful night, warm and quiet, with just the slightest breeze occasionally bringing forth a hint of the cargo being loaded and unloaded from the ships. I loved evenings like this, loved both the solitude and possibilities for the future brought forth by the calm. I thought of Cat—and wondered if she'd ever been aboard a ship. I thought of Finch—and how soon he'd be starting a new life. I thought of Elgin Settlement—and how much I was looking forward to being home. Then, just as the Sultana came to view, I thought of something else: how I'd have to settle with Taggart before any of my dreams had a chance to come true.

So much was still uncertain, but there were a few things I did know. I knew life was glorious. I knew I was grateful for all the blessings of my existence, even though I didn't deserve such favor. I knew I needed to make the best of what time I had left on this earth. And, standing there on the dock and looking across

Lake Erie to the horizon beyond, for the very first time I realized I needed Cat—that I wanted us to join our lives. There was so much to do—so much I hoped to do—and it was all starting now.

I walked to the plank connecting the *Sultana* to the dock and called out, "Permission to come aboard!"

With permission granted, I looked one last time back up the hill toward the Hubbards' home, then moved ahead, my steps careful but determined, ready for all that lay before me.

....

Chapter 13

Safe Haven

Elgin Settlement, Ontario, Canada

An hour before sunrise and while darkness still provided fair cover, we said our heartfelt farewells to the Hubbards and set off for the harbor. When we were sure we weren't being watched, we made our way to the *Sultana* and were escorted aboard by Captain Appleby's brother, Gilman, a short, stocky man with a portly chest. He took us below deck to the main cargo area and instructed us to remain seated behind large barrels of flour and grains until the ship was well away from port.

Lake Erie was typically swept by storms and strong waves through the month of May, but we were lucky. Other than a sudden squall that erupted the first mid-day, the first half of the crossing was without incident. The only casualty was Tasby's stomach, the contents of which made their way overboard just as the storm was subsiding.

Toward the end of the first evening, Captain Appleby invited me to join him at his quarters for bread and brandy, the traditional Lake Erie cure for unsteady legs earned while a ship is tossed and turned in foul weather. Neither of us needed the cure, but the opportunity to visit was most welcome.

We had known each other near to six years and, in that time, even though he was old enough to be my grandfather, we had built a special bond forged by mutual purpose—and curiosity. First and foremost, we both felt privileged to serve as guides for those seeking freedom. At the same time, the worlds of land and water we traversed could not have been more different, and our curiosity about each other's domain often kept us talking well through the night. I was fascinated by travel across water and wanted to learn as much as I could about the workings of ships. Captain Appleby seldom went ashore and desired as many details as I could provide about both the towns and landscape I brought passengers through on my journeys. For both of us, the exchange of information about method of travel and points of geography was always a time of fascination, of wonder—and great joy.

However, we seldom spoke of the true reason our paths had crossed. I knew he abhorred the institution of slavery, but he never shared with me what brought him to his belief or why he risked his ship and livelihood to transport runaways to Canadian soil. All I really knew about him was he was once captain of a ship captured and burned by the British. Other than that, he was a man of mystery. He also never asked me to share my views on slavery or anything else about my background, which made our time together all the more relaxing. I knew he had heard stories of some of my adventures, but to his credit he never asked me to recount them. Still, each voyage seemed to strengthen our friendship, a friendship we both badly needed, especially because our work prevented us from becoming close to many others.

We spotted Port Burwell near to noon our second day into the voyage. The process of docking was surprisingly fast, and it was no time at all before Tasby and I had again thanked Captain Appleby for his assistance and made our way ashore. My first act was to find a boy with whom I could send ahead a message to Oshie Turnbull, the proprietor of the local livery. It had become my custom to leave our horses with Oshie while travelling south to collect passengers. He fed, exercised, and curried them exceptionally well, so much so that I came to learn I could count on him having our mounts ready at a moment's notice upon return. I paid him handsomely for his efforts and was never in the least disappointed by him.

My message specified for him to make ready horses and provisions for two riders—not three. Captain Appleby and Finch had taken an immediate liking to each other. As the captain was in need of a good hand and Finch had no family left to speak of and had taken on an immediate love for the water, both agreed that Finch would remain and begin his new life aboard the Sultana. This filled me to happiness—for the both of them.

Once we had retrieved our horses, Tasby and I immediately set out for Elgin Settlement, an easy ride of just over a day's time. I considered Elgin my home—or as near close to a home that I'd had since leaving my family in Virginia. Elgin was known as a place of hopes and dreams for those fortunate enough to enter its boundaries. The settlement was originally founded by Reverend William King as a safe haven for runaways. The land, initially nine thousand acres, had been purchased by Reverend King with the help of the Presbyterian Church and a group of Canadian abolitionists he had brought together whose membership was, by design, both black and white. All began with the understanding the Canadian legal authorities would welcome all the new inhabitants with open arms.

As it turned out, the welcome was there, but the Canadians could do very little to block the legal reach of the Fugitive Slave Act and to protect those coming to their soil. By point of law, slave catchers from the United States still had every legal right to make the crossing to Canada and recapture and return slaves to their masters to the south. I had been doing my best, in the time between my own journeys, to train those new to the settlement in the use of firearms so they'd at least be able to put up a good show of resistance if slave catchers were suddenly found about. Those who received the training formed a line of defense, but we were still badly in need of additional weapons, of all types, for many others. A year or so before I had decided a portion of my funds from all my excursions would be set aside for this cause.

Fortunately, Elgin Settlement also had a natural ring of defense around it. It was about a dozen miles from Chatham, the largest town of the region. The terrain between the two was dotted by rough logging trails and dense pine forests, not the easiest ground to cross for those bent on tracking down runaways. Furthermore, the residents of the settlement never minded that the outside terrain made the settlement something of an island. Their "island," carved from what had once been wilderness undesirable to even the most rugged of trappers, was now a place where all men were truly equal and free to pursue their dreams.

From the time its first settlers arrived, in the year of our Lord 1849, the settlement had grown to nearly eight hundred inhabitants, most of whom were experiencing freedom for the first time in their lives. They came from Mississippi, Georgia, Tennessee, Kentucky—nearly every state hosting the institution of slavery. They may have come from different geographic origins, but once at Elgin, all proudly became part of a world new and full of promise. They took care of and watched over each other and the settlement in ways I found nearly beyond description. Whenever a new arrival let out word he needed help putting up a cabin or barn, scores of neighbors would be waiting the next morning with tools, food, and the desire to offer all assistance possible. Whenever there was a well to be dug, teams of residents would often work days until buckets of water could be drawn. If a resident fell to hard times for whatever reason, from crop failure to illness, others were there at once offering aid and comfort. The most amazing event of all to me occurred when a decision was made to erect the first church for the settlement. Once the necessary land had been secured and cleared, so many joined in the work that the building was completed in a mere four days, including the windows, doors, and pews. Elgin Settlement had become more than just a haven for runaways; it was now "home" to all, home to body, spirit, and dreams.

When first news of the settlement got to southern states, not a soul there believed it had the slightest chance of success. After all, slaves were thought to be ignorant, lazy, shiftless animals who could do little more than tote-and-fetch. However, soon enough, and much to their horror, their former chattel used and built upon the skills they had learned in bondage to create a settlement of which all could be proud. Many set up trade as blacksmiths, cabinetmakers, livery keepers, stonemasons, coopersmiths, saw-mill operators, and shoe cobblers. Still others tilled the soil and harvested lumber. When each was allowed to share skills freely and openly with others, the settlement flourished. Not a soul professed to know what the future would hold for the settlement, but many felt, in their hearts, as I did—that through continued sharing of purpose and goals, the best was yet to come. And I was proud and grateful to be part of it.

The settlement also thrived and flourished because the Elgin Association had come up with a list of rules they consid-ered absolute. Those found to be violating these rules were asked either to change their ways—or get themselves out. These rules were strict, but were also—as even a lawbreaker like myself could understand—necessary to build the type of future all desired. One was that land could be owned only by runaways or those who had already achieved legal freedom—and no land could simply be "leased" to others. Another rule dictated the mini-mum size of homes and the distance each was to be constructed from the road passing in front. In addition to being a certain size, each home also had to have a front porch and a garden area. Many said these were for reasons of aesthetics, but it didn't take much thought to realize the true purpose was to help build a common spirit of accomplishment among the settlers, a worthy goal indeed.

I was proud to be, at least to the present, the only white resi-dent of the settlement, albeit an infrequent one. I wasn't allowed to own my own land because of the rules of ownership, so I had provided the funds for Tasby to purchase the ground where our cabin now stood. Our agreement for this partnership was simple enough: if I died before he did—and there was a mighty good chance of that—he'd have his own property. In the meantime, however, I could live there as his "guest" during my time at the settlement. I suspected some others knew of this arrangement, but no complaints ever came my way.

I felt good and comfortable calling this settlement my home because I knew many of its residents. I had brought many of them there myself, so I felt genuinely part of the local family. There were also more selfish motives for staying. Slave catchers were after me, and I knew my neighbors thought highly enough of my efforts for the cause they'd do everything in their power to protect me. With this circle of safety about me, I felt a security and peace I knew nowhere else. At the same time—and I made no apology to anyone for it—my best customers, those who had built up their fortunes since achieving their freedom and were interested in having relatives brought north, were right close at hand. Therefore, the landscape was also perfect for me and my trade.

There were a few, perhaps more than I realized, who felt I was wrong to accept money for my work, but the price of freedom was never cheap—and growing higher all the time. It took a tidy sum to purchase the weapons and provisions I required to make the excursions. It also took funds to prepare the elaborate ruses I frequently used to get in the good graces of local towns-folk where I was to acquire my passengers. Even more money was needed to make the return trips—because so much was typically left behind as part of my ruses. How I used the funds and my reasons for accepting them may have been misunderstood by a good many, but I felt not a speck of guilt for any of my actions. For taking money for my services, I may eventually burn in Hell. But for now, I'm content and happy with the risk.

Tasby had nearly driven me mad during the ride to Elgin by repeating over and over to me his version of our recent adventures. At one point, I interrupted him and said, "Let me ask you something. Was I not there with you? So, how's it I recall the same events not even a whit as you do?" He didn't reply. Instead, he just stared at me blankly a few moments before picking up where he left off, speaking even more rapidly than before I had stopped him. To my great relief, then, Elgin Settlement came to view just as the clouds moved clear of the afternoon sun. The settlement appeared so calm, so quiet, so peaceful. Off in the distance, directly to my left and near to the river, I could see a whisp of smoke rising from the chimney of our cabin. I was home—at last—and ready to be so.

"Didn't know if we'd ever to see it again," Tasby said, removing his hat and wiping his brow. "Beautiful, ain't it?"

"Most beautiful thing I've ever seen," I replied, kicking my horse to a gallop. Then, turning back to Tasby, I shouted, "Last one back takes care of the horses!"

It was a game we played upon every return to the settlement, and I always won, although I suspected Tasby purposely held back to allow my victory. I also assumed part of the reason he was so gracious had to do with the fact I employed a woman to take care of the cabin and our belongings the times we were away, and through the years he had tried with all his might to bring us together. I imagined he believed—rather, hoped—I'd eventually discover I was in love with her. So he very likely held back during our races to the cabin in order to give me a few moments alone with her.

Her name was Serena. I had brought her and her mother to their freedom five years previously, but the mother had died shortly after our arrival. Serena was but seventeen at the time and, truthfully, I had no idea what to do with her after her mother passed. There were precious few jobs in the settlement at the time for a girl of that age, especially one on her own, so I hired her myself and gave her quarter in our cabin. Doing so did raise a few eyebrows among the more devout of the settlement, but most also understood Tasby and I would be away most of the time, and that seemed to mollify them at least somewhat.

By any measure a man could devise, Serena was a remarkable beauty. She was tall and willowy, and her complexion was light and smooth. Her hair was raven-black and full to curl. In the five years I had known her, she had grown from a gangly girl to a breathtaking young woman. However, as attractive as she was and as good of spirit as she turned out to be, my heart still belonged to another, a fact I regularly shared with Serena, and which she always chose to ignore.

This time I made it to the cabin not more than three lengths before Tasby. I fully expected him to keep back, but it was soon apparent why he had followed so closely.

"More woman trouble for you here, I 'spect," he said, laughing softly and shaking his head. "Don't want to miss this. When you gonna learn?"

"Now, let's not start all that again," I shot back. "You were a peck of trouble and misery to me at the Spread Eagle. If you so much as...."

Before I could finish my words, the door to the cabin swung open and Serena ran out to greet us.

"Praise be!" she shouted, raising her arms. "Knew you'd come today. Just knew it. Get down from there right now!"

The minute my foot hit the ground she lunged forward, wrapped her arms around me, and kissed me fully on the lips.

"Told you so!" Tasby called over as he started leading the horses out back. "You in big trouble now."

When I could finally step back from Serena, I said, "I'm glad to see you, too—but you really shouldn't do that. What will people say?"

"Know exactly what they'll say. They'll say you should be my man. I know it—and you know it. At least you should know it by now."

"Serena," I said, not exactly sure how to place all into words this time. "You're a wonderful soul. I know that. But...."

She cut me off, placing a finger to her lips and leading me to the porch. "Enough time for talk later on. Don't take much to see you been in the saddle too long. Pull over that chair and rest your bones. I'll see to your comforts."

Just then Tasby walked back around to the porch.

"What about the horses?" I asked. "You couldn't have put

'em up that fast. Nobody's that good."

"Forget them horses," he said. "There's six pies coolin' in the back window. Six! I need them more than our horses need grain!"

Serena smiled and said, "Those be for the church gatherin' this Sabbath. My work was to make some pies. Used the preserved cherries, blueberries, peaches, and pears. Think they came out mostly to good, too."

Tasby looked crestfallen—until she said, "Don't think we fall to Hades if them pies didn't make it to the gatherin'. Tell you what we do. You go over to where they're puttin' up a new meetin' hall. Lucius and Henry are there, and I know they've been waitin' to see you two. Go get 'em, and whisper them they can come over now for pies and coffee—and maybe something a little stronger if we keep it quiet. Now get yourself movin'!"

"Yes, Ma'am," Tasby replied, running back to bed down the horses. "Don't you eat that cherry one while I gone!"

As soon as he departed, Serena turned back to me and said, "Now, let's see—where were we?"

She moved toward me, leaning up to kiss me again.

"Now you wait a minute, young lady," I said, backing away. "This isn't right."

"Then just one more kiss, and I'll leave you to peace," she replied. "Just one?"

I was trapped, and I knew it. Knew it good.

....

To my relief, it wasn't but fifteen minutes later I heard loud and hurried footsteps on the front porch. The whole time Tasby was away I felt like a greased hog being chased around a pen.

"John, so good to see you," Lucius said as I opened the door and stepped out. He firmly shook my hand and asked, "Any troubles the way back?"

I was about to reply when Henry ran forward, wrapped his arms around me, and said, "Was really worried this time. Thought that wound might kill you off. Doc must have used all his magic up this time."

"He did just that," I said, smiling. Then, pointing to Tasby, I added, "Even saved his sorry life, though I'm not sure he did us any favors by that. Had to listen to his stories all the way back here. That almost killed me!"

Both then patted Tasby on the back and said, at the same time, "Welcome home."

"Don't know what his complaint be," Tasby said, shaking a fist at me. "If hadn't been for me, he'd never made it close to back here. Saved his backside agin."

Our laughter was interrupted by Serena, who came out with a tray heaped with slices of pie.

"Better get 'em before the flies do," she commanded. "Well, what you waitin' for? Get yourselves seated and dig in. I'll get the coffee and better see you eatin' when I come back. Worked like a dog gettin' 'em cooked, so want to see some smiles in with them chews."

We didn't have to be asked twice. I had half my blueberry slice down before she was back with the coffee pot.

Between bites, we shared with each other details of our return journeys. Tasby and I recounted our time at the Spread Eagle, with Tasby embellishing at every turn of words. I kept waiting for him to bring up the subject of Cat but was grateful he chose not to. I imagined he didn't because he wasn't about to upset Serena, the "hand that fed him" on this day. When I got to the subject of Finch, I chose not to provide many details about how I managed to get him away from the slaver. It wasn't that I didn't want them to know more. I felt it was enough they knew he had found a new life with Captain Appleby and would likely be of help to us in future crossings of Lake Erie.

After we had finished with our account, I asked Lucius to tell us how our most recent passengers were coming along at the settlement. I knew something was amiss when he and Henry looked first at each other, then to the ground.

"What is it?" I asked. "Tell me."

"Most are doin' just fine," Lucius replied, still avoiding my eyes. "It's just that...."

When he didn't continue, Henry finally spoke. "It's Delia. You remember how she was to go back to that man what sent for her? It's sure we'll never know the full of it, but she decided she couldn't be with him. Wouldn't be with him."

He looked off to the distance.

"Well, where is she?" I asked. "She need help?"

"Not any more," Lucius said, his voice now low, soft. "She's finally free. The last night on the trail she snuck to the woods and cut through her wrists. Was gone before anyone found her. Wish I could believe she's at peace now. Just don't know. All I can figure is she just didn't want to belong to anyone again. Now she won't."

"Of all that group, I thought she might end up the strongest," I said, shaking my head.

"Hard for someone to understand who hasn't felt chains," Henry said. "Maybe she strong, or maybe she just too broken. The Lord will know."

"And the others?" I asked. "What of them?"

"All doin' just fine," Lucius said, firmly. "They'll have no troubles here."

Serena reappeared with more coffee. We then continued our sharing of news. Lucius informed me Toby wanted to come along with us on our next excursion—that he wanted to help all he could with the cause. I had been thinking of going south as a buyer of horses during my next venture, and as it appeared Toby knew as much about them as anyone I'd ever met, I was not opposed.

"Tell him to come talk to me," I said to Lucius. "I believe we might be able to use him."

I also asked Henry to begin the next morning with the collection of the rest of our fees from those who had hired us to bring back our most recent passengers so that all could receive their share of the profits. Henry would put all his effort into this as he needed his share to purchase additional machinery for the print shop. Lucius said he needed a new pistol. Tasby chimed in that he needed his share for new clothing to make himself "even more beautiful than I already be!" His pronouncement was so in his character we didn't even laugh. Instead, we all just nodded in agreement.

Finally, in addition to the shocking tale of Delia, another bit of news took me completely by surprise. Just as I reached for another piece of pie, Lucius nudged Henry in the ribs and said, "Go on—might as well tell him now."

"Tell me what?" I asked, stuffing my mouth again.

"Mr. John," Henry said, firmly, evenly. "Got something to say—but won't come easy."

He cleared his throat, stood up, and spoke again at Lucius' urging, "You see, between our travels I've been seeing a young woman who works at the general store."

He paused, so I urged him to continue.

"The whole of it is, I've decided to marry her, so I believe I won't be going with you any more—if you'll put your blessing to it. Think I'll sink my roots here and start my family."

I started to respond, but he interrupted me. "I know I owe to you much more than I could ever repay, so I don't feel the best about this. I just think it's time for me. Can you understand?"

As I looked at him, my emotions were so mixed. On the one hand, I was caught completely off guard by the news. On the other, I was always so worried about him during our travels I often had tried to keep him back at the settlement. He was like a young brother to me. Because of his skills as a printer, he was also one of the most important warriors in the cause of securing freedom for others. In the end, though, even as my thoughts swirled, I wanted only what would bring the most happiness for him. With my heart full of respect and love, I leaned forward, placed my hand to his shoulder, and said, "This is your home. This is where you can build your life. With all my being, I wish you every happiness a man can find."

Henry stepped closer and embraced me. I didn't pull back. I was happy for him, and he understood it so. We'd been though so much together, nothing else needed to be said.

We spent the rest of the evening listening to Tasby recount to Serena, over and over, with greater embellishment each time, how he had held off the whole town of West Liberty while the rest of us made our escape. When we'd all finally had enough of that, Lucius managed to get in enough words to ask me when we'd be getting prepared for our next excursion. I suggested we take a week and a half to rest and provision ourselves, which was met with joyous approval. Then I asked Henry to get word out around the settlement that on the morning of Wednesday next I'd be at the main inn to interview those who desired us to bring back their loved ones. I knew he wouldn't be traveling with us this time, but I did ask him if he'd sit in with Lucius and me when we conducted the interviews. He said he'd be proud to.

It was getting late, so Lucius and Henry thanked Serena for her pies and hospitality and departed. Even though he believed none of us were aware, we all knew Tasby had a sweetheart on the other side of the settlement. While heading toward the door, he announced that he was going to visit a "friend" and not to wait up for him. Serena and I smiled but kept silent as he closed the door behind him.

I was so tired all I wanted to do was crawl into bed. I said goodnight to Serena, walked to my bedroom, quickly stripped down, and practically dove under the covers.

I was just starting to drift off when I heard a knock at the door, followed by Serena's whisper, "Can I come in?"

I rolled slightly to my right and pretended to be sound asleep.

I heard Serena sigh and tiptoe back down the hall toward her own room.

Even though I was on the other side of exhaustion, thoughts of Cat, the western territory, and Taggart whirled through my head. It took me a long time to fall asleep.

....

Chapter 14

Price of Freedom

THE NEXT WEEK FLEW BY because there was so much for all of us to do. Henry kept busy collecting funds from those who had hired us to bring back their loved ones during our last excursion. While he did so, he was able to visit with our newly arrived passengers to find out how they were getting along. According to Henry, all, and especially Lucy, had taken to their lives in Elgin so well he hardly recognized any of them. Isaac Zorn, the innkeeper from New Glasgow who had asked us to return Delia to him, was grieving her loss. Much to my surprise, he still insisted upon providing us the funds he had promised. Whether he acted from guilt or love he still held for her, I could not tell.

When Henry had finished with the collections, he opened the print shop and prepared two sets of papers for Toby so he could join us on our next foray south. One set of papers indicated he was my slave, purchased in Nashville for the sum of $900; these documents would suffice for our time in states still holding fast to slavery. The other papers indicated Toby had been set free the previous year by his owner in Jackson, Mississippi; these were prepared in case we were questioned by slave catchers or legal officials during our time north of the slave states. One afternoon I asked him again if he was certain he wanted to risk all to journey with us, and as long as I live, I'll never forget his response: "Mr. John, I'd feel myself a powerful coward if I didn't do my best to help others to here. Just wouldn't be right." I admired his strength of conviction and his courage. At the same time, I wasn't sure he knew what he was in for. In slave states, he'd have to, at times, take both physical and verbal abuse from me and Lucius in order for our ruse to play out without suspicion. Even for a former slave, such treatment would be horrible.

Lucius busied himself throughout the week, obtaining the supplies we'd need for our next journey—from food to clothing to tack for our mounts. He was meticulous to the point of obsessive in his preparations. For this I was grateful; I could not recall a single time he had failed us in this regard. He did, however, always seem to bring more than just a little above what we actually needed, so I often joked with him he must have been with Noah when the ark was made ready for journey.

There was plenty to keep myself to task. I always considered my weapons part and parcel with my line of work—and took great care with both their purchase and maintenance. I had heard of a new "pocket gun" that was now available through a merchant in Chatham, so I spent one day riding there to examine it to determine if it might prove useful to me. Pocket guns were smaller, much lighter, and typically of a lesser caliber than the pistols carried by most men. The one I traveled to see, a Colt 31 caliber six-shot revolver, was reputed to be deadly up to thirty yards. It was smaller than the older 1851 Navy Colt and not half its weight. This was significant because in the heat of battle, the process of reloading the chambers was quite lengthy. Any time lost in this process could lead to the enemy achieving advantage. The lighter the gun, the more of them could be carried on one's person, either in holsters or secreted within a coat. The proprietor of the general store allowed me to step out back to fire one so I could check for fit and feel. The new weapon seemed it belonged to my hand. I purchased six, three for me and one each for Tasby, Lucius, and Toby.

Back in Elgin Settlement, I called upon Josiah Baker, owner of the largest livery. Before I had brought him to his freedom, he had served with a tailor in Kimbrough, South Carolina. That work taught him the skills required to make the long, duster coats favored by those who spent long stretches in the saddle. They were called "dusters" because of their length; most stopped just above the heel of the boot. Their length kept trail dust from settling to the rider, a welcome relief for those covering great distances. At the same time, I wore dusters for another more practical reason. Their size allowed for numerous pockets to be sewn inside, each capable of housing pistols and knives. If I knew a fight to be drawing near, it wasn't uncommon for me to carry as many as six or seven pistols and a knife or two inside my coat. The advantage to carrying this many weapons was that I did not have to spend time reloading during the heat of conflict. I merely had to grasp another loaded pistol. As my former coat met with an untimely demise during our last journey, I badly needed another. Josiah said he'd have one ready for me in two days.

Josiah was also a gifted leathersmith. I had him apply this skill to the manufacture of special belts I could wear under my coat. These belts were designed to hold extra pistol cylinders in case I had to make time to reload. The cost of Josiah's work was high, but I never felt cheated. His handiwork had saved my life on more than one occasion.

I also had work to attend to of the evenings, but my work at the cabin was not as productive as it could have been. Serena took every opportunity to try to engage me in conversation and distract me. I tried again and again to explain how my heart belonged to another, but her reply was always the same: "You just think it so!" She'd then storm from the room, only to return a few minutes later with coffee and pie. If nothing else, she was persistent.

When I wasn't eating or trying to fight off her advances, I spent the bulk of my time preparing letters to be sent to those operating depots I frequented. I did so to let them know a general range of time I might show up to their doorstep during my next venture. I knew if these letters fell to the wrong hands, the information within could lead to traps for me and those who were at the depots. Therefore, they were written in a simple code only I and the keepers of the depots understood. I wrote the notes in such a manner the first letter of the first word of each sentence, when put to order, built the true message. On the surface, the letters were rambling and at times incoherent to all but those who understood the code. My letter to the Reverend Rankin, of Ripley, Ohio, began thusly:

> Can I express how much I've missed visiting with you? Oh, I believe not. Most nights I pine for our conversations. In the daylight, the desire is even greater. Night, however, is terrible! Getting together soon must be a priority for both of us. Some visit we must learn to play checkers to help pass the time. On rainy nights, that would occupy us nicely. On any night, such competition would be good for us both. Next visit we shall undertake this. Just you wait and see. Others will be jealous of our frivolity. However, we shall not care. No, we will be full of joy and challenge!

The initial letters, in row—COMING SOON JOHN—told all. I never signed the letters. I didn't have to. I prepared such notes for the Reverend Rankin, the Haines in Alliance, the Keltons in Columbus, the Hubbards in Ashtabula, and even Levi Coffin in Cincinnati, whom all referred to as the "President" of the Underground Railroad, a title he had earned time and again through leadership and courage. I didn't yet know where my next journey would take me, but I felt better knowing at least a scattering of depots would be on alert should I need their assistance. At the same time, I also prepared a note to be delivered to Cat. However, the content of that letter was much different....

With all of us to our duties, the week folded quickly. Too quickly for me. I had hoped for an afternoon or two of fishing, my favorite way to relax and escape thoughts of the cause for at least a few moments. However, there never seemed to be enough time—and the time between journeys felt to be ever shrinking. Still, I could not complain. There was still so much I wanted for the cause.

And now for me. And for Cat.

....

The morning of the interviews dawned bright but with the crisp-
ness of early summer. As was my custom, I walked to the Elgin
Hotel, where I'd visit with those wishing us to bring their loved
ones back to the settlement. When I turned the last corner and
set my eyes upon the building, I could see at once Henry had
been successful in getting word around: a long line of those
hopeful for my services drew along the full length of the front
walk. As I walked past, each in turn reached out to touch me,
many saying, "God bless you" or "Lord protect you." I knew I
could not help them all, so I avoided their eyes as much as possible. I kept mine to the ground ahead of me and replied to each,
"Thank you—thank you."

Lucius and Henry were waiting for me inside the main
entrance.

"This way, John," Lucius said, motioning me to the main
dining area off to the right. All the tables were empty, their chairs
tilted forward against them. There would be no customers and
no food prepared this morning. On the day of interviews, the
proprietors of the hotel ceased all other operation out of respect
for those coming to inquire about my services and those yet to be
set free. There was a solemn atmosphere about the room and, at
the same time, more than a touch of anticipation and excitement.

Henry and I sat at the table farthest from the entrance. He
placed several sheets of blank paper before him, paper he would
use for the gathering of information related to each case we
heard. I stood and walked to the closest window, opening it just
enough to allow the cool breeze to enter.

As soon as I sat back down, Lucius called over, "Ready for
the first?"

Nodding to Henry, then to Lucius, I said, "Let's begin."

For the next two hours we listened to those pleading for the
deliverance of their parents, spouses, children, and other close
relatives. All brought small tokens of appreciation for us, and I

was always touched deeply by this. They brought everything from quilts to handmade knives to bunches of flowers. These were not bribes; they were genuine offerings of thanks, for past ventures and those yet to come. All were worthy of my assistance, but I could not take them all, a fact that weighed heavy to my heart.

One case in particular, that of a man desiring us to free his wife and three children from what he described as the most brutal of owners, was of special interest to me because the location of his family was in close proximity to several of the other cases placed before us earlier. Gathering passengers in a tight geographic area was most desirable—and easiest to arrange. In addition, I wasn't ashamed to admit to Henry I'd take great pleasure in giving that slave owner a taste of his own whip.

Henry and I always discussed the merits of each case between interviews and how much of a fee we might ask for each. As we held these exchanges, he made note of both on special charts he had designed. The fees depended upon many variables: the distance and how long the journey might take, whether we knew the location might require bribes for legal authorities or other officials, potential danger involved, the cost of the ruse which would have to be used, and how much in the way of weapons and other goods we might have to leave behind in the event of a hasty exit. There were also other variables in the more "humanitarian" sector as well, and at times these did overpower our decisions. However, I never let the others forget one of my favorite expressions, one I had learned from my father: "Emotions and money do not mix." It was cold, but it was also true as rain.

We had almost decided upon which we'd accept when a large man with a square head and deeply-set eyes gently brushed Lucius to the side and marched heavily to the table. I recognized him immediately. He was Sampson Taylor, known in Elgin as the most financially successful of all those who had come to the settlement. By his own hand and without a dollar to his name, Sampson had built what had become the largest sawmill of not just the settlement, but the entire region as well. He was not a churchgoer and kept mostly to himself, but through his accomplishments he still retained the highest amount of respect from all.

Before sitting down, he removed three cloth bags from his right pocket and dropped them to the table. The resulting sound indicated all were heavy with coin.

"Sixteen hundred there," he said, sitting and pointing toward the table. "All yours—if you bring my nieces to me."

I started to tell him the sum was nearly four times greater than any fee we'd ever accepted, but he curtly interrupted, "B'fore I run off, promised my brother at his deathbed I'd find a way to get them. Aim to keep that promise. They close-age sisters—'spect now near on to twenty. Just got word they still at Paris, Kentucky."

Then, he stood again, hovered over us, and said, his voice rising, "You'll do it for me."

By the look of his face, I could tell it was, at the same time, a challenge, a command—and a dare. I also admired his bravado. It was how I hoped I could have held myself if the tables had been turned. Therefore, I was not offended by his manner—not in the least. To the contrary, I felt respect and admiration for him.

And then there was the money before us....

"Tell you what I'll do," I replied, looking right to his eyes as I kicked Henry's leg under the table. "I'd be honored to deliver them, but it will cost you more than this."

He raised an eyebrow and sat back to his chair. I then continued, "I'll accept your money, but you also have to give me your word you'll provide the lumber, and any funds yet needed, for the construction of the new meeting house. That work is going slowly—too slowly—and you can settle that. If you're in agreement with that, we have a deal."

I stood, pushed back my chair, and extended my hand. Sampson stared at me for a few moments, stood, and firmly grasped my hand.

"They're right 'bout you," he said. "Said I ought count my

fingers after shakin' with you to make sure you don't end up with some."

"They are right," I replied, shaking his hand again. "No doubt about that. But, I'm good to my word and my work, so I'm tolerated. I never ask for more—nor do I deserve more."

I motioned to Henry. "We'll need some information and descriptions. I'll leave you two to that. Need to stretch my legs."

As I started for the door, Sampson grabbed my arm and said, "Thank you."

"Ain't done nothin' yet," I replied. "You can thank me later."

Lucius, again standing at the doorway, nodded his head and pointed to a white man, still a relatively uncommon sight in the settlement, sitting in a chair on the front porch. As I drew closer, Lucius whispered, "He wanted to be last. Insisted on it. Said he had money to weigh you down."

"Really?" I said, taking stock of him. He was tall and lean, with the attire and bearing of a man born to wealth. "What's his name?"

"Wouldn't say," Lucius replied. "Said he'd only talk with you. Don't like the look of him."

"I don't either," I replied, "but it might be interesting to see what he has to offer. Henry'll be a spell with Mr. Taylor, so I'll meet this gentleman on the side porch. Give me a minute to get settled, then bring him around."

"Okay," he said, shaking his head. "Don't think it wise, though."

"We'll see," I said.

A few minutes later Lucius brought him to the porch and indicated he was to sit in a rocking chair directly across from me. I stood and said, "I hear you'd like a word with me. It's been a long morning, so please state your business quickly."

He removed his hat and said, "Name's Oliver Boyle, from Asheville, North Carolina, and I'm a businessman—same, I hear, as you. Believe we have something in common."

"What would that be?" I asked, rocking back in my chair.

"Money—and a desire for more."

"You have my attention," I said. "Continue, Mr. Boyle."

At first his voice held a cockiness, a swagger. However, it didn't take long for the true emotion behind his words to reveal itself. He was nervous, anxious—much more so than he should have been for simple business dealing. Maybe Lucius had been right in suggesting Mr. Boyle held for us nothing but trouble.

"Word of this settlement has reached as far to the south as where I live, and as I've heard about it, I'm of the belief it has a fair future in store. Therefore, as a businessman, I'm here to purchase land on which to develop a profitable commerce. At the same time, because of the distance to my home, I'm seeking a partner here, one who can keep watch to our operations while I'm away."

"And just what type of commerce would this be?" I asked, noting how quickly sweat was soaking through his shirt.

"As much as this settlement has grown, there are a number of goods and services that require a fair amount of travel to acquire. I hear the merchants of Chatham are less than enthusiastic to conduct their trade with black businessmen. Well, that's to their loss—and potentially to the heart of our gain."

When he paused, I said, "Do continue. You still have my ears."

"Then, Sir, if there were suppliers and merchants nearby who'd be eager for the trade, my guess would be everyone here would frequent them as needed. As the settlement grows, which I am sure it will, so then will the profit from commerce."

"Makes some sense," I said, "but why are you coming to me? I don't own land around the settlement. I have nothing to sell. The Reverend King would be a much better resource than I in a matter of this sort."

Mr. Boyle mopped his brow with his handkerchief. "You are a man holding great respect among the locals. I, on the other hand, am a stranger, an unknown. A man of your reputation surely would have connections to those who do own the land I seek and would be better equipped for the negotiation of purchase. You also know those who could be hired to construct the places of business that would be required."

Smiling weakly, he added, "And besides, Reverend King is a black man. Rather my business be with you. I'm sure you understand."

Lucius looked over at me, shaking his head and raising his eyes. I, feigning agreement, nodded in response.

Mr. Boyle wiped his brow again. "For your contribution to the venture, for your local considerations, I'd offer you a hand-some percentage of the profits from same. Does this interest you?"

I didn't answer right away. Instead, I studied his face, which had grown crimson, and his breathing, which had become short and labored. As he rocked faster and faster in his chair, he appeared a man on verge of illness. He looked away from me so I could not see his eyes.

Finally, I leaned forward and said, "I would be interested—except for one thing."

He coughed loudly before asking, "What, Sir, would that be?"

Catching his eye at last, I added, "You may take offense at what I'm about to say, and if that turns to the case, I ask you to leave this place at once."

Through the years I had acquired the sharp skills of the liar, so it was not difficult for me to detect one myself, especially the amateur as now sat before me. I leaned even closer to him and said, "I don't believe a word you've uttered. Not a one. Do you care to share your real purpose for being here, or would you rather leave now? I'll leave that choice to you."

Lucius, who had been listening intently, drew back his coat and placed a hand to his revolver, a movement captured by Mr. Boyle, whose face was suddenly drained of its color. He stopped rocking and started to stand, but his knees buckled and he fell back, heavily. In one motion, he drew his hands to his face and began sobbing, deeply. Lucius looked at me, shrugging his shoulders. I nodded—and indicated he keep close hold to his weapon.

"You remain here with Lucius," I said, standing. "I'll leave you a moment with your thoughts while I fetch us some coffee."

I purposely took my time, and when I returned several minutes later, Lucius was seated on the railing, sharpening a knife on a small wetstone he kept in his boot. As he did so, he was listening intently to the crackling voice of Mr. Boyle.

As I approached, Lucius stood up, walked over to me, and said, "You better hear this. We've now trouble by the pound."

I sat back in my rocker and urged Mr. Boyle to continue. He began his narrative, pausing every so often to catch his breath and compose himself.

"Said he'd kill my children and sell off my wife if I didn't find you, and I believe him. But more than that, I believe he will do all that no matter what actions I take. That's why I'm choosing to risk all by drawing you into this, by revealing myself to you."

He wiped tears from the corner of his eyes and continued, "I'm now completely at your mercy, Sir. I'm asking—no, I'm begging for your help. I don't know what you can do, but you're my only hope to rid myself of him."

"Who?" I asked, already believing I knew the answer. I needed to hear him say it.

"Taggart. Wilson Taggart. Didn't say why he wanted you so bad, but he's out to have you—or Hell itself in the process. Asked me to find you, gain your confidence, and discover, somehow, when you'd be back south again. Told me that if I didn't succeed, my family would...."

Here his voice trailed off again as he looked far out to the horizon, as if looking there for comfort or strength. Finding neither he placed his face again in his hands.

"Then, a trap?" I asked, reaching over to pull away his hands. "Through you, that's what he's aimin' for, yes?"

"Yes," he replied. "Just said to find your plans. Said he'd do the rest."

"How'd you find me?" I asked, sharply. "Does he know I'm here? Tell me the truth."

"Taggart said he had suspicions you came here, but he wasn't sure. Sent me to find out. Once across Lake Erie, didn't take me long to hear of a 'Messiah' who brought slaves to their freedom here. Took a chance they were speaking of you and came to see for myself."

"And you've sent no letters or word back to this point, right?"

He nodded he hadn't, brushed aside more tears, and continued, "If I don't have something to tell him, all will be lost. Everything. My family..... What can I do?"

"We'll think of something," I said, trying to be as reassuring as I could. However, I was growing less and less fond of Mr. Boyle and his plight as the seconds ticked by.

"For now, this is what we'll do," I said, finally. "I'll see you have a room here for the night. A black man owns this hotel, but I think you'll be able to stand the circumstances for a few hours. You get some rest—and try to calm yourself best you can. I've more business to attend to, but I'll return at dusk. By that time, I'll think up some course of action."

I smiled thinly. "You might as well trust me. Don't see as you have much choice because you were right about one thing: he will kill you and your family, and take pleasure in it, no matter what you do. You were wise to confide in me. Not sure yet if I can help, but if I can't, then we all die. You never forget that."

He nodded.

"Then get yourself inside and ask for a room. Tell them I sent you. Up, now. Let's be at it."

As he entered the hotel lobby, Lucius turned to me and asked, "What do you make of this? Think we can trust him?"

"Not in the slightest," I said, flatly. "Not an ounce of honesty or courage in him far as I can see. But we can use that to our advantage. I've no doubt he'll end up dead somehow, but before that happens, we should be able to use him to bait Taggart."

"How you reckon?"

"Don't know yet, but I'll study on it. There's a way, I'm sure. There has to be."

"There better be," Lucius added. "Boyle being here means Taggart will soon know where we always hole-up after. Don't like the thought of that. Not a whit."

"Me, either," I said. "So we best figure out something—and fast. In the meantime, please keep an eye on him to make sure he doesn't wander off before I return tonight."

"And if he decides to leave?"

"Then follow him—and see he doesn't make it very far. Get my meaning?

"Perfectly," Lucius replied. "And it'd be to my pleasure."

....

The better part of the rest of the day was spent providing directions for Henry and Tasby. Henry was to secure us maps for our route to and from Paris, Kentucky, and print the rest of the paperwork we'd need along the way. I asked Tasby to work his way from merchant to merchant to purchase the remaining goods we'd need to take along with us. By the end of the afternoon, both had accomplished their tasks.

For the remaining part of the afternoon, I thought long and hard about how best to use Mr. Boyle to advantage. I knew he'd need quite a story to tell upon his return or Taggart would kill him at once. I didn't want that to happen. It wasn't I was concerned for Mr. Boyle. I wasn't. I was concerned he'd be put to grave before serving my purposes. I finally came up with a plan I hoped would at least buy Boyle some time—and buy enough for me to come up with a plan of my own. As gutless as Boyle had already shown himself to me, I knew there'd be a chance he'd return home, fall to emotion, foolishly throw himself upon the mercy of Taggart, and reveal all we'd discussed of the morning. I knew I couldn't trust Boyle as far as I could throw him. Whatever plan I came up with, I'd have to account for Boyle's lack of nerve—and Taggart's cold-blooded nature. Such a plan would not come easily.

By design, to make Boyle suffer more, I waited a good half hour past dark before returning to the hotel. Lucius and he were both back at the side porch, sipping at steaming cups of coffee. Both stood as I walked up.

"Ease yourselves back down," I said, pulling a rocker close.

Without wasting any more time, I began, "Here's what we're going to do...."

I shared how our best plan would be to tell Taggart that Boyle had, indeed, gained my confidence and I actually bragged about having several forays back to the south in the planning. At the same time, Boyle was to say I agreed to contact him when a venture took me close to Ashville so we'd be able to conclude our business—and he would immediately send word to Taggart. I allowed it wasn't the best plan in the world, but it was the only one I could think of that would buy him time, time that might save his family. I gave no more specifics. At this point, I knew it was wise not to. Boyle seemed greatly relieved and offered to buy us a round of drinks if we'd lead him to the nearest saloon. When we informed him no liquor was allowed in the settlement, he replied, "Not much of a place to live, is it?"

"Depends upon what you're looking for," I said. "Give that some thought."

I knew he wouldn't. By the look of his eyes, my best guess was his thoughts had already turned to other ways of saving his own skin. That was fine with me. I needed him to remain alive—for at least a little while longer.

"Tomorrow morning I'll find a man to ride with you back to Port Burwell. Don't want anything to happen to you."

"You won't regret helping me," he said, excitedly extending his hand. "I'll make it worth your while. I'll pay you. You'll see."

I shook his hand in turn. "Let's first wait and see if we're all lucky enough to remain above the grave. If that happens—if we somehow end up with Taggart no longer a problem—then we can talk of money. For now, you need to leave here tomorrow morning and get what we discussed back to him. You can do that without breaking down during the telling?"

He nodded slowly but didn't say anything. Instead, he shook

my hand again, then Lucius', and hurriedly walked back inside. When he had gone, I turned to Lucius and said, "Find a good man to go with him tomorrow, a man we can count on, if you have my meaning."

"I do, and I know of such a man. I'll see it done."

"Good. We'll give him a day headstart and get about our own business the morning after. Everything will be ready by then."

As I started to leave, Lucius said, "John, I've a question."

"Go right ahead."

"It's the job you agreed to this morning. I know that's a bushel of money, but why'd you take it? Just two passengers? We never done like this before."

"I took it for what that money can provide. We can never bring back all the passengers we'd like. Not if we lived a thousand years. It's a fact I've learned I have to live with or I'd go completely mad. That money will provide weapons for the settlement, new homes for those who can't afford them, new beginnings for those who show up with nothing but rags and whip marks on their backs."

I smiled. "And you and I aren't getting any younger, my friend. Our usefulness to the cause is closer to the end than the beginning. And it isn't just Taggart and other men like him who make me feel so. I'm not afraid—just feeling a touch more practical these days. There may not be many more journeys for us. If that's the case, then Sampson's money becomes all the more important. Do you understand?"

"I do," he said. "I'm also mighty toward curious about what's to become of Taggart. I think I'll tag along for a spell to see what grows. Knowing you, what's left will at least be an adventure."

"That I can promise you," I replied. "An adventure of a lifetime."

We both exited the porch without another word. There are times when silence is of greatest value.

This was such a time.

....

Serena was seated on the porch when I finally made it back to the cabin.

"You leaving again soon, ain't you?" she asked, lowering her head and looking away.

"I have to. You know that, and you'd be disappointed in me if I didn't."

"But so soon? Can't have you for just few more weeks? You like a spirit—here and gone b'fore can get my arms to you."

"It's for the best—for both of us," I replied.

"Might be for you, but ain't never for me."

She stepped toward me. "I love you so. B'lieve you know that. Always will. This heart won't let me otherwise."

"You're everything a man could want. I...."

She interrupted me and asked, her tone terse, "Then why you not love me? It still her? That why?"

"It's true I care for her. I've told you that before. But, that's not all. There's so much more I have to do, and you can't go with me. You just can't."

"'Cause of this, ain't it?" she asked, tapping her arm. "'Cause of my skin?"

"I won't lie to you," I replied. "That's a part of it. It's not why my heart is as it is, but that keeps you from being able to travel with me most everywhere I need to go."

"I'd be happy be yours just when you here," she said, her tone almost to point of begging. "Be a good wife to you. Best you ever have."

"I know you would. I do. It just isn't the time—at least for now."

I was building false hope, but she was suffering, and I couldn't stand it. So, I took her into my arms, held her close, and whispered to her, "I make no promises, but the time may some-day come. No way to tell yet. Until then, all must stay as it is. It must, and I hope you understand that."

"I don't," she said, choking back tears. "Never will. But, I smart 'nough to know can't change you now. Won't give up, though. Can't. Hope you understand that."

"I do," I replied. "Honestly, I do."

Believing the moment finally right, I brought up what I'd been thinking about for some time. "I do worry about you while I'm away, so I've asked someone to keep watch over you. His name's Mumphry. Just brought him up from Kentucky. Good man. Strong. Smart. He'll be by at least every other day to make sure all is well. I think you two will get along just fine."

"Tryin' to throw me off?" she said, her eyes widening. "Won't work. You tell him keep away. Don't need him. Don't want."

"He's just to help when needed. I'll feel better knowing he's around. So, be nice to him for me. Please?"

She didn't respond. Instead, she backed away. "Well, if you ain't goin' to propose to me tonight, might as well eat sometin'. Got ham and greens—and fresh bread. Maybe you get full belly, you change your mind."

I just shook my head and smiled. "You'll never give up, will you?"

"Never!"

I believed her.

Hand in hand we walked up the steps and into the cabin.

....

Chapter 15

Building a Ruse

Paris, Kentucky

OUR JOURNEY TO PARIS, KENTUCKY, was generally peaceful and even somewhat relaxing. That is, it was if one didn't count the many tales of heroics offered up by Tasby, who now had a fresh audience in Toby. These were told over and over again, each time with even more embellishment. Toby listened wide-eyed and mouth dropped at every account. As usual, I had been present at most of the events described, but my recollections were not of the same world. On top of all, his manner of delivery was constantly punctuated by dramatic gestures and an expression Tasby had picked up back at Elgin: "Why, chaw me up, head to foot, if I ain't truthin'!" He uttered that so often I began to believe Lucius would shoot him from the saddle.

Toby didn't care for silence either. When Tasby wasn't building adventures, Toby tried matching him by repeatedly going over the anatomy of a horse, all while leaning dangerously down and pointing to each: hoof well, pastern, fetlock, cannon loney, forearm, elbow, tendon joint. When he tired of that, he started in on explaining the various types of saddles and tack: plantation saddle, English saddle, trail saddle, sweetwater bit, Kimberwich, snaffle, long shank. By the end of the second day, I gave Lucius a look he understood: "If you shoot Tasby, I'll get Toby." At one stop to rest the horses, Lucius even came up to me and said, "Sure miss Henry. Least he didn't foam at the mouth so." I heartily agreed.

At the same time, I was trying my best to come up with a plan to get at Taggart, but I couldn't settle on anything without enormous risk. However, I vowed to keep at it. At this point, I had no other choice. With the large sum of money we'd earn from this trip and take back to the settlement, I'd be able to take as much time as I needed to find my pursuer. So much depended on this venture.

I never liked taking the same route twice on our way back south, so this time we made our way along a new trail at the eastern edge of Ohio before dropping down into Kentucky. From there we traveled the main road to Mount Sterling, where we purchased a wagon and such tack as Toby advised to make us appear as professional horse buyers. I also purchased "commerce clothes" for my work ahead. After provisioning ourselves so, we continued to Paris and camped in a dry wash to the west of town just as darkness was falling. We had made our destination in remarkable time, just five days.

The next morning, just after dawn broke, Lucius and I left Tasby and Toby with the wagon and made our way to town. The Paris Hotel was directly across from the bank and offered a perfect vantage point for our purposes. There, we entered the dining area and chose a table next to the window, where we took a light breakfast of eggs and coffee while waiting for the bank to open its doors for the business of the day.

Lucius sopped up the last of the sticky yoke of his eggs with a piece of bread, plopped it into his mouth, and then struggled to ask, "How long we gonna wait? Can't plant ourselves here too long b'fore some start starin' at us, you know."

"Waiting's always the hardest." I replied, signaling our waiter to bring us more coffee. "Don't imagine too long, though. Those with money aren't lazy, so they're usually the first to the bank of a morning. We'll find someone soon enough. I'm sure of that."

"I hope so," he said. "This chair's worse than the saddle." He swallowed the last of his breakfast with a wash of coffee. "And besides, don't think I can stand much longer lookin' at you in those clothes. You look a dandy."

"I'm supposed to," I said, tugging at my collar. "That—and a man with pockets full of money and connections to more. I believe I look the part quite well."

"You look a dandy," he repeated, shaking his head.

"I miss my coat, though—and the trappings inside," I replied. "But, I'm still heeled enough if trouble shows its face."

"Your boots?" Lucius asked, quietly.

"Pistol in one. Knife in the other. And another blade here, in my sleeve. Wouldn't want to fall in a river today. I weigh enough to sink right to the bottom."

Lucius laughed and went back to his coffee just as I looked through the window and saw a likely candidate walking toward the bank. He was a tall, older man near to sixty with thick, graying sideburns. He was wearing the clothing of a gentleman and possessed the confident gait of a man clear to mission. I couldn't see her face, but a woman was walking with him, her hand on his arm to the right.

"I believe they'll do," I said, standing. "Stay here long as you like, but if I leave with them, follow us—and keep out of sight."

"I'll find a place to sit outside. Day's warmin' up, so just as soon be in the sun."

"Suit yourself," I said, straightening my suspenders and brushing my hair back. "I've work to do."

"And you love it—love this part of it—don't you?" Lucius asked.

I didn't reply. I was already focused on my mark.

There were a few waiting for assistance inside the bank, and I was mightily grateful for the time it would purchase for conversation. I walked behind the older gentleman, pretended to stumble, and fell forward, righting myself by resting my hand against his left shoulder.

"Oh, I beg your pardon!" I said, backing away. "I am so, so sorry. Must have caught my boot on the edge of this board."

I tapped the floor repeatedly before continuing, "I'm not generally this clumsy. I beg your forgiveness, Sir."

He nodded, ran a hand across his shoulder to straighten his coat, and turned away.

The woman with him turned to me, shaking her head slightly, "You must forgive father. Wouldn't offer two words to a stranger if his very life depended upon it."

Her father glared at her but remained silent. The daughter wasn't what most would have called beautiful, but she was a handsome woman with full eyes and lips. She wasn't overly plump, but her ample proportions made me think she didn't like to miss meals. Her cheeks were round and soft, and her light, blondish hair curled slightly below her shoulders.

"If that truly is the case," I said, bowing slightly, "then it would be a crime for me to remain a stranger. Please allow me to introduce myself. I'm John Fairborn, of the Oxford Fairborns. I'll be in town for a while as I'm currently serving as agent for Mr. Abel Lancaster and several of his associates. You may have heard of Mr. Lancaster."

The mention of the name drew the father's attention, and he again turned toward me. "What would that business be?" he asked, his face now full to attention.

"You know Mr. Lancaster personally—or by reputation?" I asked, hoping for the latter as I had actually never met Mr. Lancaster myself and only used his name because of its reputation for success in every enterprise it touched.

"I know of him," he said, flatly. "Most do." Then, he repeated, his voice more firm this time, "And your business?"

"Father!" his daughter scolded. "Business—right here in public? Rude is rude. Shame on you."

Finally seeing the opening I was waiting for, I jumped in, "Miss, you are very likely to think me the rude one—but I just have to say something. And please feel free to slap me if you wish; I know I'll deserve it. I've been on the road quite a long time now, and I just want you to know you are the most breathtaking sight

I've seen my whole way here. Why, the flowers of early summer have nothing on you. I'm sincere in my words and mean no disrespect of any type to you. I'm merely making an observation. I realize I should keep my thoughts inside, but I can't help myself. I never can when I'm caught off guard by such beauty."

It was plain compliments were not common for her, so she stared at me blankly, as if unsure how to respond. She then fanned herself, the motion of her hand increasing rapidly.

I didn't give her a chance to find her words. I turned to her father and said, "And I apologize to you, Sir, for my boldness, true as my words may have been. And also for my earlier act of clumsy."

He started to speak, but he also appeared flustered and more than slightly confused. I continued, attempting to distract him from my comments about his daughter. "My business, Sir, is to make a profit for Mr. Lancaster, something of which he has become accustomed, as you may well know. I'd be most happy to share details of the whole enterprise with you at a more convenient time, as your daughter is correct. This is no place to discuss business."

Here I lowered my voice to just above a whisper. "But the short of it is we—that is, Mr. Lancaster and his associates—have come up with a plan to find profit in those making their way to the west. It is, to my way of thought, a plan of genius, a plan my family endorsed and were glad to join from the beginning."

I glanced at those in line ahead of us, and turned back to him. "That is all I should say here. I believe you understand why."

The daughter, still fanning herself, stepped forward and said, a smile finally forming, "I see you're as bad as Father when it comes to public discussion of business. Shame on you, too."

She playfully poked me with her fan. "And you *were* rude to shower those words to me. And that in public, too." Here with a flourish, she waved her hand at those around us in the bank.

Then, turning to her father, she said, "Two peas in a pod, I see. Heaven help us all. That's just what this town needs. Still, I doubt much will ever change for either of you. That seems clear enough to me already. Only thing to do, I suppose, is get you both to yourselves so you can continue counting your money."

At this point we were growing to be the center of attention in the bank, attention the woman obviously relished. "Mr. Fairborn of Oxford," she announced, "this is my father, Charles Conklin. My name is Amy. We've a place to the west of here, and you'd be most welcome to come dine with us this evening, if you aren't previously engaged. I believe you and Father would find conversation to the liking of both. Well, Mr. Fairborn, will you accept the invitation?"

Mr. Conklin, obviously used to his daughter's boldness in such matters, looked at me and rolled his eyes. "Please do."

"I accept," I said, again bowing slightly. "And I'm deeply honored to do so. At what time would you like me to arrive?"

Amy stepped in front of her father and said, "Seven. We dine early—because commerce has him up with the chickens each morning. I hope that is acceptable to you."

"I'm always reminded of, and firmly believe in, Benjamin Franklin's wise words: 'Early to bed, early to rise, makes a man, healthy, wealthy, and wise.' So, I personally find no fault with your father's habits."

"I knew it!" she replied. "Two peas in a pod. It's plain you will enjoy each other's company. Why, I might not get a single word in at all tonight."

Mr. Conklin and I glanced at each other and smiled.

We both knew there was little chance of that.

....

Lucius and I spent the rest of the afternoon spreading word we were looking to purchase horses of the best quality. When questioned as to the reason, we kept our responses simple: We were planning to take them to Missouri and Kansas Territory to sell to those making their way west. For most, the idea of families uprooting and moving westward through untamed territories known for crude trails, unpredictable weather, and savages lurking behind every tree and bush was the height of foolishness. However, there were others, although a decided minority, who secretly wished they could do so themselves, and they were quick to recommend farms and plantations we might visit in our search for the horses.

Our last stop of the day was the town saloon, where we purchased a round of drinks for all present. These were funds well spent as I was also then able to talk of my plan to those who would have listened eagerly to a "fire and brimstone" sermon if a drop of alcohol was at its conclusion. From experience, I knew this audience would announce our venture across the town most quickly. At that point, I was very happy with how all was unfolding. That is, I was until we stepped from the saloon.

In an instant, my breath caught. I instinctively bent down and, with as little motion as possible, drew the pistol from my boot and placed it in my trouser pocket, my finger finding the trigger at the same time. There, at the hitching rail directly across the street, two riders stood staring at us. After a matter of mere seconds, they mounted their horses, eased them back a few steps, and urged them at a slow walk past us. For a moment, the riders continued gazing intently at us. Then, they lowered their hats, tilted their heads to the side, and moved on, finally kicking their mounts to a gallop as they neared the edge of town.

Lucius turned to me and said, "Taggart's men. No doubt 'bout it. Seen the one just b'fore they pinned us down that day. Never forget that ugly face. They may have placed us, too. Want me to go after 'em?"

"No—don't think so. We *should* go after 'em, and we *should* take care of 'em—but we can't risk a fight just yet. Don't have the time for one thing. We won't be here that long if all goes to plan. No, we'll just have to trust to luck they didn't recognize us and will have to work quicker is all. Then, we better get away from here like the flames of Hell are at our heels."

"What if they did place us? Think any chance they'd be back?"

"They won't if he's not around. Wouldn't risk it. So, I expect we'll know one way or the other soon enough."

"And what if he's here?"

" I don't think he is. I just don't feel it. Think he'd have been with 'em here in town. He's not one to stay out on the trail with a saloon this close by."

"Seems we might be riskin' awful lot on just what your gut says."

"I know," I said smiling weakly. "I better not be wrong. Not this time."

Lucius didn't reply. Instead, he pointed toward our horses. His meaning was clear: we had precious little time to waste.

"When we get to the horses, do it quickly and without drawing attention—but get your pistols from the saddlebags. I'll do the same. Even if they did recognize us, I still don't think they'd try to drop down on us, but we best be prepared just in case."

"I'll be ready. You can count on that."

"I know," I said. "You always are, and for that I'm grateful."

I took a final glance at the riders fading in the distance. "Now let's go. We've much to do."

....

With the seeds of our ruse firmly planted, Lucius and I rode back to camp to check on Tasby and Toby and prepare them for upcoming events. Now that dinner with a respectable family had been secured, the next step for me was to ask the Conklins, in the course of the evening, if it might be possible for them to help me locate a suitable place for my "slaves" to be kept while I conducted business in the town. Once Tasby and Toby were quartered such, it would make it easy for them to question the slaves in the area and find the exact location of the passengers we were seeking. When they made contact with and prepared them for the journey ahead, our plan would then, I hoped, unfold smoothly and rapidly.

As we entered camp, Tasby, never one to be shy in such

matters, howled at us, "We kept out here in the sun all the day long. Near to burn up in this heat. Near to die, I s'pose. What took so long in that town? Bet you was drinkin' and looking to women, too, wasn't you?"

"You hear that?" I said to Lucius. "Such talk from slaves!"

"I'd say we shoot one of 'em," he replied, drolly. "And I know which one."

Toby grinned and said, "I've felt the whip enough in my days. Keepin' my mouth shut is what I aim to do."

"That's a good slave," Lucius said, laughing aloud. "Hope some of that rubs off on the other one, too."

Tasby helped Lucius down from his horse and said, "Well, you just try sittin' here in the blazin' sun with nothin' to do all them hours. See how you'd to like it."

"Okay, enough teasing," I said, dismounting and motioning everyone to gather close. "We've not got the luxury of time. And, likely even less than first planned—now that we may have been spotted."

I quickly relayed to Tasby and Toby the events of the day and asked them to keep extra watch in case Taggart's men showed up again. I'd work quickly as possible to get them either to the Conklin plantation or another just as suitable for our purposes. Tasby was experienced in my methods, so I asked him to explain later to Toby how they'd work to discover the whereabouts of our passengers—and what they'd need to do in preparation after that.

When we finished our discussion, I took Lucius to the side and said, "After what we saw today, I'd like you to come with me tonight and stay with the horses while I'm in their home. I'd be more to ease if I knew you were watching my back."

"Was plannin' on it. You just weave your stories—and leave the rest to me. Nothin' will get by me."

"Thank you," I said, placing my hand on his shoulder. "Tonight then should go smooth as ever."

Lucius spit a stream of tobacco to the ground and said, "Do it quickly. Your gut might not be growlin', but mine has a odd feelin'. I think we best be gone from here fast as lightning."

"You may be right at that," I said.

Lucius grunted his approval and looked off to the horizon, first scanning east and then far off to the west. I could guess the meaning of the look on his face. We knew Taggart had men searching for us, but what we didn't know was where he was holed-up while waiting for news. As there was a chance his men had recognized us, I hoped I was right and he wasn't close by. However, no matter what rock he was under, we still had work to do, and nothing—not even Taggart—was going to keep us from it.

....

Earlier in the day I had asked specific directions to the Conklin plantation. The reply, from an elderly hired man at the stable, was plain enough: "Just ride west 'till ya see nothin' but fields of young tobacco shootin' up. Then, keep on 'till ya see the biggest house a body ever saw. That's them. If ya miss it, ya be blind."

The man was right. When the Conklins' home finally came to view, I was awestruck—and I'd seen some mighty grand homes in my day. A dozen columns, each about eight feet apart, held the roof of the front porch. The main part of the structure consisted of two floors of rooms—with a somewhat smaller third floor centered just above the second. Tall, rectangular windows were evenly spaced between the columns and reflected the late evening sun.

A tall, slender black man walked over to take the reins of our horses as we finally dismounted. Before I could thank him, Miss Amy stepped out to the porch and said, "Glad you're on time. Father never is. At least I've discovered one way you two are different. Bodes well for the evening, I'd say."

"And a good evening to you," I said, tipping my hat. "What a magnificent home. You're still the beauty of the area, and I'll stick by those words, but this falls in not too far behind. Absolutely magnificent!"

"You do like to spoon out your flattery, don't you?" she said, walking down the steps to shake my hand. "The question in my mind is whether you're sincere—or just like most all other men I've known."

"Trust me," Lucius suddenly cut in. "He's not like anyone you've ever known b'fore. That's the truth of the matter."

Amy looked at Lucius before turning to me, a questioning look on her face.

I nodded toward Lucius. "He's my protection. I've been known to carry quite large sums of cash for my dealings, and he's always with me to make sure I'm not parted from those. This is Lucius, and with your permission, he'll wait with the horses while I'm here."

He bowed slightly toward her and backed away. She barely acknowledged him, her face empty of emotion, then returned her attention to me.

"Father's been anxious to visit with you, so I expect we better hurry in. And if you don't find my words too bold, I'm not ashamed to admit I've been looking forward as well to what few words he'll let us put together."

"No, I don't find it too bold at all. As a matter of fact, I was counting the minutes until we'd be together again. I hope you don't find *that* too bold."

"Flattery again," she said, smiling and leading me up the steps. "You just keep that up and see what it gets you."

"You've now made it a challenge," I replied.

Amy swatted me again with her fan and led me into the house. Once inside, she motioned me to follow through an entryway with polished marble floors and recessed areas in the walls that housed magnificently cast busts of historical figures, several of which I recognized—Caesar, Pliny, and Socrates. We continued down a long corridor lined with the history of the Conklin family shown in portraits of dower-faced women and stern-faced men. Off to our right, as we walked past the parlor, I noted no expense had been spared in acquiring the furnishings—lamps with gold-embossed bases, ornate silver candelabras, high-backed oak chairs of the highest grain and quality, and even decorative and colorful tapestries.

This was even better than I had hoped for.

We finally came to Mr. Conklin's study. He was seated at a polished mahogany desk, a large glass of brandy in his hand. Behind him shelves of books lined the walls. When we entered, he stood, shook my hand, and pointed to his glass and then at me.

"Not just yet, Sir—but thank you," I said. "Maybe later."

"Father likes his brandy just a little too much if you ask me," Amy interrupted.

"And my daughter likes the sound of her own voice a little too much—if you ask me," he said. "She's never at a loss for words."

"I like that in a woman," I said. "Good conversation is hard to come by these days, and if a man finds it in a beautiful woman, so much the better."

"Women were quiet when I was a young man," he replied.

"But that was back before men discovered fire," Amy shot back, frowning. "Things have changed just a mite since."

"Too much so," he continued. "Why, I remember when...."

Mr. Conklin stopped in mid-thought when a young black woman entered the room and announced dinner was ready.

"We're saved by the food—thank goodness," Amy said, walking over to take my arm again. "Otherwise, we'd have to sit through another sermon on what a fool Adam was to keep Eve around."

Mr. Conklin just shook his head and said to me, softly, "Better watch out for her. That's all I'm going to say." He then smiled and motioned us to follow him to the dining room, which, as we entered, I noted was at least twice the size of the whole of my cabin.

Over the course of the next hour, as we enjoyed a grand spread of chicken, early peas and carrots, sweet potatoes, and an assortment of fresh breads, I barely fit two words into the conversation that turned back and forth between father and daughter. Mr. Conklin's wife had died when Amy was but ten years old, and he had yet to find anyone who could come close to filling his heart with the same love and affection. I also found out the plantation had been handed down through Mr. Conklin's grandfather and father—and that the grounds consisted of nearly six thousand acres mostly put in with cotton and tobacco—but a fair-sized parcel of land was also used for everything related to sorghum production. By all indications, the Conklins were among the wealthiest of families in the region, a fact of which Mr. Conklin was mightily proud.

Much to her horror, Mr. Conklin also went on and on about his daughter's failings—everything from the amount of time it took her to dress of a morning to the fact she had an opinion about every subject that came before her. He meant his stories to be humorous, and in fact his words indicated more pride in his daughter than disappointment, but it was still clear he believed she would be much to the better if a husband who could control her came along. The way he eyed me as he told his stories made it clear he was sizing me up as a potential candidate for the position.

When I finally saw an opening to get into the conversation, Amy said something that caught me completely off guard. "Father and I disagree about most things these days, but I try to understand his views. Truly I do. However, there is one area we've been having words about where I believe we could use the perspective of someone from outside these walls. Could I trouble you for your views to it?"

"Whatever I can do to help, I'm your humble servant," I replied, glad finally to get in a few words.

"Amy!" Mr. Conklin shouted. "We don't need to air that discussion with Mr. Fairborn."

"And why not?" she retorted, loudly, boldly. "I'm going to ask him."

"I don't want to come between a father and his..."—was all

I could get out before Amy continued. "I've been trying to get Father to draw papers to grant freedom to our slaves after his passing. I feel if they've been loyal and devoted servants, they deserve to be rewarded."

She paused only slightly before continuing, even louder this time, "It would be the right, and Christian, thing to do!"

Mr. Conklin rubbed his temples before throwing into the discussion, "You just don't understand what would happen—the ramifications that would fall. They can't take care of themselves. We have to do that. If we set them free, where would they go? What would they do? They'd all be starved out or dead in three months. That's true, and you know it deep down. Why, I think...."

"Hogwash!" Amy interrupted. "Most would likely just keep working for us. Wouldn't have to provide much more than room and board. We do that now anyway, and they'd be happy and have incentive to work even more if we also paid them something, which we can afford to do."

Then, turning to me, she asked, "What are your views on this, Mr. Fairborn? Be truthful now."

I took a few moments to study the faces of both. Amy was full of steam, her breathing coming in rapid bursts. It was clear she was firm in her thoughts on the matter—and wasn't interested in what others had to say. Mr. Conklin, on the other hand, had pulled a kerchief from his vest and was mopping his brow. It was very clear he'd had this discussion with his daughter many times. He was also a man obviously defeated in debate—but still in control of the final decisions to be made on the subject—at least for the time being.

As I looked at them, I felt the great irony of the situation. While I didn't agree with her logic—that slaves had to earn their freedom—I was intrigued and wanted to know more of her feelings on the subject. At present, I just couldn't tell whether her views were formed by the guilt of the wealthy and spoiled or if she genuinely had feelings for our darker brothers and sisters. At the same time, I knew Mr. Conklin controlled the family fortune, some of which I hoped to take back north with me, so becoming an ally to his beliefs seemed to be the path of most advantage. Therefore, not wanting to wear out my welcome with either, I chose my words carefully before responding.

Addressing both of them, I said, "First of all, I'd consider it most kind if you'd call me John. Whenever I hear 'Mr. Fairborn,' I tend to look around for my father. I'll let a few more years pass before I feel comfortable being called such."

I continued, directing my words to Amy. "On the matter at hand, I both respect and admire your view. A Christian man could not do otherwise. It is possible one day freedom and equality will come for all. Many say this is truly what the Almighty intended. I'm just a humble man of business and am not the best authority to consult on that subject. But...."

My pause had a purpose. Out of the corner of my eye I could see Mr. Conklin fidgeting in his chair and knew it was time to shift my words toward his way of thinking.

Looking directly at him, I said, "But... I also feel this to be dangerous territory for all us southerners right now. Granting freedom for slaves might not hurt larger plantations, like this one, but for the smaller ones the loss of those working the fields would be devastating. Such action, on a wide scale, would likely cripple the South both economically and politically. So, while I sincerely respect Miss Amy's view, I also see the consequences that might result from what I'm sure she believes the humanitarian thing to do."

Before either could speak, I added, "The matter will be settled in due course. In the meantime, all sides of this discussion will have to respect the views of the others, lest all go up in flames. That, to my way of thinking, is the wise thing to do."

I didn't believe a word I said, but I knew it was the most common of arguments in the South—and Mr. Conklin would be pleased to hear it spouted again. Slavery was an evil institution—plain and simple. There was no place for it in this world, no matter the justifications provided. The facts were simple enough. The

South would not shrivel up and die if slaves were set free. The overall economy of the region was more than strong enough to survive such a change, although most would never admit to it.

Still others, especially those who did not wish to tie themselves to economic arguments, felt slavery was a "Southern Tradition" and should be kept at all costs to preserve a way of life many felt would vanish without it. These poor souls were the most ignorant of all. How could they truly believe "tradition" and "slavery" were inseparable—that tradition justified bondage and brutality? Through the years I had asked this question of many who kept slaves, but I had yet to hear an answer that made me feel anything but anger toward those believing such. All fell back to the "tradition for tradition's sake" argument, which was little better than saying we should never consider change of any type for fear of what we might discover. I'd never understand their beliefs, but at the same time, I never once had any doubts about my own. To my grave, I'd carry with me the belief slavery was the work of the Devil—and I'd never offer quarter of any type to those who aligned themselves with him.

And yet, here I was, in the middle of a splendid dinner, spouting the words of pro-slavers. The taste in my mouth was sour, but not nearly as foul as it was when I thought of the thousands of slaves feeling the slice of the whip and the hopelessness born of chains each day.

To my great surprise, neither jumped in and attacked my words. Rather, Mr. Conklin muttered, quietly, "I suppose it best we leave the matter for the present."

Amy, calmly followed with, "You'll never change my mind—either of you. And that's a fact."

As Amy turned toward the window, I said, "Mr. Conklin, I know my timing may seem inappropriate just now, but the conversation reminds me I've two of my slaves traveling with me, and I'm seeking a place for them to stay at the times they're not of service to me while I'm here. Would you be able to recommend a solution for me?"

To my relief, he suggested they be kept with his own, so I said I'd have them brought over before morning. I then turned and faced him. "I've one more matter. I'd consider it most kind if you'd give your blessing to my coming back to visit your lovely daughter tomorrow. Though I do have my own opinions, I'm always open to hearing the thoughts of others—and I'd value an opportunity to hear more of your daughter's. Sir, may I have your permission?"

"If you wish," he said, smiling. "But you best be ready for a good lashing by that tongue. Just want you to know what you're in for."

"Father!" Amy protested, her mouth falling open. "How can you say such a thing—and about your own daughter!"

Mr. Conklin again looked at me and smiled. I knew exactly what that smile meant.

Their house slaves at last brought in dessert, a crisp apple cobbler well covered with the sweetest sorghum I'd ever tasted. Soon after, Mr. Conklin called for a bottle of brandy.

"Always best to coat the stomach after a meal is what I say. John—a glass for you now?"

Before I could respond, Amy said, dryly, "Father believes brandy should be taken liberally—and at every occasion. And I mean *every*."

"I can find no fault with that," I said, raising my glass to toast both of them.

As we neared the end of our evening, I found opportunity to share with Mr. Conklin the details of my purpose for coming to the area. I relayed, with as much enthusiasm as I could, the potential profit to be gained from the provisioning of those heading to the west. I spoke first of the recent dramatic increase in the price of horses in Missouri and Kansas Territory, the two most popular jumping off points for the travelers, and what this would mean for those supplying these mounts and the wagons sold along with them. From there, I moved the conversation quickly to potential financial gains from building trading posts at strategic points along the trails west, trading posts where all variety of goods could be sold to the hardy souls.

When Mr. Conklin's manner finally suggested he was at least partially sold on the enterprise, I concluded matter-of-factly, "Because of how large this is all likely to be, Mr. Lancaster did want me to see if I could find another investor or two while through this area. Can you think of anyone experienced enough in commerce you might recommend I make visit with?"

By the look in his eyes, I could tell he took the bait—fully and completely. Mr. Conklin took another sip of his brandy and replied, "I do believe I know one."

He then looked toward Amy, who was also smiling. "Young man, I've been associated with many ventures in my day, and I have to say this one sounds among the best. The trails west are only going to become more rutted by those seeking new lives—and many of those people will carry great sums of money with them."

Mr. Conklin took another swallow of brandy, "And I believe I'd like to have some of that for myself. Would you feel comfortable petitioning Mr. Lancaster on my behalf—to see if he'd be so kind as to involve me?"

"I was hoping you'd say that," I said, raising my glass to salute him. "I believe you will find handsome profit, and I will be happy for you. At the same time, on a purely selfish level, I'll become all the richer myself—because I'll then possess more reason for finding myself back here in your lovely home."

My last words were directed toward Amy, and she knew it.

"There's just one more thing, Sir," I added. "With good fortune, I'll be able to secure from this area the full number of horses I require in a matter of days. While I'm here, as agent for Mr. Lancaster, I am authorized to draw papers to formalize the involvement of investors deemed worthy partners in our venture. And, Sir, I place you at the highest of that order."

I studied his face again and continued, "Mr. Lancaster insists upon cash from his partners—for the obvious and practical reasons—so if you are truly interested in joining us, we'll need to meet, at your convenience of course, at the bank again. While you secure the requisite funds, I'll draw up the partnership papers. Is that acceptable to you?"

Mr. Conklin replied, "It is. Let's say tomorrow as the bank opens—if that's convenient for you."

"That will be fine," I said. "I find it especially appropriate because I desire enough time in the afternoon for a buggy ride with a beautiful young woman I know in these parts. That is, if she is available."

"She is," Amy said, fanning herself again. "I'm fairly sure of it. Close to the hour of one would be splendid."

I nodded and smiled back. "Then one it shall be."

Mr. Conklin stood and excused himself. "I know when two young people should be left alone. As difficult as it is for my daughter to believe, I was once young myself and remember such things."

With that, he turned and left the room. I then took Amy by the arm and led her out to the front porch.

"I should go now—but I'd rather do anything but," I said, moving closer to her, looking deeply into her eyes. "I don't know how I'll be able to stand the time between now and tomorrow."

"You'll just have to try your best," she said, also moving closer to me. When our faces were just inches apart, I leaned forward and kissed her softly, gently—finally drawing her close and pressing our lips firmly together. She let out a low moan and dropped her fan—but did not back away. We continued, locked in embrace, until we heard horse hooves clomping toward us. At the same instant, we backed away from each other and spotted Lucius nearing the bottom of the stairs.

"I'm sorry," he said. "Please forgive me."

"I don't think we should," I said, turning back toward Amy. "What do you think?"

She smiled and replied, "Maybe forgiven just this once. But, never again."

I kissed her hand, turned, and slowly walked down to Lucius, who handed me my horse's reins.

"Till tomorrow afternoon, then," I said, climbing onto the saddle.

"Until then," she replied.

Lucius and I rode back to camp. My work, for the night, was complete.

....

Chapter 16

Waiting Game

Signal Point, Tennessee

W‍ARREN L‍EWIS’ H‍ORSE W‍AS W‍ELL-L‍ATHERED and breathing short bursts when he came over a long rise and found Wilson Taggart and two of his men just off the main trail and back against a high canebrake along Morton’s Creek. As Warren moved closer, he first saw a black man, tied at the ankles, dangling from the branch of a towering oak tree. To the right, he saw another man staked out next to a roaring fire. Wilson Taggart was standing over this man, a blazing hot iron with a small “r” brazed at the end, in his right hand.

“Hold him down good, boys,” Taggart commanded. “Don’t let his head move—nary an inch.”

One of Taggart’s men straddled the man’s legs and pressed the full of his weight to keep him from squirming side to side. The other, a small man wearing filthy rags and with streaks of dirt several directions across his face, stepped forward and mashed his boot roughly on the staked man’s hair, pinning his head to the side so that he was unable to move at all.

“Please, Suh!” the staked man cried out. “Have mercy to me. Beg you, Suh! Won’t ever run a’gin. Promise you!”

“If you do, I’ll know it,” Taggart replied, gruffly. “This here’s my mark, and if I see it again, as I did on him, you’ll end the same. That I promise you.”

He pointed to the runaway, now motionless, hanging limply

from the tree branch. His throat had been cut, and he had been dead for some time. Blood had dripped from his tattered shirt and trousers to the soft dirt below, where it had formed small, ruby puddles.

"Hold him tight now," Taggart said, bending down and placing the glowing iron firmly to the staked man's right cheek. The sizzle of steel to flesh could be heard, followed by a small puff of smoke rising directly above. The man let out a high-pitched scream that carried several seconds. His whole body then went limp as he fell to unconsciousness. The "r" was burned raven black, deep into his cheek just over from the tip of his upper lip.

Taggart stood again and without looking, flung the iron back toward the fire. He laughed heartily and said, "You can let go of him now. Won't be goin' anywhere. Bring that packhorse over here and tie him across the saddle—feet to hands. Doesn't deserve more for the ride back."

He kicked the limp man once for good measure. "He's worth three hundred, so guess we'll have to keep him breathin'—but let's not make it easy. Want all at the plantation to see what's become of him."

"What about this 'un?" the small man asked, pointing the direction of the tree.

"Has value, too," Taggart replied. "Cut him down. We'll take him back so the others can see what happens the second time I see the mark. Always love that show. They get sick and wail and...."

Just then he saw Warren stepping down from his horse and moving toward him. To the others he commanded, "Get 'em tied down good—and do it fast b'fore I take the whip to you. And don't you think I won't!"

Taggart then motioned Warren to follow him toward the canebrake. When they were out of earshot of the others, Warren turned and asked, "What you doin' here? Thought you were still waitin' for news in Chattanooga."

"Easy money," Taggart replied. "Close by—and couldn't pass it up."

Then, his expression hardening, he asked, "Why are *you* here? Any word?"

"Maybe," Warren replied, taking off his hat and fanning away the heat of the day.

"What do you mean 'maybe'?" Taggart said, his voice turning to a growl.

"Don't know for sure. Just received a wire from Tolson and McMurphy. They were over to Paris and saw a couple of men they thought might run with Fairfield. They never seen 'em before, but the reason I come to see you is one was some close to the description on the posters. Just thought you should know is all."

"Paris," Taggart muttered under his breath as he turned away from Warren. "He's worked Kentucky too much the past two years. Be surprised if it was him."

Turning back to Warren, he said, "Since we're not sure, I'll stay. You go. Take these two with you. I'm sick to the sight of 'em. Neither has the brain of a hog. Keep 'em on point and maybe they'll get picked off. That'd do us all a favor."

Warren rolled his eyes and shook his head. "Why them? Ain't worth the gunpowder it'd take to blow their heads off."

Taggart shrugged his shoulders and replied, "If you get tired of 'em, shoot 'em. Fine with me."

Then, squatting and clearing a small area in the dirt, Taggart picked up a stick and started the outline of a map. "Let's see now. Paris is here. If it is him, he'll likely cross the Ohio up here, at Ripley. Got both Reverend Rankin and that old black-devil John Parker there. He'd likely stop and shelter with one of 'em if my guess to be right. So, here's what I want you to do."

Poking his stick in the ground just north and east of his mark for Ripley, he continued, "You get there quick as you can and camp off the main trail. Send one of these idiots back to Ripley and see if he can find out anything. Doesn't actually matter if he does or don't, but that'll get his smell away from you for a time anyway. If Fairfield's on the move, he'll eventually get your direction. You take note of everyone who passes. If you get the slightest notion a group might be right, jump 'em and find out. If it ain't them, just let 'em pass and say you was lookin' for someone else."

He broke the stick roughly across his knee. "If it's him, take him. If it's him and you don't take him, then I'll take you. Have my meaning?"

Warren did. He nodded sharply and backed away.

"Good," Taggart said, also standing. "Soon as those two are done tying everything off, take 'em with you back to town and get supplies you'll need. Then head toward Ripley yet today. Don't want any time wasted. Might be close this time."

"And you?" Warren asked.

Somebody's got to take these back to their plantation and collect the reward. If we send one of that scum, he'd like as not run off, and we'd never see 'em or the money again. No, I'll go myself. I better."

He grimaced. "If I had feeling it was really him, I'd be off with you. But since we don't know more, I best head back later to Chattanooga and wait for other news in case it comes. We've men everywhere now. If I missed him b'cause I was off on a goose chase, would never forgive myself."

"If it is him, I'll get 'em," Warren interrupted, his words clipped, cold.

"I know you will," Taggart replied, pressing his right hand to a pistol in his belt.

His meaning was clear to Warren. "I won't let you down," Warren said.

Taggart just stroked the handle of his gun and smirked. Warren didn't need to see or hear anything else.

Taggart turned and yelled to the others, "Be done in five minutes or I'll shoot your ears off!"

Both looked up, stopped their work a few seconds, then doubled their pace.

"Wish me luck," Warren said, walking toward his horse.

"Don't believe in luck," Taggart replied. "Believe in this."

He drew his pistol, cocked the hammer, and pointed it at Warren's head.

Warren stepped to the side, ducked slightly, and screamed toward his new traveling companions, "Hurry up! Now!"

Taggart jerked his arm to the right and fired a shot directly over their heads. Both immediately dove down and clawed at the ground.

"I expect they'll be ready by time you're in the saddle," Taggart said, smiling broadly. "Just needed a little persuadin' is all."

All got his point.

Perfectly.

....

Chapter 17

Sweet Confidence

OUR MEETING AT THE BANK went more smoothly than I had expected. I arrived shortly before Mr. Conklin and secured from the bank manager a table toward the rear where we might conduct our business. Thanks to the superb printing work of Henry, I had with me an impressive array of contracts and forms to draw from for the new "partnership." As a matter of fact, Henry's documents were so good, so professional in style, that there were moments I almost believed I was entering into legal negotiations.

After leading Mr. Conklin through the typical language of such paperwork, I approached him with the sum he would immediately have to provide to be involved in the venture: $2,000. To my surprise, he didn't blanch. Instead, he put on a small, round pair of spectacles, drew the papers close to his face, studied them intently for a few minutes, and finally replied, simply, "Looks acceptable to me. Where do I sign?"

We completed our business in less than twenty minutes. Mr. Conklin was all smiles as we left the bank. So was I, and for a very different reason. I had his money in my pocket.

With the first major portion of the day's work completed, the next order of business belonged to Tasby and Toby, who were searching for the whereabouts of our passengers. While they attended to that, I had to prepare for a buggy ride with Miss Amy.

The appointed time, one in the afternoon, came soon enough. I hired a buggy from the livery and drew to the Conklin home a few minutes early. Amy was already waiting for me on the porch, her hand clutched to the handle of a large basket. She possessed not a lick of that "Southern shyness" typically found in women of these parts.

"You're a man on time," she said loudly as I stepped from the buggy.

"Would have come earlier," I said, taking the basket from her hand, "but I didn't want to appear too anxious."

As I placed the basket in the buggy, I said, "Shouldn't say it, but your beauty draws my thoughts so much now when I'm away from you. Saying so is definitely not proper, but I'm not a man to waste much time. I hope you're discovering that already."

"I am," she said, stepping forward and kissing me lightly on the cheek. "And I'm not a woman to waste time. I'm guessing you're also already finding that conclusion. Am I right?"

"I've a notion that's so. Now, since we're both in agreement about the importance of the clock, I'd be honored to begin our ride. As I'm not familiar with the area, I'll bow to your judgment. In which direction would you like us to travel?"

"If you've the time, I'd like you to see some of Rosedale. That's what my father calls our little place—in memory of my mother, Rose Emily Conklin."

"Again, I'd be deeply honored. Let's be off."

Once we were comfortably seated and on our way, Amy said, proudly, "Can't see it all in a day. Father tried it once and ended up sleeping under a tree in the rain. He's still teased about that."

"What I've seen so far is stunningly beautiful," I said, motioning to a small lake and a dense grove of oak trees off to our left. You and your father are very lucky to have a place like this to call home."

"Luck had very little to do with it," she replied, curtly. "My grandfather and his father fought Indians, drought, and squatters for every inch of Rosedale. This has our blood in it. I love it so—I do—and don't know if I could ever leave it."

She then lowered her voice and asked me, almost in a whisper, "And your home? What's it like?"

I knew what she wanted to hear, so I replied, doing my best to add a touch of exasperation and sadness to my words, "Don't really have one now. I attend to my business so much I haven't given a great deal of thought to finding a permanent place to call home. I guess you could say, at least for now, I'm a ship without a port. If the Good Lord ever blesses me with a wife, then of course I'd want to plant some roots. Just hasn't happened yet, is all."

Amy smiled and placed her hand on my arm. "You'll find a good woman. I just have a feeling about that."

Over the next half hour, she did her best to audition for the role. She wasn't bashful in the least about sharing the memorable moments from her childhood and upbringing. At one point, she even described how she'd be favored by her father, in terms of dowry and land, if she were to marry. I noted she watched my eyes carefully as she came to that part, apparently trying to determine if the business side of me was interested in the potential windfall nuptials would bring. I knew it best to stay close to the middle of the road, so I said, "It will be a lucky man who takes you for his wife—in so many ways. That I know already."

At that point, I thought it best to change the subject of our conversation, so I asked, "We've come quite a far piece, and I see ahead a fork in the road. What shall we do?"

"I'd like you to see my special place, a place I came every chance I had when I was a girl. It's just over that rise. Stay to the left. We'll be there shortly."

Once over the rise, I immediately saw why she favored the area most of all. Ahead of us ran a branch of the Clearwater River, a river fitting of its name as one could see through its spring-fed water down to its colorful, rocky bottom. Stately oak and maple trees, their leaves still maturing in the early summer sun, lined the river's banks on both sides. Just before the trees on our side of the river, a field of early wheat, intersected by the road, swished and swayed in the breeze.

"Let's stop over there," Amy directed, pointing left to a small clearing at the edge of the river. "I like to sit there and watch the water flowing by. Every time I come here, I lose myself in thought, and the hours just seem to melt away before me."

I eased the horses to a halt, hopped to the ground, then helped her from the buggy. "I can most certainly see why," I said. "Most beautiful place I've seen in a long, long time. Thank you for sharing this with me, Miss Amy. Beauty gives beauty. I'm not sure life gets better than that for a man."

"Now you stop that flattery or I'm going to insist we leave at once!" she said, her voice rising.

I knew she wasn't serious, but I played along. "Yes, Miss," I said. "I'll do my best to stop, but now I've two areas of beauty to distract me. You'll just have to allow for that."

Amy swatted me again with her fan and said, "Well, I brought one distraction that will hold the attention of most men. Here—take this basket and start for that clearing. I'll spread a quilt so we don't muss our clothes, and you set that on the edge of it to keep the breeze from blowing everything away."

"And what is in the basket?" I asked.

"Food. Food for distraction," she replied, laughing. "Thought we'd have a bite and enjoy the scenery. Think you could stand that?"

"I believe you know the answer to that," I said, taking her arm.

"You men are all alike. When food shows up, all other thoughts go up with the air."

"Not all," I said, drawing her close and kissing her lightly on the lips.

"That'll be enough of that, Sir," she said, backing away, a smile betraying her real thoughts. "Sit! Not another word from you—or anything else—until I have our meal ready. You understand?"

I nodded and sat heavily on the quilt. While Amy prepared plates of chicken legs, butter beans, and apple and pear slices, I kept quiet and took in our surroundings. It wasn't long, however, before my thoughts turned to Cat. This was exactly the type of outing I ached for with her—and hoped we'd soon have. In the meantime, however, I was here with Amy Conklin, a woman I was using to help achieve my purpose. For a moment I asked myself if I felt guilty about what I was doing. The answer, quick to come to my thoughts, was simple enough: "No—not in the least." I was here to bring souls to their freedom and continue the cause. To me, whatever I did along that path was completely justifiable.

When Amy handed a plate to me, I said, "Thank you. You're too kind. I don't get food good as this very often. And, this is the first time I've had the chance to be with a beautiful woman in surroundings like this, too. Why, Miss Amy, you just spoil a man. You truly do."

"Eat!" she said, pointing to my plate. "Your words are kind. Too kind. You just concentrate on that chicken now."

"I'll try," I said, sighing. "But you're so pretty."

"You stop that!" she scolded, reaching over to squeeze my arm. Eat!"

We ate in silence a few minutes, both of us enjoying the rhythmic sound of the small rapids in the river before us. Soon, a small raft floated by. Two young boys sitting with their legs dangling in the water as they held tight to their fishing poles looked up and waved wildly when they saw us. We waved back and laughed as one, losing his balance, nearly fell into the water. His friend grabbed the back of his shirt just in time to keep him from a good dunking.

Amy then offered another chicken leg, which I gladly accepted. I set it on my plate, turned to her, and asked, "Miss Amy, if I may be so bold, I'd very much like to ask you something. Last night you shared a very interesting perspective on the issue of slavery. How'd you ever get to such a notion?"

She smiled and replied, "And here I thought you might be sitting there trying to come up with other ways to woo me. Instead, you ask me about my politics. Well, I guess I have no one but myself to blame for this. Father always says men don't pursue women who speak their minds."

"That's not it at all," I said, softly, moving closer to her and brushing her curls back from her shoulder. "I'm not most men—and I hope you're also getting to know that. I value a woman's perspective. I do. I'd just like to know more about you is all. And, this just happens to be a subject I've been wrestling with myself of late. Both of the boys with me now are long-serving to me, and I've questioned more than once what would happen to them should I meet an untimely demise. If that were to occur, would they be deserving of freedom for their past work? Should they be rewarded in this fashion? Or, should they be kept in bondage for a new master after me? What are your thoughts on the matter?"

"Don't get me wrong," she began. "I'm not one of those abolitionists who believe slavery is wrong and unnatural. I know the dark race is inferior to us. I've seen that all my life. Still, I believe slaves can be educated to do at least some occupations—and especially those that people of our upbringing don't favor. Like fieldwork, caring for animals, and hard manual labor. They have an aptitude for that. It's born in them. Still, I don't think anything is wrong with—how'd you put it?—rewarding some for honest and loyal servitude, specially those capable of working on their own."

She gave a self-satisfied smile, and continued, "And besides, even though I'm a woman, I understand some of the world of commerce. That is, freeing some for loyal servitude will make the rest of them believe it's a possibility for them as well. It won't be, but they won't know it—and will work harder and won't revolt or cause trouble. My father always says, 'A happy slave is a productive slave.' So, if freeing some will make the rest hopeful and happy, then I say it all makes good sense in all directions."

Her voice trailed off as she handed me another piece of bread. She looked up at me and, as I studied her face, I couldn't say I was shocked by her views. If anything, I was only mildly surprised by how articulately she presented them. To me, she had revealed her very nature quite plainly. I had hoped her heart to be a touch more compassionate. It wasn't. She was like an apple: absolutely beautiful on one side, but with the hole of a worm on the other.

"You are a remarkable woman," I said, leaning forward and gently kissing her again. "What a catch you'll be for some lucky man."

"How has your luck been running?" she asked, coyly backing away from me.

"Pretty fair. I have to say I've been favored by good fortune a time or two in life," I said. "We'll just have to wait and see if that continues."

She blushed again and turned to face the river. At that moment, it occurred to me just how much the two of us really were alike. She believed freeing a few slaves would create the illusion of freedom being attainable for all. Therefore, she was not above building a lie to accomplish a goal. And here I sat—weaving my own web of deception to lure in people like her so that my beliefs could be carried forth. Deception was firmly rooted in each our hearts. I knew I was right to use deception—just as I was sure she felt the same way. Any way the pie was sliced, we were both nothing but liars, each of us doing so to foster our individual agendas. For that reason alone, I was certain there would be, in due time, a place in Hades for both of us. But, for the time being, I wasn't going to let the thought bother me, especially because I was sure of one thing: I was a better liar than she was—and in a battle of wits with her and others like her, I'd always win the day.

At the same time, another thought came to me. My father was fond of saying, "Always make the other side believe you respect their views—even if you abhor them; more than one battle has been won with a well-chosen kind word delivered to an adversary." With this advice in mind. I eased closer, drew her into my arms, and kissed her passionately until we were both near breathless. She formed herself to me and drew me down to the quilt.

Her voice husky, her breaths coming in gasps, she said, "I know a place we can go. More private there. Can walk to it. Leave everything here. Nobody will bother...."

I drew her close and ran my hand along her cheek before kissing her again, first on her neck and then back to her full, warm lips. Just as I was about to accept her invitation, we were both startled by the sound of a rider rapidly approaching. I quickly stood up, and as I did so, I instinctively drew a revolver from my left boot and prepared to fire if need be. However, when the rider finally came to view, I lowered my weapon and let out a loud, deep breath.

It was Lucius.

He drew his horse up before us and said, his voice tense, "Boss, glad I finally found you. There be problems."

He looked at Amy, then back to me, his expression telling me he was about to choose his words carefully. "Mr. Conklin wants Miss Amy back home right away. Right now. Doesn't feel it safe for her out here, not even with you."

"What's it about?" Amy asked, standing and grabbing hold of my arm.

Pointing to me, he said, "Mr. Conklin wants you to join the posse...."

"What posse?" Amy asked, obviously upset by Lucius' untimely interruption.

"Abolitionist named Carstairs was spotted this morning. Stole some slaves down to Lane City—and shot their master. Don't know if he'll live. Most doubt it, so makes Carstairs a murderer—and the posse says fit for a rope. Some farmers just to the east of here jumped him couple hours back and got the slaves—but he got off from 'em. Carstairs shot one of them, too. Not for sure, but seems like Carstairs took a wound."

Lucius paused to catch his breath before going on, "We can catch him if a posse gets up right away. Mr. Conklin's already put up a $200 bounty—dead or alive. He asked we come along. That is, after gettin' Miss Amy safe home."

I turned to Amy and shrugged my shoulders. "Seems your father's wishes must be honored. I'm so sorry about that. We'll just have to continue where we left off soon as we can. And I pray it's soon."

"Me, too," she said, peering disgustedly at Lucius. "Soon would suit me."

"Sorry, Miss Amy," Lucius said, removing his hat. "Your father's orders were strict. Want me to help you gather up everything?"

"No, thank you," she replied, curtly. "You've already done enough."

She turned to me. "See, it's exactly what I was saying before. If we give some their freedom, this wouldn't happen. And a white man nearly killed. I hope they catch that low down abolitionist and hang him from the highest tree they can find."

This "low down abolitionist" knew she wasn't really angry with Carstairs. She was angry we didn't get to her private spot, a spot where she, no doubt, believed her future would have been secured. I resisted the temptation to tease her. Instead, I kissed her on the cheek and said, "We'll come back here soon. This shouldn't take long."

With Lucius in tow, the ride back to the Conklin home was a quiet one—for all of us.

....

After delivering Amy to the safety of her home, Lucius and I set off for town to see if we could catch the posse before they started their search. On the way there, Lucius asked me, "Think we know this Carstairs? He one of us—or just some poor man suddenly got religion?"

"Haven't heard anyone using that name before, but that doesn't mean much," I replied. "How many names have we used?"

Lucius nodded. "That's so—but we still better see if we can find him first. If he's caught by the others and sees us and knows us, he might try avoiding the noose by calling us out. Yep, we better be first. Where you think he'll head?"

"The terrain 'round here is pines and rolling hills to the south. If this Carstairs is experienced, he'll go that direction to throw everyone off his trail. If he's new to the game, he'll make a mistake and either go straight north or west, the shorter ways to the closest depots. Either north or west would put him in more open land—and the posse would probably run him down for sure. Whoever he is, you're right—we better find him first."

"And if we're lucky and do find him first—then what?" Lucius asked.

"Hopefully, our luck will continue and I'll come up with a plan. In the meantime, when we find the posse, follow my lead."

I spotted Mr. Conklin as soon as we entered town. He was standing on a large box next to the entrance of the saloon. About a dozen men, all armed with rifles, stood around him, waiting for his next words. As we dismounted, I could finally hear what he was saying.

In a dramatic voice, with his arms moving back and forth to punctuate his high points, he said, "Men, you know what we have to do. Can't have this... this *scourge* touch our town in any way. We've all seen what can happen when these rabble-rousing abolitionist scum put ideas in the heads of our darkies. Why, the minute they believe they can just run off, our very lives are at peril. Surely you remember the women and children who were killed in the insurrection last year in Jackson. Do we want that to happen here?"

I knew about the ever-expanding legend of what had happened in Jackson. The popular story told of three slaves who tried to run off from their plantation and while doing so set fire to a barn in which a farmer's wife and their three children were tending to their cows and other stock. The wife and children perished in that fire, and the slaves responsible were tortured—and then hanged—for all in the town to see. However, I had it on good authority, from a friend living nearby to Jackson, that the truth of the matter was some different from the legend being created. According to my friend, it was the slaves who were cornered in the barn and one of the posse threw a torch into the hay mow to try to smoke them out. What the posse didn't know was that the wife and children were also huddled inside, hiding from the runaways. When the bodies were discovered, a story had to be created to make the whole situation the fault of the slaves—and not the real killers that day. As Mr. Conklin whipped his posse into a frenzy, I nodded when he again referred to Jackson—but kept my mouth shut.

That is, I kept mum until he started in with specific orders about how the posse should form and proceed with the pursuit.

"Pardon me, Mr. Conklin," I interrupted. "If you don't mind, I've a suggestion to add. I've been on the chase for runaways a good dozen times or more, so I've some experience in these matters. Your plans are sound, but I'd like to add, with your permission of course, something else to them."

I paused and noticed all eyes were now directly on me. Mr. Conklin leaned forward and said, "Go on. I'd—we'd all—welcome your experience. After all, we all want the same thing—to see this man strung up before sundown."

"In that case," I continued, "here's what I suggest. In my short time here, I've noted the hills and dense woods to the south of town. Many would guess he'd head straight north as fast as he could spur his horse, but these abolitionists are getting smarter. My money says he's heading away from where he figures we'll go, which means he's probably well on his way into the hills. I'll take Lucius, and we'll make tracks quick as we can back east and then directly south toward the river. I think we can easily beat him there—that is, if I'm right and he's going that way. Then, if most of you will fan out and slowly make your way that direction, Lucius and I can flank him and force him right into your laps."

I looked around at the attentive members of the posse. "At the same time, just in case I'm wrong, the rest of you can still start north and snare him before he gets too far. By covering both directions, We'll get this man before sundown."

There were plenty of nods in the crowd as a low murmur moved toward me. Mr. Conklin gave his approval. "Sounds like a wise plan to me. We'll bow to your experience and do exactly that. Jim—Dale—Brownie—you three put your heads together and decide how to get your men spread out in a line and headed south toward the river so you can help work John's trap. I'll join Charlie's men, and we'll cover directly north while y'all are doing that. We'll get him. And I don't think it'll take long."

Then, turning to me, he asked, "How soon you ready to start?"

"Right away," I replied. "Lucius and I will be at the river in an hour or so, and then we'll make enough noise to raise the dead as we measure the area. If we spot him, we'll fire two shots, wait a few seconds, and then add a third. If you men coming south hear that, come chargin' fast as you can. Oh—one more thing— if you hear a single shot, don't rush ahead. Don't forget there'll likely be hunters in the area. Let's not end up cornering one of those by mistake. No, listen for two shots—and then the third one. Everyone understand?"

"Then let's mount up and have off!" Mr. Conklin shouted. "Want this over as quick as possible."

Lucius and I were off at a gallop toward the east. Once out of sight, I pulled up and motioned Lucius to do the same. "We'll wait here five or ten minutes while they all get far enough south they can't see us. Wasn't that tough to split them up, was it? Then, we'll double back and head northwest. The more I think about it, I don't think this Carstairs is experienced or smart enough to head south, and I doubt he'd be stupid enough to go directly north, where everyone would expect. No, I imagine he's frightened enough he'll fade some to the west first to try throwing everyone from his trail, especially if he's taken a wound, and that's where we're likely to find him. With most of the posse to the south and Conklin and the others straight north, we stand a good chance of finding him first. He won't be moving that fast, especially if he's hurt. And if he is, he might even look for some cover. We'll poke around that direction and see what we come up with."

"What 'bout the posse and Conklin? Aren't they goin' to think it mighty strange when they find out we went off that direction?"

"We'll just tell them we came across a blood trail, followed it, and must have missed them on the way across. None of 'em looked smart enough to think otherwise."

Lucius smiled and shook his head.

"What?" I said, smiling back. "They look smart to you? Just a bunch of country boys playin' lawmen, by my measure."

"Hope you're right," he replied. "I sure hope so."

....

For the better part of the next hour Lucius and I combed the countryside to the northwest. We thought we had found Carstairs' trail at one point, but it turned out to be nothing more than the tracks of a wild mustang we finally spotted along the treeline.

Shortly after that, however, Lucius tapped me on the arm and pointed to a barn in the valley below. Off to the left of it were the charred remains of what had at once been a very large cabin. Still farther to the left, we could see the movement of a horse tied just inside a dense grove of trees.

No sooner had Lucius asked, "What you think?"—when the dull crack of a small caliber pistol shot echoed up toward us.

"You get around back," I called to Lucius as I dismounted, tied off my horse, and cautiously made my way through the tall grass toward the barn. Once to the door, I quietly pried it open just enough to see inside. In the middle of the barn stood a man, his back to me and holding a gun, leaning heavily against the ladder leading up to the loft. I looked down and saw a body stretched out on the ground below him. The standing man sighed and grabbed his shoulder, dropping the pistol in the process. That was the opening I was waiting for.

Throwing open the door, I shouted, cocking the hammer of my pistol at the same time, "Don't move or you're dead where you stand! Hold steady!"

When he started to bolt, Lucius entered the rear door and shoved his gun in the man's face, which brought him to a sudden and immediate halt. I walked up behind him and checked his pockets and boots for other weapons. Finding none, I swung him around and said, "Who are you? You kill this man? Be quick now or I'll shoot you between the eyes and you'll fall right on top of him. You want that?"

Blood was trickling down his arm as he started to speak, "I... I ... didn't mean to. He jumped at me. Had a knife—cut me, here. Didn't see my gun. I just raised my arm and fired. I didn't mean...."

"Better look at this," Lucius said to me, using the toe of his boot to point at a tin star on the dead man's vest bearing the words "Deputy—Lane City."

"You Carstairs?" I asked, moving closer and studying his eyes.

He didn't respond. Instead, he looked down at the body, covered his mouth, bent down, and threw up on a small pile of hay to the side.

"Doubt they heard the shot," Lucius said, moving to the door at the front of the barn and peering out. "They'd be too far off for that, but there might be others roamin' 'round. Better be fast 'bout this."

"I agree, " I said, pulling Carstair's up by his shirt. "Listen to me," I said, sharply, turning him around again to face me. "I'm only going to say this once, and you better pay attention if you value your life even a whit."

He eyes were hollow and his breathing rapid and loud. It also appeared he was on the verge of being sick again, but there was no time for that. With my left hand I grabbed his cheeks and squeezed them—hard. I then shook his face back and forth until he finally looked into my eyes.

"Get your clothes off. Strip. Everything. And do it right now."

"What you going to do to me?" he said, his voice now hoarse and low. "Why you want me to...?"

I cut him off. "I'll explain as we go. You just start with those trousers. Lucius—you help him. Looks like he'll fall and faint if you don't."

As Lucius moved forward and helped him out of his clothes, he pointed to the body at their feet and said, "One shot. Right through the neck. There's a scattergun under him, through his belt."

"Good," I said. "Fetch it out and hand it to me. It's our good fortune --shotgun will be perfect."

Carstairs, still to the point of falling down, quickly snapped to attention when I cocked both hammers of the shotgun. "Oh, please don't shoot me!" he cried. "Please don't!"

"If you don't shut up, he will," Lucius said roughly as he pulled off Carstairs' right boot. "And don't you think he won't."

"Now, you two strip that deputy—and don't leave a stitch on him."

"You!" I shouted, again gaining Carstairs' attention again. "Put those clothes on the instant they're removed. Get started!"

It took just a minute or two more before Carstairs looked the part of a deputy, complete with tin badge above his heart—and the body on the floor looked every bit a lousy, good-for-nothing, dead as a keg of nails abolitionist.

"Here's what we're about now," I said, handing Lucius the shotgun as I bent down and arranged the body in a seated position against a post. "Mr. Carstairs, you're going to use that shotgun and shoot the remains of this poor creature in the face. Get it right up there close so not much'll be left."

"Do what?" Carstairs asked, covering his mouth again, close to heaving.

"Don't you dare!" I commanded. "No time for that. You better make this look good or you'll be hanging from a tree by nightfall."

"I don't understand," he said, leaning back and nearly falling down.

Lucius righted him and said, evenly, "Simple. Posse will be here soon enough. This man will be you—and you're now a deputy from Lane City. Should work just fine. Just need to wipe away his face is all. Then won't have to worry about any descriptions passed along the way. You follow now?"

He nodded slowly, then asked, "But why are you doing this for me? Why aren't you going to shoot me?"

I cut in and said, bluntly, "Because it just may be our beliefs are similar and maybe I'll need to call on you for a favor one of these days. So, I'm going to give you your life, and you're going to promise to repay a debt if I call upon you. Would you say that's a fair trade?"

Carstairs fell back again, this time from relief. When he finally righted himself, he said, quietly, "All you'll need to do is call on me. I swear—I'll do whatever you want. I swear it."

"I'll count on it," I said, again looking deep into his eyes. "I know you won't let me down."

He nodded weakly.

"One more thing—where you live?" I asked. "Don't lie to me now. If you do, I'll know it. Tell me where."

"Down to Camden, Tennessee," he replied, swallowing hard. Got a little place there—with my wife. I'm working with the cause because...."

"Don't want to hear about it now," I said. "I'm sure you have your reasons. You can tell me later when we're not so... rushed."

"What's your full name?" I then asked sharply, squinting.

"Jeremy... Jeremy Carstairs."

"Then, Jeremy Carstairs of Camden, Tennessee, get close now. Make ready."

Lucius interrupted us and said, "Enough gabbin'. Time's slippin' away. Best be on with it. "

He handed Carstairs the shotgun and said, "You know what needs to be done."

Carstairs looked at me for a moment before turning and firing both barrels. The effect was exactly what we'd hoped for.

"One more thing," Lucius said, as he picked up a piece of firewood and whacked Carstairs on the shoulder, reopening his wound. Too stunned to say anything, he instantly dropped to his knees as blood gushed down the front of his vest and across his new badge.

"There," Lucius said, matter-of-factly. "That should do it. Wounds you got from the abolitionist. Will get you loads of sympathy, no doubt. And likely a round of drinks."

"Sorry about that," I said to Carstairs, moving over to wipe some of the blood across his cheek. "This will be a nice touch. You'll look like you put up a good tussle before you put him down."

I paused and added, "Lucius, get that rope over by the far stall. We'll tie his legs and find a sturdy limb outside to hang him from—upside down. We'll hang him high enough to make sure there's nothing left to identify. And besides, a posse always loves a show, so let's give 'em one."

Then, turning to Carstairs, I said, "While we get this ready, let's talk about our story and make sure we all give the same account. We'll keep it simple—and straightforward. No need to embelish. The body will speak volumes."

Carstairs, still shaking his head, bent back down and, hands trembling, tied the rope to the legs. "I killed this man twice," he said. "Twice!"

"He was for slavery," I said, flatly. "Don't you lose any sleep over it. He was the Devil, and it ain't no harm to kill the Devil. Not even twice. You remember that."

"Who are you? he asked. "Just who are you?"

"I'm... we're the men who just saved your life. We'll leave it at that for now. When one day I call upon you for a favor, and that day likely will come, I'll use the name Mr. Paris. That's where we are now. Just outside the town of Paris. You got that?"

He nodded, flinched in pain, and rubbed his shoulder again.

"Good," I said, motioning toward the door. "Let's haul him out, string him up, and fire shots for the posse. Someone will be back this way by now. Everyone ready?"

We dragged our story along with the body out into the sunlight and hoisted it into a maple tree. Lucius then fired the shots to alert the posse.

Half of them rushed over the hill in less than five minutes. Once dismounted, the men barely listened to our story as they stood staring up at the body. They had what they wanted.

So did we.

....

Chapter 18

Favor Earned

THE MINUTE WE ARRIVED BACK to town, Mr. Conklin, with the rest of the posse in tow, instigated a celebration the likes of which I had never seen before. Holding court at the saloon, he bought round after round of drinks for anyone and everyone who would listen to the tale of the capture, a tale I embellished more and more as the time went along. I insisted it was actually the deputy who deserved most of the credit, but I made sure to include how Lucius and I provided the split-second distraction that allowed the deputy to get the drop on the slave stealer and blast him with the shotgun. I did my best to keep focus upon myself because I didn't want Carstairs, who sat quietly through each telling, to say much of anything for fear he'd slip up in his version. I was the practiced liar, and I'd have no problem holding the attention of a group of this type. Each time I finished a telling, Mr. Conklin slapped me on the back, shook my hand, and shouted, "Death to all abolitionists and those who favor 'em!" The irony was not lost on Carstairs, who soon looked the part of a man once again ready to lose the contents of his belly.

The deceased's body was also brought back to town and hung for all to see from the roof of the stable. Mr. Conklin casually mentioned he was of a mind to keep it there until it rotted— as a cautionary tale for those who were leaning toward similar sympathies.

Finally, Mr. Conklin punctuated the festivities by dropping on the counter, quite dramatically, a poke containing two hundred dollars in gold, the reward promised for capture of the abolitionist. I quickly scooped up half—and handed the rest to Carstairs. I explained it was only fair to share the purse, given what each of us had gone through. Mr. Conklin said that was perfectly fine with him. At first Carstairs didn't want to touch his share. However, after a few minutes, he picked it up and stuck it in his trouser pocket. At that moment I guessed maybe, just maybe, there was yet hope for him.

A few minutes later I noticed Tasby standing at the window of the saloon. As soon as he was sure he had my attention, he motioned me to come outside. I excused myself and met him at the hitching rail.

"Found 'em—both of 'em," he said while bending down and examining the hoof of his horse. "But there be a problem. They bein' sent tomorrow to work fields at a farm miles south of here."

"That's not a problem," I said, also pretending to study the hoof. "We'll go tonight. Just after midnight. I've done all I need to here—and Taggart may be close—so might as well be off soon as we can."

I gave him enough of Mr. Conklin's reward money to purchase two good horses and asked that he get to the stable quickly as he could to obtain them.

"One more thing," I said, standing up and checking the tightness of the saddle ties. "Soon as you get the horses, go back to our passengers and get 'em ready. Then, choose the place where we'll meet up. After you decide, send Toby back to camp to let me know where and when. And, whatever you do, make sure they get there on time. I've got an itch on my neck that says it's time to go—now."

"I know," Tasby said quietly. "Done this b'fore. Will take care of everything."

"I know you will," I responded, stroking the horse's mane. "I have full confidence in you."

"Then it 'bout time," he said, smiling.

"Get going," I said, helping him into the saddle. "We haven't much time."

....

As soon as Tasby was out of sight, I reentered the saloon for one more dramatic retelling of the story. At the conclusion, I was again cheered. It was an odd celebration, a celebration of a man's death, that brought everyone in the room to mutual joy and an affirmation of a way of life. I laughed like everyone else, at the appropriate times, but deep inside I couldn't stop myself from thinking how much more enjoyable it would have been to run to the door, throw an oil lamp back into the room, and watch everyone in it roast alive.

When the wave of cheers finally wore down, I pulled Mr. Conklin aside. I told him my slave had just informed me a message had come saying a plantation owner down near Lexington was interested in selling a large group of horses, horses I badly needed to help carry forth my commerce and, therefore, increase the profits we'd all share. I said I was sorry I needed to rush off—but the call of the dollar was echoing in my ears. He understood completely. He was already counting his profits. I also asked him to pass along my regards to Miss Amy and to let her know I'd be returning as soon as my business transaction could be completed. The crowd wasn't eager to let me go, but Mr. Conklin stepped in and started his own retelling of the story, which seemed to appease them. To my relief, Carstairs had slipped out with me and was right at my heels as I stepped from the saloon.

"What now?" he asked, grabbing me by the arm.

"You disappear just as fast as you can," I said. "Get on that horse and ride like your life depends on it, which it does. Go back home to Camden and let all this die down. Don't go anywhere for several weeks until it does."

He was still frightened and confused, which I knew I could use to advantage. I took hold of his hand, shook it firmly, and said, lowering my voice, "And don't you forget you owe me a favor. I'm not sure when I'll call, but it'll most likely be sooner than later.

Remember, I'll use the name Mr. Paris and I'll be counting on you, so don't let me down."

Carstairs seemed to understand. His grip tightened as we shook hands. "I've one other thought for you to chew on. I now know where you live, if you get my meaning."

"I do. I won't. I...I won't forget what you've done for me. I'll be ready."

"Then off with you," I said, motioning for him to mount up. "Don't stop until tomorrow morning. That should have you far enough away."

Without another word, he nodded and eased back his horse.

"Watch to your back," I said, waving him off.

"I intend to," he replied. "You do the same."

Not a minute later, he was at the edge of town—then gone.

My thoughts were already moving in the direction of all still to be accomplished before we could begin our journey. The first order of business was Tasby getting our passengers ready, and he was already off managing that. The second was getting rid of the wagon we brought along. We'd have to move quickly, so taking it back with us was out of the question. At the same time, we couldn't just leave it out at our camp where it might draw suspicion to us after it was finally discovered our passengers were gone from their plantation.

As soon as we were back to camp, I asked Lucius to help me pull from the wagon the bedrolls and food supplies we'd need. Then, I sent him to town to leave the wagon at the livery, where he was to explain we felt it best to keep it there for a few weeks while we were off looking at the stock near Lexington. From my experience, livery owners were among the best of gossips, so I was counting on him to help spread our cover story. They almost always seemed just a step or two away from being stone broke, so I felt better knowing he'd eventually be able to sell the wagon and the rest of our supplies for a handsome profit when we didn't return.

As soon as all were off to complete their tasks, I sat in the shade of a large weeping willow tree and unrolled my maps to study them one last time. All along I had planned for us to head directly north from Paris, skirt the towns of Fairview and Helena, and cross the Ohio River just to the west of Maysville, where the water at this time of year would still be shallow enough for us to hold tight to our mounts and walk across. I liked this route because at the crossing area we'd, hopefully, be able to see the glow of a lantern in the window of a home on the Ohio side situated high on a hill known as Liberty Point. That home belonged to the Reverend John Rankin, a staunch abolitionist of the first order. That light in the window would indicate it was safe to cross—that slave catchers were nowhere in the area. At his home we'd be able to rest up, take a good meal or two—his wife was the best cook this side of Virginia—and pick up word about any potential dangers or problems at depots farther ahead of us on our journey.

I had known Reverend Rankin, and enjoyed his hospitality when needed, for nearly five years. He was a man not to mince words, and he always made it abundantly clear he didn't care for me or my methods. At the same time, he never hesitated opening his door for me because he said he had "cautious respect" for me. Like most other abolitionists, he believed the cause should be carried forward without violence of any kind. In our often lengthy discussions on the matter, I did my best to convince him I respected and admired what he was doing in providing safe haven for travelers and information to those bringing them to safe territory. At the same time, I tried to get him to understand it often took violent means to break the chains holding the passengers in bondage. To this point, my efforts had gone for naught, and I had the feeling he would never see my perspective. He was a gentleman and a gentle man—but when caught up in the fever of his beliefs, he was something to behold. As I studied the maps, I knew I was just a couple of days from being able to engage him in debate once again—and the thought made me smile.

But before that could happen, all had to fall to place. I rolled up my maps, placed them in my saddlebags, and then said a prayer.

Reverend Rankin would have liked that.

....

Chapter 19

Without a Trace

TASBY HAD CHOSEN THE SAME barn where we had caught up with Carstairs as our meeting place. His reasoning was sound enough: there was no reason for anyone from the town to return to the barn, so it offered the greatest safety of any other place in the area. I was proud of him for thinking of this, and I let him know it.

As soon as I met our passengers, Laura and Liza, I knew we were in for trouble. They were close to the age of twenty, were of mixed blood and quite attractive. Obviously, they had already gained the interest of Tasby and Toby. As I listened to them alternately flattering and then ordering Tasby and Toby around, I could see they were intelligent and strong young women.

"I'm your conductor," I said, reaching out to shake their hands when I was finally able to gain their attention.

After glaring at Tasby and Toby and ordering them to ready the horses, I went on, "Normally I have a long speech I give to my passengers before we begin a journey, but we need to be off— can't take the time. Plus, I have the feeling you can take care of yourselves."

Here I paused, shook my head, and glared again at Tasby and Toby, which caused both girls to giggle softly.

"I'm not going to reveal any details about the route we'll be taking, but I believe you should know who has arranged for your freedom."

"Your uncle, Sampson Taylor, who has been free a goodly number of years, made arrangements for me to bring you to him."

They both gasped and held each other tightly. "He promised your father he'd do so if he ever had the means. Our journey will be a long one, but you'll be reunited with family when we get to our destination. That's all I've to say for now—except you must follow my orders without question while we make our way. Understand?"

Laura and Liza nodded, tears spilling from their eyes.

"Time for us to go. Know how to ride?" I asked, pointing toward their mounts.

"We do," Laura, the slightly taller and older of the two, replied. "Don't have to worry about us keeping up. Won't fall back, Sir."

Her confidence was impressive, and I smiled in response. "Good. Lucius, you take the point and get us out of these woods. I'll stay back with our passengers and these... these swollen heart boys."

I pointed at Tasby and Toby. "You two are pathetic. One would think you've never seen women before. Don't want you two all moony and distracted more than usual. Keep your minds on the trail and the trees around us. Our lives might depend upon it."

When Tasby and started to speak, I cut him off. "Keep your mouth closed and your eyes focused to the woods."

"You, too," I added, directing my words to Toby.

Laura and Liza giggled and kicked their horses, leaving Tasby and Toby to swallow their dust. I just shook my head and followed.

....

Just after midnight we exited the woods, picked up the main trail, and headed straight toward Ruddels Mills. We'd be safe after Ruddels Mills because few people traveled the uneven, rocky, wagon-wheel rutted former logging path from that town up to Maysville, to the west of which I hoped we'd be able cross the Ohio. Most making their way through this part of the countryside skirted east to join a newer and much smoother road linking the larger towns in the region, so I was counting on us meeting few others on the road.

At the same time, I felt at least a small measure of additional security because of documents Henry had prepared for me to bring along. These papers declared all four to be my slaves—and Lucius to be responsible for them in the case of my untimely demise. Still, even with a lightly traveled road ahead of us and "legal" documents in my pocket, I remained vigilant as ever to my surroundings, especially as I knew Tasby and Toby were still distracted lookouts because of our passengers.

We rode in silence most of the night. The only excitement occurred when Toby lost his balance while leaning over to whisper something to Laura and fell straight to the ground, landing with a thud that jolted all to attention. When we saw he wasn't shot or otherwise hurt, all roared with laughter until I reminded them sound traveled a great distance down the road at the middle of night. Still, even while scolding the others, I couldn't help but smile myself. Toby was a man blinded by his emotions, a fact not lost on Laura, who scolded him and urged him to keep his words and his gaze to himself.

When the first light of the morning sun started to appear, we were, to my surprise and delight, farther along than I'd hoped we'd be. An hour or so previous I had spotted the lights of Maysville off to our right. At that point, I directed us northwest until we came to the south bank of the Ohio River. We stayed along the bank for several more miles until we saw, back off the road and into a thick stand of trees, a stone chimney, a lonely reminder of the spot where a large cabin once stood. I had known its occupants, Carl and Caroline Miller. They were staunch abolitionists who had been burned out by slavers after being caught in the aid of runaways. They had somehow managed to escape with their lives—but were never heard from again. Now, in a great irony, the area behind where their cabin once stood offered the perfect cover for those on the run.

"Let's get ourselves as far back in those trees as we can. We'll secret ourselves here today, take rest, and, Lord willing, make our crossing tonight."

I then addressed my words specifically to Laura, Liza, and Toby. "We can't be seen by anyone going past, so after we get the horses settled, I don't want anyone moving around. Get to the ground and try to sleep some. There might be riders coming our directions from Paris, so we must be on guard for that, as well. Once the rest of you are settled, Lucius and I will take turns standing watch. There's a pretty steep stone bluff just off to the left behind us. From that vantage point, we'll be able to see anything moving from all directions around. Now, pay close attention. Listen like your lives depend upon it. If, somehow, we should be discovered, Lucius and I will make plenty of cover fire while Tasby'll lead the rest of you toward the river. If it comes to that, make your way across quick as you can and keep going west to the town of Ripley. If you get safely that far, one of two things will happen. Tasby will help you find the closest safe house—or you'll be captured and, well, you know what would follow. You understand all this?"

When they nodded, I said, "Good—then get back to the trees and get bedded down. Lucius, cover their tracks as they go, then try to rest some yourself. I'll stand the first watch and come rouse you in two hours or so."

As I expected would happen, soon as all were in cover, Tasby and Toby fell all over themselves preparing bedrolls for our passengers. Laura and Liza just stood there, laughing softly, as they watched two grown men acting like they were little more than twelve years old. At least they were quiet while they tugged and pulled at the blankets, so I let them alone

In short order Lucius walked toward me and said, "Glad you're standin' first watch. I'm tired 'nough to die."

"I'm not worried about you dying," I said, smiling. "Remember what you always say to me?—'only the good die young.'"

"Funny," he growled, sitting and leaning against a large oak.

I was just about to rib him more when I realized he was already off into sleep. I saw no fault with it. He'd earned his rest, many times over.

I didn't mind taking the watch. I was never able to sleep much before crossing the Ohio. I imagined it was the anticipation as much as anything that kept me going. Plus, when along this stretch of the river, I knew I'd shortly be having a verbal tussle with a man I deeply admired, the Reverend John Rankin. Our exchanges always brought me the greatest joy—and, at the same time, frustration—and he felt the same way.

As I kept eye toward the path below my perch, I thought once again about just how blessed we of the cause were to have a man like Reverend Rankin among our ranks. With all he had gone through in his younger years, I would not have blamed him if he'd lit out for the West—and left the cause to smolder on without him.

Back in 1826 he had written what many, myself included, now considered the "Bible of Abolitionism," a book titled *Letters on American Slavery.* The book was a rallying cry for those who wanted to abolish the evil institution of slavery. At the same time, for those holding pro-slavery views, it represented the need to stand firm and build even greater defense for what they believed to be the natural order in life. In short, his book created the highest of fences on both sides of the argument, a fact which made him a very unpopular man in many circles. The notoriety also placed a target firmly to the middle of his back. Many times his life and family were put at risk when slave hunters tried storming his home when they thought him to be harboring their runaways. However, he was able to protect his home, high on the bluff overlooking the Ohio River and nearly impregnable on all sides, because of the steep terrain surrounding it. And he did it without ever taking a life, a fact he threw in my face at every opportunity.

Through the years, since the publication of his book, Reverend Rankin had become what many, myself included, considered a study in remarkable contradictions. He was a short man, standing at not quite five and a half feet. However, the voice coming from that slight frame, especially while preaching the gospel, was clear, booming, and powerful, which made for thunderous effect as scripture rolled from his tongue. He was fond of entertaining guests at his home, but as evenings wore along, his demeanor would often change suddenly from genial host to somber preacher—and he'd urge his guests to leave early. Even though he reached out in every manner to help those in need, many of the local residents, tired of his constant tirades against consumption of alcohol and the evils of dancing, threw rocks, sticks, and whatever else they could fit to their hands at him as he made his way down the main streets of Ripley. Reverend Rankin was nearly always neatly dressed and well-shaved, yet more than once I found him rolling in the dirt and leaves outside of his home as he wrestled with interpretation of a passage in the Bible.

To most, these seeming contradictions painted a picture of a single-minded, rabid-in-belief preacher who saw no other side to issues other than his own. It was easy to understand how they came to this conclusion, but they could not have been further from the truth. Beneath his gruff exterior resided one of the biggest and best hearts I'd ever known. More importantly, his work with the cause was invaluable, especially as his home served as one of the first havens of safety for those making their way to the north and to freedom. He did this at the constant risk of his life. And soon, if all went according to plan, I'd be holding battle with him once again. I couldn't wait.

The hours flew past as I stood my watch. The only person I spotted moving along the road below appeared to be a peddler in a rickety wagon about to lose a wheel. Other than that, all was quiet. At one point, I looked down on the rest of our group, still deep in slumber. I knew I, too, needed a short rest, so I woke Lucius and instructed him to serve as my relief. Reluctantly, he started up the bluff, but not before turning and saying, "Sun's not even straight up. You shorted my sleep!" I very likely did, but my body was crying for rest, so I wasn't going to let him make me feel guilty. As soon as my head touched the ground, I was gone.

Just before dusk, Tasby started kicking the bottom of my boots, which, through instinct, jolted me awake and caused me to draw two pistols in the air.

"Whoa there!" Tasby shouted. "Just me! Don't you fire on me! Wake up!"

The others laughed, but I didn't. Tasby had come close to a couple of nice-sized holes in his chest. We weren't across the river yet, and I couldn't let down my guard.

When I was awake enough to address the group, I called them together.

"We'll wait about another half hour," I began. "Then, Lucius and I will ride ahead to a point where we'll be able to ford the river. While we're there, we'll be looking for a sign it's safe to cross. to the home of a dear friend"

"Reverend hate you," Tasby interrupted, the pitch of his voice rising. "Surprised if he ain't shootin' you b'fore we get to his door!"

"Well, he might at that," I conceded. "Then again, even if he shoots me, he'll take in the rest of you."

I could see my passengers deserved some explanation, so I chose my words carefully.

"What Tasby was trying to say is while the Good Reverend and I have vowed to fight slavery and all who favor it, our methods of doing so are vastly different."

"That's puttin' it mildly, don't you think?" Lucius joined in.

By now Laura and Liza were staring intently at me as if waiting for me to explain all to them. I knew there was no time for that, so I gave them just the shorter version.

"We're going to the home of the Reverend John Rankin, one of the first abolitionists in this area to offer shelter for those on their way to freedom. He's a good man—a kind man—and at times a severe man. He'll welcome you warmly, but don't be surprised if he makes a stab at redeeming your souls. That's just the way he is, and we'll all have to put up with it if it comes to that."

"Ain't never 'deemed your soul," Tasby chuckled. "Never will, I 'spect. Lost cause, likely."

"I wouldn't laugh too much if I were you," I said, staring at him icily. "When I get down below, there'll be a chair right next to me for you."

I turned back to the young women. "His home will be your first place of rest in free territory. If all is safe, we'll take a meal there and rest up some more before continuing north. He has a hidden cellar beneath his parlor floor, and after we dine, that's where you'll have to hide. It'll be dark and likely some damp this time of the year but you'll be safe, and that's what's important now."

As a final reminder, I added, "And, if he starts in on your souls, understand he is doing so because he believes it will help you—and agree with him on everything—even if you don't."

"You can talk all about your souls and such later," Lucius interrupted. "John, we best make ourselves ready and be off. Tasby, Toby—keep your eyes and ears to the road—and not on them." He nodded toward Laura and Liza before continuing, "We'll make sure all's safe then come back to get you."

"Couldn't have said it better myself," I said, patting Lucius on the back. "All of you stay low and out of sight. And no talking!"

All nodded as Lucius and I left the group and walked our horses through the woods and out to the road.

"I have a bad feeling in my gut," Lucius said, rubbing his stomach.

"You think someone's following us?" I asked, looking up and down the road before we mounted.

"No—it's not that," he replied. "I'm worried about what's up ahead. Somethin' just doesn't feel right. Can't put it to words."

"I get that feeling every time we cross the river," I said, trying to comfort him. "Every time. Never fails. My stomach's always in knots. Don't you worry. We'll make it. I know we will."

"Glad for your confidence," he said. "But, somethin' don't feel right to me."

"You'll feel better when we see the lantern," I replied. "My heart pounds nearly through my chest every time I see it. You'll see. We'll be fine."

"Sure hope so."

I didn't want to admit it, but I was feeling the same and was hoping the look on my face wouldn't reveal me. Our journey up from Paris had been smooth. Too smooth. Still, we were just a few miles from free territory, and my heart smiled at the thought.

We rode in silence along the riverbank until we came to a half-burned dock where a ferry had once done a brisk business carrying passengers to and from Kentucky and Ohio. Even though there wasn't a speck of truth to it, a rumor grew that the ferry was being used to transport runaways to their freedom. One moonless night a vigilante group torched the station and the dock, both of which continued to smolder for three days, sending thick, black clouds of smoke high into the sky. Some said the fire burned so long because it was an omen, a sign that the fire of abolitionism couldn't be snuffed out. Others said the smoke represented the resolve of those who vowed to keep slavery a natural part of life. In the end, however, the passing of the ferry service would lead to something of great importance. From the thicket where the dock had once thrived, one had a clear and unobstructed view of the Rankin home high on the bluff directly across the river. If a lantern burned bright in the parlor window, it was safe to cross; if the windows held nothing but darkness, danger lay ahead.

Once we were through the thicket and could see across the river, our eyes caught it at the same time. The light from the window seemed to be beaming directly toward us.

Lucius and I looked at each other and exhaled deeply.

"You're always saying I worry too much." he said, shaking his head. "Guess you're right at that. Best I go get our passengers so we can run 'em across. Can taste Mrs. Rankin's cookin' already. That, alone, is 'nough to get me to the other side."

"Me, too," I said. At the same time, I couldn't take my eyes off the road behind us. Like Lucius, I felt something was off. I didn't know what it was, but I decided we'd take every precaution we could—and then some—as we continued our journey. "I'll stay here and keep watch down the other direction. If I see anyone, I'll come fast as I can to warn you. Otherwise, I'll be waiting right here for your return. Don't take too long. Like you, I'm ready for Mr. Rankin's table."

Lucius tipped his hat—and was off.

I dismounted, tied off my horse, and sat on a large rock by the side of the road. No matter how many times I prepared for a crossing, these moments remained the treasures of my life.

I knew, deep down, this was likely to be one of the last times I'd be able to experience this. I was a marked man, with a large enough bounty on my head that every pistolero in the South was laying for me. I wasn't worried for myself. I figured I still had a fair share of my nine lives left and the Lord had been very good to me, a fact I still held in the highest of mystery. No, it wasn't for my personal safety I worried so. I knew if I stayed to the cause, I'd be putting others at incredible risk. Just by association with me, others would fall into increasing peril—and I couldn't live with myself knowing this was so. At the same time, I couldn't give up the cause. It was too deep within me to ever consider such a thought. I knew now, as I looked at the glow of Reverend Rankin's lantern, I'd have to find a way to continue my special services without leading to the destruction of others.

How I was to accomplish this, I still did not know for sure. Oh, I'd had dreams for quite some time of helping out in the West, helping those running that direction to freedom. Maybe that was the answer. All I knew for certain now was a change was coming, and it would likely be a change like no other I'd ever experienced. The thought was both exciting and dreadful, which is the way I suppose all new adventures worth their salt begin. Only time would tell what was in store for me. For now, I'd just have to trust in myself and the cause.

For that much, I was resolved.

....

Chapter 20

Light of Freedom

Ripley, Ohio

THE CROSSING WAS THE SMOOTHEST I'd ever experienced. The current was slow, and we encountered no quickmud or drop-offs the whole way across. The water was so shallow the horses didn't spook once. Even my passengers seemed to enjoy the cool water. Lucius went ahead of the rest of us and, once on the other bank, looked around to make sure no one else was in the area. When he deemed all to be safe, he motioned us to follow along.

We made our way ahead, slowly, cautiously, as quietly as we could. When we approached the bottom of Liberty Hill, I had Lucius stay with the rest of our group in a densely wooded area while I made my way up the long, steep incline toward the Rankin home. Even with the lantern shining brightly in the window, there remained the possibility of a trap ahead, so I had to make sure all was safe before I dared ask them to follow.

Not wanting to take any unnecessary chances, I decided it best to circle around the hill and make my way up from the rear. It took a quarter hour to reach the small, flat stretch of ground behind their home. From the edge of their garden, I could see into the back of the summer kitchen, which was also brightly lit. I finally saw Mrs. Rankin moving slowly back and forth in front of the window. It looked as if she were removing bowls from a cabinet and placing them on a sideboard. At least that's what my growling stomach wanted to believe.

I watched long enough to be sure she was in no distress of any kind, then started walking toward the back door. Off to my left, I heard the sharp snap of a twig, followed by a booming voice: "Who goes there! Stand and be discovered!"

I was taken so much by surprise I had just started reaching inside my coat for a pistol when the voice called out, "Oh, it's you! What in the name of Creation are you doing here?"

It was Reverend Rankin, hands on hips, snarling at me.

"Well, I'm glad to see you, too, Reverend," I said, extending my hand. He didn't take it. Instead, he turned and walked toward the house.

When I just stood there, he turned and asked, "You might as well follow me. I've never seen it to fail. You always show up just as Jean has a meal to the table. You're like a dog once fed who never leaves again. Well, you coming?"

"Reverend, you just took a year off my life. What are you doing out here?"

"Talking to the Lord. Trying to make sense of a verse. What did you think I was doing?"

"I should have known," I replied. "Same old habits, right?"

"And I take it your habits haven't changed a whit, have they?" he said, sharply.

"No, they haven't—least ways not in the way you'd like. I'm a lost cause,."

"If anyone were to be a lost cause, and I'm not convinced that is ever so, then you, Sir, would most definitely be the one."

"I'll take that as a compliment," I said, finally loosening my grip on my pistol. "But, I'm guessing you likely didn't mean it so."

"I didn't," he replied, flatly. "What are you doing here? Working again?"

"I've passengers below. May I have your permission to bring them up?"

"Figured you did. Otherwise, you wouldn't be hiding in my garden. If you stepped on any of Mrs. Rankin's tomatoes, she'll take a switch to you."

I smiled. He didn't. "Go get them," he commanded. "You'll be safe—safe as one can be in these dark times. I'll tell her to hold the meal. Don't make it long to happen. I've to eat—and then back to the woods to ready tomorrow's sermon. Time's not to waste, you know."

Reverend Rankin was a stern man with thin lips, an icy stare that could appear in an instant, and bright grey-blue eyes. Yet, under this severe countenance resided a heart full to the brim with love and kindness toward all God's creatures and a man ideally suited for the ever-present dangers of the cause. He may not have cared at times for me or my methods, but I still held him in the highest of esteem. Men like him came along seldom, and we were blessed to have him on our side.

"I'll be back soon as I can," I replied. "Please tell Mrs. Rankin we're grateful she'll wait on us."

He grunted, turned away, and stepped to his porch. As he opened the door, the smell of freshly boiled vegetables swept toward me. That was all the inspiration I needed to be back down the incline in a shot.

"It's all right," I said, nearly out of breath, to Lucius and the others upon my return. "And food's on the table. We better hurry, though. Reverend Rankin does not like to be kept waiting."

No sooner had the word "food" left my lips when everyone started gathering belongings and readying themselves for the climb. All were as hungry as I—and needed no more prodding.

....

Mrs. Rankin was out on the porch and fanning herself with her apron when we finally arrived. She was yet another of the contradictions in Reverend Rankin's life. Whereas he was most generally somber, she was full of the joy of life, even though, out of respect for him, her outward displays were few. However, when out of his sight, she had a sunny disposition and a ready smile, and I cherished the moments we were able to spend together. At such times, she was a woman transformed.

"Hot enough to roast peanuts," she said, stepping forward and hugging me tightly. "Good to see you, Johnny. It has been much too long."

Tasby broke into a smile and started clearing his throat. The look I gave him quickly restored him to order, and he took two steps back.

Mrs. Rankin, for some reason unknown to me, a couple years back had taken to calling me Johnny. There wasn't another living soul on the earth I would have allowed to do so. Anyone else would have received a knife in the eye—or worse. But Jean I couldn't refuse; I could refuse her nothing. She was a woman of the finest cloth in every sense, and she, unlike her husband, was fond of me. That alone earned her the freedom to call me whatever she liked.

When she finally backed away, she looked past me and said, "Who'd you bring me this time?"

"You know Lucius and Tasby," I began. Both stepped forward and tipped their hats.

"And behind them?" she asked, moving forward.

"Laura and Liza are my passengers this journey. They're sisters, and I'm to see them to their uncle. The fine man next to them is Toby. He came along to offer his expertise and help to our enterprise. All of you—I'd like to introduce you to Reverend Rankin's wife, Jean.

"You're welcome to my home," she said, warmly shaking the hand of each. "We'll visit inside as we break bread together. All of you could use a fair meal. Doubt very much Johnny fed you so much as a morsel along the way. Am I correct?"

"I for a fact could take a meal," Tasby spoke up. "Let me to that table!"

"If I recall, you're always ready for a meal," Jean said, smiling and shaking her head. "Well, come on. What are you waiting for? Food's no doubt getting cold."

As we entered their home, we were all taken aback by the swarm of activity that greeted us. In addition to serving as a balance for her husband's solemn nature, Jean was also quite good at something else: raising children. John and Jean were the parents of thirteen, several already away from home finding their places in the world. Still, I counted no fewer than seven children of all ages milling about as each performed a responsibility in getting tables ready for the meal. It was always difficult to tell which ones actually belonged to the Rankins because nearly every visit they seemed to have an extra body or two they had taken in because of one tragedy or another. I spotted near the fireplace a young woman I remembered to be called Kitty McCaskey. Kitty was a former slave to whom they had granted shelter. When no one came to track her down and take her back south, the Rankins decided to have her stay on with them and become one of their own. That was kind and generous of them, but she was also very much earning her keep; she was partly responsible for making sure the children kept to the straight and narrow, a task that could not have been easy, from a volume standpoint alone.

Three long tables had been moved together so that all, including those of my group, could be seated together. Steaming bowls of vegetables were spread at intervals from one end to the other, and a platter of venison steaks sat halfway in between. A finer table I had not seen in years.

When we were seated, Reverend Rankin asked all to hold hands with those next to them. He followed with the blessing, which lasted upward of five minutes. I was holding Tasby and Lucius' hands, and by the time the "Amen" came around, my own hands were covered with sweat. However, such was a small price to pay for the delicious meal that followed.

While we ate, conversations all around grew to the point it was difficult to hear anything being said, even by the person closest at hand. At these times, Reverend Rankin would loudly clear his throat and offer a thought from the Bible for all to study, which caused all talk to cease. As a matter of fact, every time he spoke, their home became quiet as a church, which I'm sure was his main intent all along.

At one point, when conversation was at a particularly high pitch, he cleared his throat and shouted, "'But I say unto you, Love your enemies, bless them that curse you, do good to them that hate you, and pray for them which despitefully use you, and persecute you'—Matthew 5 and 44. I'd like to hear what thoughts any of you may have of this. Speak up now."

One of their sons, Thomas, stood stiffly and said, looking straight ahead and not at his father, "I believe the meaning is we are all God's children and are worthy of His love, no matter our sins and transgressions."

We all nodded our approval, and even Reverend Rankin seemed pleased because he nodded toward the child, which was about all the outward expression he was given to in such situations. I was very much taken by surprise by what happened next. Liza, who hadn't said more than a dozen words our whole journey, asked, her voice soft, "May I speak, Sir?"

When Jean reached over and squeezed her hand, Liza continued, "I know this part. Think often to it."

Here she paused, eased her chair back slowly, stood, and said, loudly this time, her eyes to Reverend Rankin, "Though we be beat, whipp'd, and told we not be worth shucks, we musn't wish no harm come to anyone—or we be no better than they. We must turn other cheek, even if our thoughts be hot."

"Very good, child—excellent!" Reverend Rankin said, a smile coming to his lips.

When the rest of us saw this, there were wide grins and deep smiles all around, which we all tried to conceal—but failed.

"There'll be none of that in this house," he scolded us as Liza sat back down. "Scripture is not to be laughed at."

At that moment, one of the children they had taken in, a young girl I guessed to be near the age of six, quickly spoke up. "Oh, we're not laughing at that, Sir. We're laughing at you."

The words were so innocent, so full of the highest measure of respect and love.

Still, the entire room was instantly full of laughter.

Reverend Rankin, blushing crimson, stood up, walked to the front window, and stared intently outside.

There was nothing more he could say.

No doubt much to his relief, Jean quickly turned the conversation back toward me. "Johnny," she said, her voice even, direct, "is it true what I just heard—that you recently made off with twenty-eight slaves by stealing an undertaker's carriage and forming everyone into a block-long funeral procession? And right through the center of that town in broad daylight?"

Tasby piped up and said, "It were more like fifty-eight, and Johnny sat up on that wagon all dressed up and lookin' like Death hisself. Stole the undertaker's clothes—and a coffin, too! Let on like there was a body inside being took to a grave down by the river. Whole town just let us pass."

Here he picked up his fork again and pointed it straight at me. "Only when we were to the river, we all swum across and got ourselves free. You never seen the likes 'afore. Looked so pretty even I b'lieved we was totin' a dead man."

"This true?" Jean asked, disbelief forming to her face.

"Some of it," I said glaring at Tasby, who just smiled. "It was more like twenty-three, and there wasn't much of a worry about it at all. Even the worst of white folks will usually pause to pay last respects. And how were they to know we weren't taking some poor soul to his final resting place? We just kept our heads high and marched right on through. They never suspected a thing."

Jean shook her head and smiled. The others round table followed her lead, and soon the room was again filled with the sounds of laughter. That is, until Reverend Rankin finally turned away from the window and said, severely, "And I suppose you left no compensation for that poor undertaker. Am I right? You robbed him and likely took away his means of making a living. The Good Book says 'Thou shalt not steal'—or have you ever truly known that?"

"Oh, he know it all right," Tasby interrupted. "He just don't b'lieve it, is all."

"And you need to shut that mouth of yours," I said.

Reverend Rankin must have thought my words were directed to him because he suddenly turned toward me, stomped a boot heavily to the floor, and shouted, "Be not rash with thy mouth, and let not thine heart be hasty to utter any thing before God: for God is in heaven, and thou upon earth; therefore, let thy words be few!' Ecclesiastes, 5 and 2. It's plain to me you don't...."

I did my best to cut him off, but the words were already flying from his mouth when I stood and started toward him, hoping to calm him down. Fortunately for us all, Jean jumped between us, extended her arms to keep us apart, and said, above both of our voices, "There'll be no more of this! Not in my home! You two stop this—and I mean right now."

Turning to Reverend Rankin, she said, calmly, "Johnny wasn't talking to you. He wasn't." Turning to me, she continued, "But I'm not defending you. He's right, and you know it. Stealing is not something we preach in this home. Wouldn't hurt you to ask forgiveness for that, no matter what you feel the circumstances of the act. Now sit down—both of you. Shame on you. You're both grown men and should know better than to behave so in front of the children."

With those last words, she had us, and she knew it. Fine examples we were on this night.

"I apologize," I said to her. I next nodded toward Reverend Rankin, who grunted and turned toward the window again. Jean just sighed and motioned for me to return to my seat.

"We'll have a sweet treat now," she said while waving Kitty to follow her to the kitchen. "And no more talking while it's being served. A little reflection will do us all good right now. Agreed?"

We all waited quietly until Mrs. Rankin and Kitty emerged from the kitchen carrying two warm apple pies.

Her pies were so delicious it was easy to stay quiet through every last bite.

....

After we had finished eating and while the others cleared the tables, Reverend Rankin invited me to go outside to talk and take in the evening air. I knew from past visits this was his way of getting me alone so he could try working on my soul.

I followed quietly as he led us down the path toward his vegetable garden. When he finally stopped and turned around to face me, I decided on this night I'd have the first words.

"You'll never admit it, Reverend, but you like me—and you know it."

"Why do you say that?"

"Because without men like me, you'd have nothing to do, nothing to keep you going. That's why."

"You flatter yourself. I do what I do because it's right."

"Same with me," I said, boldly.

"Your results are to be commended, but certainly not your path. How you get to the conclusion is not, and never will be, right."

"What about 'An eye for an eye' and 'Render unto Caesar the things that are Caesar's'?" I asked. "Seem fitting to me."

"Don't you make scripture your excuse. Don't you dare hide behind it. People have done that for centuries, and look where we are now."

"My point exactly," I replied. "Just look where we are. I don't offer it as an excuse. I mean it as a rallying cry."

"And you'll likely burn for it one day," he said, coldly.

If that ends up my fate, then so be it. When a cause is right, sacrifices have to be made. If I'm one, then I'll go gladly."

"I hope you're not comparing yourself to Christ," he said, dropping his head and staring to the ground. "If you are...."

"Don't worry—I'm not. I'm as far from that as a man can be, and I know it. There are just different types of sacrifices. That's what I mean. I do my part—and am glad to suffer what consequences may come. I feel good—feel clean—at the end of the day. Nothing will ever change that, will ever change me."

He looked up, and I caught his eye. "Still, I know you take me as a challenge, and for that I'm grateful. With you at my back,

I feel most fortunate."

He interrupted me and said, "You could work the cause without the violence, the killings."

"I could, but I wouldn't accomplish even half of what I do. I'm good at the violence, and a man should always follow his strengths."

"Your strength is also your weakness, and you do know that deep down. Remember, 'He who lives by the sword....'"

I cut him off and said, "I know—but my sword is what I have—is a part of me. I can't change that, and I wouldn't if I could. So many are still chained and fettered."

We fell silent, each to our own thoughts. He wasn't going to change his views, and I knew I could not. We were at a standoff again, as always. Yet, beneath all our arguments, I still felt a bond with him I had never felt with another man. He was a good man, one who was a true believer in every sense of that word.

"We might as well go back inside," he finally said. "There's a chill to the air tonight. Always happens when the wind blows from the south across the river."

He was making small talk, his way of saying we'd just have to continue our truce and stand together, no matter our differences, for the cause. I knew what he was doing, smiled, and offered my hand.

"Would be pleased if you'd take it," I said.

He moved toward me, shook his head, and gripped my hand.

"Don't worry," I said, laughing softly. "You won't be struck by lightning."

"Are you sure of that, my son? Because I'm certainly not."

I put my arm around his shoulder as we headed for the house together.

As we neared the porch, he stopped me, his voice deadly serious, "There's one more thing I'd like to bring to your attention this night. The bounty on you has doubled. You'll have a difficult time staying ahead of danger now. I worry about that, as should you."

"Reverend, you could turn me in for the reward. Think of what you could do for the cause with that kind of money. Would be a lot."

"I'm no Judas," he said, slowly.

Stepping to the porch, he turned to me one last time and said, dryly, "Still, don't tempt me...."

I stood there, shocked, and smiled.

Reverend Rankin opened the door, turned to me, and said, "Still coming inside?"

I couldn't think of a single word to say. I nodded and followed him in.

....

Chapter 21

Deadly Recognition

Redoak Junction, Ohio

WARREN LEWIS, TAGGART'S TWO "IDIOTS," and a man called Judd, an elderly, one-eyed tracker they'd hired on outside of Maysville, were camped, just as Taggart had instructed, about seven miles north and east of Ripley. They had taken shelter, such as it was, behind a large pile of rocks far enough off the main road they wouldn't easily be spotted by those traveling to and from Ripley.

On this pitch-black, moonless night, three parties had slowly made their way by them, but none had resembled the group they were looking for. As the hours past midnight ticked by, Warren's men grew increasingly restless. To ease their boredom, Karl and Wilbur were throwing their knives and wagering which could come closest to hitting Judd's left boot. Judd, who had plopped himself down on the ground and was supposed to be keeping watch behind them, had fallen sound asleep against a large cottonwood tree. On their fourth round of throwing, Karl's knife skittered across the dirt, finding its mark on Judd's calf just above the boot. Judd, startled from his slumber, let out a sharp yelp, which was followed immediately by high-pitched laughter from the knife throwers.

Warren, in a tone ripe with disgust, commanded them to silence. He reminded them, for the third time, how any type of sound would carry a great distance down the road in front of them.

"Stop the foolery," he said, growing quieter yet remaining sharp and focused. "Y'all know what's to happen if we don't get this man. Taggart will hang us all upside down and slit our throats. That is, that'll be all he does if he's in a mood of charity. Think of that next time you feel like laughing. A corpse don't laugh."

The others just blinked and stared back at him. "Judd—you keep yourself awake and watch that line of trees behind us. If there's to be an ambush, it'd come from there. You two—get yourselves over beyond those rocks yonder. Keep low—and don't want to hear a single word out of either of you or I'll take that knife and cut out your tongues."

Warren stooped down, picked up Karl's knife, slammed it into the ground, and calmly added, "Or, I might just shoot you and watch you squirm at my feet. Doesn't matter to me. If you aren't going to help me, I might as well be done with you."

Heads down and appropriately chastised, the men started for their positions when Warren ordered them to stop and face him one last time. "Oh, there's one more thing. Don't know why I forgot to mention it before, but the bounty to this man is large enough all of you will get an extra $200 each—if we get him. Taggart swore that. You might think about how you'd spend that kind of money. Maybe that will keep you awake."

Wilbur started to speak but clamped his hand over his mouth. However, his smile was still evident to all. The others followed suit and also nodded their understanding to Warren, who pointed to each and said, "Then off to your posts. Stay alert. That money ain't gonna do us no good if we're dead."

As Warren watched his men moving slowly to position, he shook his head. His life could depend upon their vigilance, and the thought made him shudder.

"Don't know how it could be worse," he muttered to himself. "These idiots with me—and Taggart behind me. What'd I do to deserve this?"

He shook his head one last time and headed for his spot in the rocks.

....

Just before the hour of three, off to the south, Warren heard another group of travelers approaching. This hour of the night those on the trail were either lost or on the run from something, so he strained to hear their movements. By the sound of the irregular clomping of horse hooves, he could tell they had no wagons with them. The more he listened, the more he believed the group possibly to number four or five—but certainly not much larger than that. As they came closer, he could tell they were moving slowly, deliberately, cautiously.

Judd had again fallen asleep, so Warren picked up a small stone and flung it at his head, where it found its mark at his right temple. He jerked upright, letting out a low moan as he raised a hand to rub the wound. Karl and Wilbur were awake but engrossed in a game of cards behind a stack of rocks blocking their view of the road. Warren cleared his throat loud enough to gain their attention and motioned them to come near.

When all had gathered round, he whispered, "Might be nothin'. Then again, this might be your extra two hundred coming our way."

He pointed down the road. "Group of riders be here any minute. Here's what we're to do. We'll make it look like a holdup. I'll put this kerchief across my face, jump out, and tell 'em to drop their weapons. You'll be behind me with them in your sights. If it's them, I'll give a call to fire. If it ain't, I'll tell 'em we were expecting someone else—and let them pass."

"Why not take their money anyway?" Karl whined. "Might as well for our effort."

Warren glared at him and replied, "'Cause we don't want 'em to bring back the law, and they'd do that if we picked 'em clean. If we let 'em pass, we'll have nothin' to worry about. They'll just be scared but won't stop anywhere."

As the men moved back to their positions, he warned, "And nobody fire off a round but I command it. If you don't follow my orders, I'll shoot you myself. Now get behind me and make ready. I hear 'em coming up fast now."

....

With Laura, Liza, and Toby following close behind, Lucius slowed as he spotted the pile of rocks to his right, a perfect place, he thought, for an ambush. No sooner had the thought taken form when a masked man jumped from behind a bush and shouted, "Hold fast—your money or your life!"

His shout spooked Lucius' horse, which drew back suddenly, nearly throwing him to the ground. As soon as he had righted himself, he shouted to the masked man, "Have mercy! We're but poor travelers makin' to home. We've nothin' but the clothes on our backs."

"We'll see 'bout that," Warren said, inching closer, his pistol aimed directly at Lucius' head. "Drop your weapons—and let's see those hands raised. Get 'em up—high as you can. Do it now!"

"Do as he says," Lucius called to the others. "Put up no fight. We've nothin' for 'em, and they'll find this soon enough."

"You keep your mouth shut," Warren commanded. "No more words from you unless I say so—or I'll shoot you dead. Understand me?"

Lucius nodded and raised his hands even higher. The others followed suit.

"Now here's what you're to do," Warren commanded. "Dismount on this side of your horses—so I can see your every move. Do it slow, like molasses. When you're down, my men will look you over. Empty your pockets, too. We might or might not keep your goods. That depends. We're looking for someone. If you ain't them, you've nothin' to fear and might live to a ripe old age. Now get down!

Warren turned to his men. "Get to it. Check 'em good."

As Lucius and the others started dismounting, Warren checked their faces, the real aim behind their actions. Lucius looked familiar to him, but he also knew he was not John

Fairfield. Still, it bothered him as he was certain he had seen him somewhere before—but where?

"And who are they?" Warren asked Lucius, while pointing to Laura, Liza, and Toby. "They runaways? You abolitionist?"

"They're my property. Got papers to prove it," Lucius replied, reaching inside his coat.

"Hold there!" Warren shouted, cocking the hammer of his pistol. "What you reachin' for? Let's take a look."

He pulled back the lapel of Lucius' coat and saw a small bundle of papers in the inside pocket.

"Take them," Lucius said. "You'll see all is right."

"Maybe," Warren replied, again studying Lucius' face. "I seen you before. I better figure out where that to be, or I just might have to drop you here. Don't want to ride away and still be thinkin' about that with you behind me."

"Maybe if you drop the mask I'll be able to help," Lucius said, softly. "Otherwise, I could have no idea."

"That's a gamble for you," Warren said, grinning. "'Cause if you do recognize me and it's not good for both of us, I'll definitely have to blow a hole in you."

"Don't see as I have much choice, do I? Gamble I'll have to take. Go ahead. If you're of a mind, pull the mask."

Warren, lowering his pistol, eased down the kerchief, slowly revealing his features. When his face was full to view, Lucius, his eyes first darting to the left to acknowledge something in his line of vision, laughed softly, and said, "What I want to know is how did it take you this long?"

At the very second Warren understood his meaning and started raising his pistol again, a shot rang out. In an instant, Warren's eyes rolled back, and he fell heavily to the ground at Lucius' feet.

More shots followed so rapid-fire it was hard to tell one from the other. They were also coming from left and right of where Lucius was standing.

Before Lucius could retrieve his gun from the ground, Karl

and Wilbur fell. Karl had been shot in the back of the head and was dead before his body hit the earth. Wilbur, clutching his chest, had been hit four times. He slowly sank to a seated position, finally falling sideways, motionless on the hard ground. Judd, crawling back into the rocks, reached for his pistol just as the back of his skull was caved in. Standing over him was Laura, a sturdy tree branch clutched firmly in her hands.

No sooner had the shots ended when John and Tasby darted from cover at each end of the rocks.

"That was close," John said, nudging Karl's body with his left boot. "Check the other one, too," he called over to Tasby. "Make sure he's dead."

"Too close, if you ask me," Lucius responded, shaking his head and exhaling loudly. "A second later and I'd have quite a hole in me I expect. He finally recognized me."

"Had to make sure it was them, didn't I," John replied, smiling broadly. "Couldn't just shoot down highwaymen, could we? That wouldn't be right."

Lucius ignored him. "This one's still breathin'. Seen him b'fore. Rides with Taggart."

"Roll him over," John commanded. "See if he can still talk."

Warren was still alive—but just barely. He finally opened his eyes and asked, weakly, "How bad?"

John knelt down and inspected the wound, which was to the right of Warren's stomach. "Blood's thick and runnin' fast. Afraid you won't make it. If you...."

Warren cut him off, reached for John's arm, and said, gasping for air, "You're him,—ain't you? Him...."

John nodded.

Warren's eyes grew wide as he said, "Well, I'll be damned."

"Likely me, too, one of these days," John added, coldly.

Warren tried leaning up but immediately fell back. "Please... please bury me. Don't want animals to have me."

"Favor for favor," John said, leaning down closer to his face. "Who sent you?" Who was it? I've got to know."

Coughing loudly, Warren replied, "Tag.... Taggart."

"Where is he?" John asked. "Close by?"

When he didn't reply, John continued, "We'll make a nice burial for you—will place you deep and even say a few Christian words."

"Chat'nooga," Warren said, weakly. Has men everywhere. He'll get you—sooner or later. Won't stop. Can't get away from him. Not just the money. You stole his pride. He can't...."

Warren coughed and choked, his breathing becoming shallower at the same time.

"Why'd you come here?" John asked, raising Warren's head from the ground and cradling it in his hand.

"Heard you might be up this way. Sent me...."

Warren coughed deeply again, his body wracked with pain. He winced sharply, and continued, "Might as well be this way. If I went back without you, he'd kill me anyway."

His eyes closed, and he was gone.

It was then Lucius heard Laura and Liza quietly crying off to their right. "Look there," he said to John. "Didn't see it...."

Laura and Liza were sitting next to Toby's motionless body. During the gunfire, he had been shot through the neck, killing him instantly.

"Gone?" John asked Tasby, who had come forward from his position in the rocks to comfort the girls. Tasby nodded, then looked down again. "We goin' to bury him, right?"

"Don't have the time," John said, his voice apologetic yet firm.

"And what about him?" Tasby asked, pointing to Warren's body. "Heard you give that man a promise."

"We promise a lot of things in the name of the cause," John said, matter-of-factly, returning his pistols to the pockets of his coat.

Turning to Lucius, he said, "Check 'em for money. Then, check their saddlebags for food, weapons, and other such truck. While you do that, we'll drag 'em behind the rocks and stip 'em down, every stitch, and pile 'em up."

"Toby, too?" Lucius asked. "He's one of us."

"He *was* one of us," John replied. "Not any more. He knew the risks. We'll just put him with the others. No time to do otherwise."

"Now wait. How can you be like this?" Tasby asked. "Not right." His words came slowly, deliberately.

"Right has nothing to do with it," John said, grimacing and grabbing his right leg. "Just practical. That's all."

Tasby looked at John's hands, which were now covered with blood. "You get hit?" he asked.

"No. When I was sneaking up from behind, I tripped and landed to a knife stuck on a raised tree root. Cut me pretty good, too."

Tasby bent down to inspect the wound. "Need sewing before long. That much be sure. It deep."

"No time for that," John said, yanking the kerchief from Warren's neck and tying it tightly around his leg. "This'll do for now." He stood up. "Get those bodies out of sight—and then walk their horses around here in all this blood to cover it up. After that, we'll send 'em back down the road to cover our tracks. Got to do it fast. Better to get off again before anyone comes along."

When no one moved, he folded his arms at his chest and said, evenly, "Want to wait for more of Taggart's men?"

That got them moving, and they attended to their assigned tasks. Finally, Laura walked over to John and said, her voice cracking, "Why you barin' those men? Ain't right—ain't Christian."

"Naked men are hard to identify, and that's to our advantage. It's practical—not personal."

"Toby deserves better," she said to John, her voice firm. "At least can we say a few words over him? We owe him that much."

"If you make it quick," he replied. "And I mean quick." He turned and began the task of pulling the rest of the bodies behind the rocks.

Laura motioned the others to step close to Toby's body. Lucius and Tasby removed their hats. When all were in place, she began, first clasping her hands and closing her eyes, "Heavenly

Father, please welcome the soul of this man to your embrace. Didn't know him long but was proud to know him. He died so we could live and be free. We leave behind his remains, but we remember his sacrifice. Amen."

As soon as she finished, John walked up to the group and said, quietly, "Leave his clothes on, but get him over with the others. Then, saddle up."

Laura looked up and said, "Thank you...."

"Just don't have time to strip him is all," John said, cutting her off. "Nothin' more than that. Get mounted."

She looked at Tasby, who shrugged his shoulders and said, softly, "We best mount up b'fore he changes his mind. He do that in a hurry sometimes."

After Lucius had dragged Toby behind the rocks, he nodded toward John, who then pointed down the road. "Follow close—and move quiet. Keep the horses the same. We've still much ground to cover before dawn."

John was right, and they all knew it: it was best they were again to the road. They didn't know what lurked behind them, but they knew the possibilities ahead—freedom and new lives for Laura and Liza—and safety, however short-lived, for the rest. With no more additional urging, all quickly fell in behind him.

They rode silently back into the moonless night.

Fairfield urged his horse even farther ahead of the others, seeking space to sort his thoughts. By way of Warren's last words, Taggart's game was now obvious to him. Fairfield also knew, more than ever before, he had to get to Taggart before Taggart got to him. But how? As John looked back at the group, he knew he had better come up with a plan—and fast. He also knew something else: if he didn't find that plan, his own end would come soon enough.

Of that, he was sure.

....

Chapter 22

Evergreen House

Alliance, Ohio

WE KEPT MOVING THE REST of the night, stopping only to water our horses and stretch the tightness from our legs. We had to keep a fast pace, especially knowing Taggart had suspected we'd be heading this direction. If there had been one group of men lying in ambush, it stood to reason more might be waiting ahead of us in the chance we escaped the first trap. We'd have to change course, would have to do the unexpected.

We had planned to seek refuge in Columbus at the home of Fernando and Sophia Kelton, two ardent supporters of the cause. Because of his thriving business concerns, they had ample warehouse space in which to secret us while we prepared for the last leg of our journey. I knew they'd welcome us with open arms. However, if Taggart had been smart enough to come up with the first part of our route, he'd most certainly figure Columbus would follow as part of our master plan. As much as I wanted to see the Keltons and find out from them the latest news of the cause, the risk of going there would be too great. All the depots there were likely being watched—and especially the Keltons'.

Therefore, I made the decision our best chance for safety would be found in skirting a fair distance to the east of Columbus and heading directly for Alliance and the home of Jonathan and Sarah Haines. Their home, known to all in the cause as "Evergreen House," was only a short distance from the Spread

Eagle Tavern, where I knew we'd find safe haven. After resting at Evergreen House, if need be we could jump aboard the train that ran from Alliance just to the south and west of Hanover, an important option considering our mounts would likely be run to the ground by then. Alliance it would be; it was the logical choice—one that I hoped would keep us alive.

As we rode along in the dark pre-dawn hours, the group remained silent, mourning Toby's death. Laura seemed affected most of all. Each time we stopped to tend the horses, she quickly headed for the closest bushes, where the contents of her stomach found the ground. I saw what she had done during the ambush. It was a very brave act—and a necessary one for the safety of our group—but it was now clear she was also suffering mightily because of it. I knew I was going to have to speak to her—and soon.

When we next stopped for water, I walked over to her, grabbed her hands roughly, and swung her before me.

"You did what you had to do," I said, louder than I should have. "No telling how many of us would be dead if you hadn't."

She didn't fight to pull away from me. Instead, she slowly eased back, looked directly at me, and said, "Didn't mind killin' him. Saw he was reachin' for his gun. No, what I hate is violence never seems to end. People still kill others 'cause of their skin. When does it end?"

She wiped her eyes. "I'm not afraid for me. Not no more. I'm afraid for those still property. If we get away, if we make it, many we left behind will suffer. They be whipped, dragged, starved— all to make 'em scared of what could happen if they try followin' us. That's what makin' me...."

"Again," I said, gently resting a hand on her shoulder, "it's what you had to do, and I want you to give it no more thought. You finished off a devil, and it ain't no harm to do so. As far as the rest, I have no answers for you. The ways some people believe on the issue will never change. I've known that a long time. But, mark my words, this is just the beginning. The country can't go on this way, one camp believing in the equality of all and the other still holding to chains and whips. It'll come to violence of the worst sort, and both will suffer for their beliefs. It's clear as a July sky. The earth will run with blood as never before. All we can do is keep fighting for what we believe—and trust in the Lord. Whatever comes, will come. Do you understand what I'm saying?"

She nodded. "I do—but I still don't understand why blood has to come. Makes no sense to me. None at all."

"Makes no sense to me, either. All I know is I'll stay with the cause as long as I draw breath. That I vow." Then, turning to address the others, I ordered, "We've been here too long. Mount and ride. Lucius and I will take the point. Tasby—you keep with the girls and watch to the rear. I want no more surprises tonight."

Tasby nodded and replied, "Not for me, too. I had 'nough. Don't you worry 'bout me watchin'."

"Then let's be off," I said. "And don't fall behind."

I didn't need to say anything else. All moved ahead before I did. Suddenly, I was the one lagging last. I kicked my horse and took the point.

....

Once Lucius and I were far enough ahead of the rest they couldn't hear us, I moved alongside of him and explained the change of route. He agreed with my reasoning, and said the Keltons would be one depot given special watch by Taggart's men. Like me, Lucius hated the thought of missing a visit with them, but he understood the danger we'd be put in—and put them in—if we stopped in Columbus. We vowed we'd just have to see them again in the future and shifted our thoughts to how far east of Columbus we'd need to go in order to throw anyone behind us from our trail.

After a few moments riding in silence, Lucius turned to me and said, "John, I better drop south and see if I can find Taggart. We can't keep two battles goin' at once. I can get him. Know I can. You don't need me here—you can get 'em ahead all right alone."

"No, old friend," I said. "I can't have you risk your life like that. You're too important to me and to the cause. If anything happens to me, you'll be the one to take my place. I'd rather we come up with a plan to catch him off guard somehow. He's too dangerous to take face to face."

Lucius started to interrupt me, but I waved him off and continued, "I haven't figured it out yet, but it'll come to me. You just stick close by—and keep yourself safe. I'll let you know when it's time for us to make our move."

"I will keep you safe," Lucius said firmly.

"I know you will," I said, reaching over to place my hand on his arm.

We rode again in silence, each lost in thoughts, until it occurred to me which route would offer the best protection.

"You remember that old logging trail that used to run close by Zane's Trace over to Somerset?" I asked. "Think it's still passable? We haven't been that way in over two years."

"Last time we rode it the ruts were deep as hoe diggin'. Not sure the horses could make it. One might break a leg."

"On the other hand, if it's fallen to even halfway fair, we'd likely not see others along the way and surely no one would follow behind. And, even if they did, they couldn't make a fast go of it. The more I think on it, I believe it'd be a wise move. You agree?"

"Already told you what I think, but I admit what you say has truth in it." Lucius shook his head. "I won't fight you on it. Never does me any good anyhow. Want me to tell the others?"

"Not yet. They've been through enough tonight. Let's let 'em alone for now. We'll talk about it when we next camp."

Lucius nodded and said, "I'll ride up ahead. Wind's shifted behind us. Hard to hear anything now. I better take a look."

With that, he was off and I was left alone with thoughts swirling in my head. Too many thoughts. Too many to sort out now. I'd have to make my best choices—and then just trust to instinct. And, I hoped, a great deal of luck....

....

It took us two days of hard riding along the rutted logging trail before we reached the outskirts of Alliance. Our stops had been few, only long enough for a short rest and bites of food. Tasby kept careful watched over our passengers. It was more and more obvious by the hour he was growing sweet on Laura. It always amazed me that feelings of the heart could show up at such a time of tension and turmoil, but the more I thought about it, I started to believe it was because of the crisis that hearts often bonded. As much as I enjoyed watching this unfold, I still thought it necessary to take Tasby aside and warn him to pay more attention to the trail behind us. He said he understood. Losing Toby was an awful reminder.

I was looking forward to our time with Jonathan and Sarah Haines. They were Quakers—but not so fixated on their religious beliefs they couldn't see the benefits of my type of work. Rather, the Haines were devoted to their faith, but they were also completely committed to the cause—and whatever methods might lead to victory. As such, they not only tolerated me and my methods, they also, much to my relief, always welcomed me with open arms. Usually by the time I reached Alliance, I was emotionally and physically drained by the challenges of my journey. At those times, good conversation and a stay at their table was the best medicine I could procure.

Their home was ideally situated to be a depot, and I always felt comfortable and safe there. They had a large but modest two-story structure on nearly a hundred and thirty acres of land just to the south of the main section of the town. A grove of pine trees protected their property on the west, and railroad tracks ran at the southern boundary. The tracks proved beneficial more than once as a short, steep grade nearby caused the train to slow just enough my passengers and I could jump aboard and ride along to safety.

The Haineses' home had an attic room just to the top of the stairs above the kitchen area. They kept this room furnished for passengers making their way through. It was on the small side, but it had a window with an expansive view to the south, the direction in which they could watch the trains moving past. It never took long for passengers to understand this view represented one of the last legs of their journey toward freedom. This room was where Laura and Liza would be hidden during our stay, and I felt great relief knowing this was just ahead.

Once we came to the grove of pines, I turned to Lucius and said, "You go ahead and look for the doll at the window. Can't take any chances. I'll stay here and keep watch."

Lucius nodded and replied, "Won't take long."

With that, he nudged his horse and was off at a gallop.

The "doll" I was referring to was one of the tools of the trade employed by the Haines. These dolls, known as Liberator Dolls, were sold at bazaars and rallies to raise funds for *The Liberator,* an abolitionist newspaper out of Boston that helped spread news of the cause far and wide. Mrs. Haines often made these herself and had them delivered to other depots along the Underground Railroad. On many occasions, these dolls had helped prevent the recapture of runaways and the deaths of their conductors. They were actually two dolls in one, sewn at the waist. On one end was the face of a white child. On the other end, instead of legs being attached, the face of a black child was found. A large, billowy skirt was attached at the middle so that when pulled down one way, the white face was showing and the black one covered up completely. Pulled the other way, the black face was revealed—and the white hidden.

These dolls were placed in full view in the main parlor window so that conductors could use them as a gauge to the danger—or safety—that might be just ahead. The face of the white child on display indicated that no danger was about. On the other hand, if the face of the black child was present, this was a warning to stay clear of the area because slavers or bounty hunters could be lurking close at hand. I had heard tell that Mrs. Haines had come up with the idea for these dolls, but I couldn't place that for a fact. All I knew was these were a clever addition to a desperate cause, especially since the meaning of lanterns in windows, such as used by Reverend Rankin, were starting to be understood by those on both sides, greatly lessening their effectiveness.

While Lucius was away, I called Laura and Liza over and told them what they needed to know about the Haineses. I described the attic room where they'd be hiding during our stay there and also gave particular emphasis to the importance of their silence while they were in that room in case visitors unexpectedly showed up to the home.

Not ten minutes later, Lucius appeared again, grinning broadly.

"Miss White was starin' through the glass at me, so I knocked to the door. Mrs. Haines told me if I didn't fetch you quick as lightning she'd take a switch to me. No doubt she will, so let's not waste time. Besides, supper's nearly on the table, and it smelled mighty fine to me."

Tasby overheard and said, "What we waitin' for? I'm 'bout starved out!"

"You're always starved out," Lucius shot back.

"I could handle a bite myself," I said. "But, we've open ground to cross before we get to their home, so I want the women covered up. Tasby, get 'em two blankets from the packhorse."

Then, addressing Laura and Liza, I continued, "Wrap 'em round you—and cover as much of your heads as you can. Then, ride along side and to the right of Tasby so anyone who might be watching from the direction of the town won't be able to draw details. Don't worry—it'll work."

"Let's go!" Tasby shouted, waving his hands high above his head. "Next stop—food!"

Lucius looked at me and groaned.

"He's right," I said, laughing softly. "And a mouth full of food will keep him quiet for at least a little while."

"Doubt it," Lucius replied.

"Me, too, but it's worth a try, don't you agree?"

Lucius groaned again and spit to the side.

"Okay—let's go," I said to the others. "Keep close, and keep quiet. Ready?"

Coming from the west, we crossed acres of open field before the home came to view. As we drew closer, I motioned for Laura and Liza to move in closer to Tasby and to cover their faces better. My guard was up those last yards, as it always was when I drew up to a depot. I kept my left hand gripped tightly to the pistol in my belt.

When Mrs. Haines stepped out to the porch, I felt a wave of relief wash over me.

"John!" she shouted. "Get your sorry self up here. I've been waitin' for you."

"And I for you," I replied, dismounting and rushing up the steps. "You're beautiful as ever," I said, taking her hands.

"And you're still the biggest liar this side of the Mississippi," she shot back. "Still, your flattery does me good. I'll allow to that."

Mrs. Haines was a handsome woman, small of frame but possessing captivating blue eyes set off by her silky, silver hair. She and Jonathan were much older than I in years—but not in spirit. The fire of her faith and the cause burned hot within her, making her bold in her words and actions. I admired her greatly and was honored to call her my friend. She was one of the best women I had ever known.

"Well, you coming inside, or do you plan to eat with the horses?" she asked, shaking a finger at all of us.

"I'm ready!" Tasby called out. "You just lead me to that table!"

"Hasn't changed a bit, has he?" she said, turning back to me.

"Sadly, no he hasn't," I said, smiling. "And how 'bout your cooking? Any better?"

"What do you mean better?" she asked, kicking me playfully on the shin. "Why, last time you nearly ate the leg off the table if I rightly recall. Seems my cookin' has always been good enough for you."

Lucius collected the reins of the horses and started walking them to the barn. "You better get yourselves inside," he said, sternly. "The pack of you make a mighty good target standing there."

He didn't have to say more. He was right. Mrs. Haines said she'd have one of their hired men stand guard while we visited. Then, after introducing Laura and Liza to Mrs. Haines, we stepped into her home and closed the door behind us.

Mrs. Haines playfully shoved Tasby and me toward the kitchen, then turned and led Laura and Liza up the steps to the attic. "Be back momentarily," she said. "Jonathan's carving the meat. Go see if he needs any help. Tell him I'll be right down and to get all the plates ready."

As we entered the kitchen, Johathan Haines, apron around his waist, stood carving at the table.

"Now, that's some sight to behold!" I said, laughing loudly.

"You watch your words or you'll be eating hay instead of this," Jonathan retorted, setting down the knife and moving forward to shake my hand. "Never known you to be particular before."

"Oh, I'm not," I replied. Then, unable to resist, I said, "Just seeing you in that getup reminds me of how far a man can fall."

He picked up the knife and waved it toward me. "One of these days...." he said, smiling. He then pulled me forward and shook my hand, careful not to stab me in the process.

"Good to see you, too," he said, finally backing away.

Then, looking as if he suddenly remembered something, he added, "We've got important news to share. Don't usually like to talk about such things at supper, but we better make an exception this time."

"I think I already know it," I replied. "But I'd like to hear your version of it."

He studied my face a few moments before saying, "I'm worried about you, John."

"Ah, you needn't," I said, picking up a stack of plates and spreading them around the table. "Everybody says I'm too mean to die. I'm starting to believe they're all about right."

He shook his head and said, "This isn't a matter to laugh at. Not at all."

Just then Mrs. Haines entered the kitchen and ordered everyone to their places. "We wait for Lucius," she commanded. "Not a blessing or a morsel in any mouth until he shows."

Tasby, stood, moved to the back door, opened it, and called out, "You jughead—get yourself to here! We waitin' on you!"

"Yes," Mrs. Haines said, softly. "He hasn't changed one bit."

We all laughed—but we also stared uncomfortably at the door until Lucius appeared. When he had finally seated himself, Jonathan provided grace, and we were all soon enjoying a heaping plate of boiled ham, butter beans, and corn bread.

Mrs. Haines stood suddenly, and all of us immediately followed suit. "Oh, sit yourselves back down!" she scolded. "I'm just going to take plates up to the girls. Go ahead and eat. Don't wait for me. Won't be long."

We acknowledged her kindness—but we also dug right in. She was the best cook in these parts, and I knew how lucky we were to be taking this meal.

When she finally returned, Jonathan put down his fork and said, "Better get to it. Lots to share with you."

Lucius and I looked up at the same time as he continued, "First off, the Hubbards were carted off again to Columbus to stand trial for harboring runaways. Nothing could be proved again, so they had to let them go. Still, the message given was clear to all: if the Hubbards keep on, they are eventually going to make a mistake. When that happens, they'll find themselves looking through iron bars for a long, long time. Sarah doesn't agree with me, but I think it time for them to move along. They've done enough already."

"He's right. I don't agree with him," Sarah said, firmly. "Not at all. None of us can give up the fight until it's over. We just can't."

"I know all about it," I said. "We were through there not all that long ago. And I side with Jonathan on this matter. I suggested they move west and help the cause from there, but I doubt they will. Both stubborn to a fault. Stubborn as mules."

"And they were doing well when you saw them?" Sarah asked. "I've been worried so about them."

"Fine," I replied. "At least for a couple of mules."

"Glad you already know about it," Johathan said. "If you're off to that direction again, best be prepared for a trap. Eyes are likely on their home all the time now."

I nodded, but before I could say anything, he continued, "I've something over in the cabinet that Levi Coffin wanted me to give to you when you next showed. He said you'd likely need it by now because money just runs through your fingers like water."

He stood, walked to the cabinet, drew out a small leather pouch, and tossed it over to me. From its weight, I knew instantly it held a substantial amount of money. I didn't open it. I placed it in my pocket and thanked him for holding it for me.

"Levi always surprises me," I said. "He's too generous. Still, it's appreciated, and I'll put it to good use."

"He knows that," Jonathan said, smiling. "He says he doesn't care for you in the least—at the same time he does something like this. If you ask me, you two are like a cat and a dog trying to share the same quilt."

Tasby stopped chewing long enough to add, "And I know which is the dog!"

Mrs. Haines laughed, spilling some of her glass of milk at the same time. She was always so prim and proper at the table this sort of thing never happened. So, what did the rest of us do? We all laughed, heartily.

She blushed in response and fanned herself with her napkin.

Jonathan drew in a deep breath and turned serious. "I've still something else to share with you."

He returned to the table with a large, folded piece of paper. Unfolding it carefully and smoothing it out, he placed it before me. It was the poster with my image and description.

"They're closing in to you, John. No doubt about it any

more. I've also heard tell a bounty hunter—I forget his name just now—has spread it along he won't rest until you're in the ground. If you were my own son, I'd tell you to run—now—and not to look back. Fair is fair. Now it's time you look out for yourself."

I pushed my plate toward the center of the table and said, "I agree with Sarah. None of us can quit until we see this through."

Then, I picked up the poster. "I know about this. Have for some time. Where'd you get it?"

Sarah looked at Jonathan, her eyes narrowing. "I don't care what she said," she practically shouted. "I'm spillin' the whole pot right now."

"Sarah, you better not..." Johathan cautioned, leaning toward her.

"What? What is it?" I asked. "Please tell me."

"It's like this," Sarah said, leaning over and taking my hand. "You know she loves you more than life itself, don't you?"

She didn't need to say anything more. "Cat!" I called out. "She gave you that poster?"

"She did," Sarah replied. "But, before you get your hackles up too high, you've got to understand why she did it. When a woman loves a man as she does you, she'll do anything to protect him."

"But how...?" was all I could get out before Sarah interrupted. "She came over by train not long ago to visit with me. She wanted me—wanted us—to try to talk some sense into you. Now, before you get mad, you think about this for a minute. Who else do you know who'd go to those lengths to save your sorry self? Anyone else?"

I had to admit I didn't. "But," I said, "she shouldn't have tried to use you to put thoughts into my head. That wasn't right."

"Right has nothing to do with it," she responded. "Love does—and love wins every time in matters like this. I'm going to give you some advice, John Fairfield, and you best be takin' it. Don't you lose that woman. You'll never find another who'll feel the same about you, and from what I gather by the look on your face, you feel a might bit the same in her direction. Am I right?"

"He crazy in love with her," Tasby said through a mouth full of butter beans.

"I suspected as much," she said, grinning. "You follow my advice now. You hear?"

"Yes, Mam," I said, bowing slightly toward her. "Whatever you say."

"Don't you be humoring me now," she said, her voice growing louder.

Thankfully, Jonathan came to my rescue and changed the subject—in a manner of speaking. "We've heard a powerful lot about you of late. If one were to believe all the stories going about, you've taken near to a thousand passengers to freedom— from every corner of the South. And according to these tales, you've killed at least two dozen along the way. On top of all this, you are now supposed to have a black woman you are keeping somewhere farther north. Just amazing what people will say, isn't it?"

He was fishing, and I knew it. However, I didn't mind. I began, "Well, it isn't true about the black woman...."

Tasby laughed so hard he nearly choked. "And as far as the rest is concerned," I continued, "legend helps with the business. If those numbers are being tossed about, I'm not going to correct them. No, Sir—I'm not. Good for my business—and good for the cause. If you want to, you can do me a favor."

Sarah asked, "And what would that be?"

The next time you hear one of these stories, tell them the numbers are actually much greater than that. Tell them it's well over a thousand now and that I've put four-dozen in front of the Almighty for judgment. Tell them that."

"You truly are a wicked man, aren't you?" Sarah said while looking at Lucius and shaking her head. Lucius just shrugged.

At this point, I just couldn't resist turning the table just a shade. "I've also heard some stories about you," I said, pointing my fork toward Sarah. "Seems you've been doing some conjuring of spirits for the local citizens—and doing it for money. You do know they used to burn witches for the same thing not all that long ago. Think they'll burn you one of these days?"

Sarah's mouth dropped open, and she started to reply when Jonathan came to her defense. "It's true Sarah does an occasional seance, but she's not trying to conjure up anything but money from the rich folk who refuse to provide funds for the cause. If we can't get the money one way, we'll get it another. That's something—that's a choice—we made a long time ago."

"I feel no guilt about this, John. I'm helping the cause first—and if I make some of these people happy in the process by telling them what they want to hear, so be it."

"Why, you faker," I scolded. "And you have the nerve to chew on my tail for all the rumors flying about me. As far as I see it, what's the difference between what you're doing and what I'm doing? I make up my tales so I can tell people what they want to hear before I steal their property. And you—you tell your own tales before stealing their money. Seems to me we're more peas in a pod than you'd care to admit."

"Now wait a minute," Jonathan said, dropping his spoon to his plate. "She isn't harming anyone—and certainly not killing anyone."

"I'm just funnin' you," I said, quickly. "No need to get riled. Just couldn't resist throwing the rag back at you is all. I have nothing but deepest respect for both of you. It does my heart good to hear that others are being—how should I say it?—creative in the name of the cause. I'll sleep just a little bit better tonight knowing that."

Jonathan and Sarah looked at each other and smiled. "Creative," Jonathan said loudly. "I like that!"

"So do I," Sarah added. "Very much."

The rest of us howled.

....

While Tasby and Lucius helped Sarah clear the supper dishes, Jonathan and I went out to the front porch and sat in the rocking chairs there. No sooner had we been seated when Jonathan said quietly, "Didn't want to say anything inside in case your passengers could hear through the cracks, but when Cat was here she said you needed to get over to see her quick as you can. She has a plan about something that might help save your life. That's all she would say. I'm a pretty fair judge of people, and from the look on her face, I could tell she was dead serious. You get to her fast. How soon you plan to leave here?"

"Tomorrow morning—early. I was going to have us jump to the train at the slowdown, but I have the feeling it's being watched. Taggart—the bounty hunter you talked about—has eyes all around now. Our horses are tired, but if we make our way some to the south before setting a course toward Hanover, we shouldn't be spotted. I'd rather take my chances that way."

"I agree with you," he said, rocking back in his chair. "The train is too risky just now. Besides, with that handsome bounty on your head, it won't just be that bounty hunter looking for your hide. You should move quickly, but there's no sense taking unnecessary chances. Head south 'till you come to Jepsen's Lake—and then head over from there. You know where that is, right?"

"I do—and thank you for the advice. I'll take it."

We rocked in silence for a few minutes until he stopped, stared at the porch floor, and said, his voice softer than before, "In my faith we don't condone killing. You know that. But, you're going to have to do something about this man. If he catches you first...."

His voice trailed off, and he closed his eyes as he started rocking again.

"I know. His men almost had us the other night. We got out of that—just barely—but it won't be long for me if I don't stop him—and soon. I think about that constantly now."

"You could just go to Canada and stay, you know."

"He'd just follow eventually," I said, shaking my head. "No, I can't hide from him. At least not for very long. We're destined to meet up again. How it ends, I don't know. All I know is one or both of us won't walk away. I suppose that's the way it should be anyway."

"What do you mean?"

"In our way, he and I aren't all that much different. There isn't room for both of us any more—and maybe not room for either."

"I still don't get your meaning."

"I don't expect you to. I don't. But, my friend, I do have a favor to ask. If I'm the one to fall, I want you to give something to Cat for me. Will you do that?"

"What is it?"

"Before I sleep tonight, I'm going to write down for you the name of someone at Elgin Settlement I'd like you to contact if I'm the one to fall. While I'm away, he watches over all my worldly possessions. If I'm not coming back, he has instructions to take half and donate it to the cause—and deliver the rest to Cat. It should make her comfortable the rest of her days. Will you do that for me?"

"You know I will," he replied. "But let's not think about that now. You were right when you said you were too mean to die. At least I hope that's the case."

"Me, too," I said.

....

Chapter 23

Baiting a Trap

Hanover, Ohio

CAT JUMPED INTO MY ARMS when she opened the back
door of the tavern and saw me standing there. Her first kiss was
so intense I staggered back, almost falling.

"I've been praying for this moment," she said, tears welling
in her eyes as we caught our balance. "I heard you might have
been killed down to Ripley. Trappers said they found bodies just
north of there—all in a pile. I knew right away it was either your
work—or it was you stacked up. Haven't been able to sleep an
hour at a time since."

"Don't you remember," I said, "I'm too mean...."

She stopped me, pressing a finger to my lips. "I know that
already, but it looks like you have my heart—for better or worse.
Probably for the worse, I'm guessing."

Then, backing away from me, she looked me over and said,
"Okay, where are you hurt this time? Tell me now. Be truthful."

I bent over and rolled my trouser leg to just above the
boot. "Well, I'm in one piece. But I do have this cut I want Dr.
Robertson to look at."

She looked at the red, festering knife wound and turned
away.

"Of course you do," she said, her voice knotted with exasperation. "I'd faint dead away if you ever showed up and weren't
shot, stabbed, or run over. Just what am I to do with you?"

"I know what I'm going to do with you," I said, stepping toward her and taking her in my arms. "How's this to begin?"

I kissed her, gently at first, then with passion. When I pulled back, she didn't say anything. Instead, she placed her head on my shoulder and held close to me.

"What?" I asked. "Not going to tease me any more? Now I'm worried about *you*."

She drew back and said, quietly, "We need to talk, but not here. I've a few things to take care of inside first. Give me half an hour—please—and then meet me at our spot down by the canal. Will you do that?"

"Let's make it a full hour," I said. "I've two passengers to get to Dr. Robertson, and I want him to look to this leg. It's startin' to trouble me. Go take care of your business. Soon as I can I'll get down there and will be waiting for you."

She kissed me, turned, and was gone.

....

I was kneeling behind a small pile of logs and adjusting the bandages Dr. Robertson had applied to my leg when I heard Cat walking down the hill toward the canal. As she approached, I stood and motioned her to come close.

"Later," she said, taking my hand and leading me farther down the bank. "We talk first."

"Okay," I said. "About what?"

"Sit down," she commanded, pointing to a small grassy area toward the edge of the bank. "As difficult as this is going to be for you, I want to keep your mouth tight and listen to me for once. Can you do that?"

I nodded as she continued, "Some of Taggart's men were through here last week. They stayed two days, scouring the countryside for you during the daylight hours. While they were here, they received word you were supposedly on your way to the Iron Works at Cumberland Furnace, Tennessee, to help with a problem brewing there involving a large group of slaves. They said the bounty on you had increased, and Taggart promised the man who brought you to him would receive the riches of a king. That got them to their horses and away from here. You should have seen the dust as they left. Like a tornado blowing through."

I stared off at the canal and turned over in my mind all she had said. Taggart was closing in from many directions at once. And, I didn't like the thought of him picking the time and place of the showdown that was to come.

Cat inched closer and took my hand. "Before they moved along, they let it slip Taggart hadn't started yet, but he was also considering making his way toward Cumberland. That is, he'd do so if he received some better confirmation you were truly set that direction. I should have paid more attention to them, but I was suffering so at the time. I was so worried you were in that stack of bodies down to Ripley."

"You believe this story?" I interrupted. "You hold truth to it? Think now. We must be sure."

"I do," she replied. "And it's much to our advantage, and if you'll close that mouth of yours again, I'll tell you why."

I smiled and said, "Then go on, my love—please."

Cat frowned as she continued, "If we could be certain Taggart would head toward Cumberland Furnace, we'd take an upper hand. That is, we'd know where he was—but he'd still not have a clue where you'd be. That's the first step."

At that instant, I thought of Mr. Boyle.

"I know someone who might be able to help with that," I said, matter-of-factly. "Met a man at Elgin who knows Taggart and, more important, how to get a message to him. That is, if he's still alive—if Taggart hasn't cut him down yet. If he's still above ground, he could be of use to us."

"Can you trust him?" Cat asked.

"Not in the least. But, he's in a fix right now. He has to either trust me—or Taggart. It's the frying pan or the fire, but I think he'll throw in with me. He'd be a fool not to. I could get word to him to let Taggart know I'm toward Cumberland."

"Good. That takes care of the first part. Still, to be safe, we'll spread around that you are, indeed, making for Tennessee. A lot of trappers through here this time of year. With a few choice words at the tavern, shouldn't be hard to get them talkin' about it. After that, it will spread like fire."

Looking right to my eyes, she added, "The next will be just as important, maybe even more so. We'll let it be known far and wide you'll be using the name Fairborne, which is what you first told me was your true name. Remember?"

"Sorry," I said, shrugging my shoulders. "I've always felt bad about that. Wish there was something I could say."

"There isn't right now," she said, "so keep quiet and just listen. We'll spread it that you're on your way there to help the slaves at the Iron Works. For the past two weeks, traveler after traveler has had on his lips what's happening down there. The story being told is the poor slaves at the Works are being abused more than imagination could hold—and that the whole area is a powder keg waiting to be set off. It would make sense someone would try to come to their aid, and we'll make it out the someone is you."

"What makes you think Taggart and the others would believe I'd get involved in this?" I asked. "What profit would there be in it for me? They know I don't go for causes. To them I have the reputation as a hired gun, plain and simple."

"Already thought of that," she replied. "We'll say one of the slaves there is kin to a rich freedman in Canada, and you're being sent there to help that slave and many of the others to their freedom—for a price, of course. A very *large* price. On top of that, we'll add that a group of wealthy abolitionists is also backing your play by throwing even more money your direction. With that much money involved, Taggart will figure you'll be there."

"So, if we do get Taggart to Cumberland, how do you propose we take care of him?" I asked.

"You're asking *me* that?" she asked, shaking her head. "You—you of pistols and knives lodged in every pocket and boot you have?"

Here, her confident voice backed off slightly. "Here's the most important part of all. We'll need a confederate in that area for this to work. If you have someone who can help make sure Taggart gets over there—and if you also have a confederate who can be counted on—then I've a plan I know will work to get us out of the quicksand we're in. You'll never have to look over your shoulder again, and maybe I won't have so many sleepless nights worrying about you. I'd give anything for both to happen. And, this plan *will* work, will get us what we most want now. It'll take some luck as well, but I just have to believe fortune will shine on us."

"Tell me—just how does all of this unfold?" I asked, leaning back and smiling, curiously. "What's to do when I get to Cumberland?"

"You're the master of the ruse," she said, smiling back. "But, I've a few ideas of my own about how to bait a trap. Now listen close."

For the next hour, Cat amazed me with a plan I'm not sure even someone of my considerable experience could have built. It wasn't a simple plan by any means but, as I heard it unfold, I also realized she was right. If we had even the slightest amount of luck on our side, it could work—and the quicksand she mentioned might soon just be a distant memory.

When she finished the last of the details, I sat back and saw her in a light I'd not been aware of before. I knew her heart to be full of love, but I hadn't suspected her also capable of such devious plotting and planning. Suddenly, I realized there was much more about Cat yet to know, and the thought made me smile.

I leaned forward and said, "We've still some work to do on this, but I'm of a mind it could work. Thank you—thank you, my love."

"What did you call me?" she asked, her voice becoming very quiet. "That's the second time today you've said that."

"My love," I repeated.

I couldn't help but notice the tears slowly sliding down her cheeks and catching at the corners of her lips. "I know I shouldn't say it," I said, "but Heaven help me—and you as well—but I do mean it. I've known it from the minute we first met. I haven't said it before—I didn't dare—because I figured it wouldn't be fair to you. I figured I'd be long under ground by now. I know this shouldn't be coming out of my mouth, but if I survive this, I want a new life with you in the Territory."

Wiping tears from her cheeks, she said, "There have to be new lives out there for us. There just have to be."

I drew her close again. "I want you to dream about those new lives for us every night. Will you do that?"

"Just you try to stop me," she said, hugging me even tighter. "I will. Every day. Every night. You'll never be away from my thoughts."

"And you'll never leave mine. Now, continue building the very best plan we possibly can. We must not allow a single error. Too much is at stake."

"Everything's at risk," she said, looking down. "Everything."

We spent much of the afternoon adding one detail to another. I decided I'd still continue on as far as Ashtabula, where I'd tell Lucius just enough of the plan to keep him from trying to talk me out of it. Then, I'd leave him and Tasby in charge of getting Laura and Liza to Elgin—and explain to them what to do with the money received for their delivery. The money I had received from Levi Coffin was all I needed for the ruse Cat and I planned. After leaving them in Ashtabula, I'd make my way straight for Cumberland Furnace while Cat did her best to spread word that Fairborne was on the move. At last, we felt we had come up with the plan most to our advantage.

"It will work," she said, confidently.

"It better," I replied. I didn't have to tell her what would happen if it didn't.

I took her hand, and we walked back up the hill toward the tavern. Along the way, it came to me if our plan didn't work out, this might be the last time we'd ever be together. Cat must have been thinking the same because she drew close, hugged me tight, and kissed me, her hair brushing my cheek.

At the back door of the tavern I stopped and let go of her hand.

"You need to be off, don't you?" she asked, her voice calm, already knowing the answer.

I didn't want to leave her, but much had to be done if the plan was to work.

"I'm afraid I do," I said, backing away.

Nothing else needed to be said. We kissed one last time. Cat then turned and walked through the door.

....

Chapter 24

Into the Furnace

Cumberland, Tennessee

FOUNDED IN 1796, THE CUMBERLAND Iron Works had first achieved national notoriety as the company that had manufactured the cannonballs used by Andrew Jackson in his defense of New Orleans during the War of 1812. With two converging reputations, it was still one of the major suppliers of armaments and building materials for the South. The first was for its quality of craftsmanship, which many considered second to none. The second was its brutal treatment of the slaves who manned nearly every station of the Works.

Slave labor was used for all the dangerous tasks, from stoking the massive furnaces to the handling of the newly created, smoldering-hot iron products. The working conditions were so hazardous that deaths within the compound were common. A constant reminder of the dangers was the large cemetery just inside and to the left of the entrance of the main compound; nearly all those resting there had lost their lives either in the creation of iron or as a result of whippings for what the supervisors judged as slothful work habits. To the slaves, who were at times literally chained to their work, the Iron Works was now known as "Death City, Tennessee." Adding to their fears was a question that had long gone without answer: What happened to slaves when they became old or physically unable to perform their duties? What they did know was the old and infirm slaves were transported out of the compound, never to be heard from again. Where they went remained a mystery, but all had their suspicions. Many believed they were simply taken away and killed. No one could prove this, but the belief was strong enough that most saw escape to freedom as their only hope for survival.

It didn't help that close on to two weeks before, five workers had perished when one of the furnaces collapsed while they were inside. The fire had been so hot the bodies were instantly cremated, their ashes mingling with each other on the black earth below the rubble. The supervisors hadn't allowed even a moment of prayer for those who had been lost. Instead, whips were brought out again, and crews of slaves worked around the clock until a new, taller, and, therefore more dangerous, furnace stood in place of the original.

After that event, in the early hours past midnight, talk in the slave quarters turned to how freedom might be achieved. They didn't fear the death that would follow if they were caught discussing such plans. They felt they had little to lose. They were so heavily watched, however, most plans for escape they came up with could not be carried out by a group of any size. Still, whenever possible, any free moments were spent forming plan after plan. Somehow, the supervisors seemed to sense this, and the whippings and beatings increased because the owners of the company believed this would keep slaves in line. Little did they know, these were only stoking the desire to escape even hotter.

On top of all, running parallel to all other events, was a rumor not known to the slaves but constantly on the minds of the owners and supervisors. Rumor had come from several sources that a group of abolitionists, led by the notorious John Fairborne, was hell-bent on stealing their slaves to freedom and blowing up the Iron Works. This Fairborne was reputed to have already led thousands of slaves to their freedom and murdered dozens of their masters along the way. Once John Fairborne's name was heard, the owners of the Works doubled security at every entrance. However, even that didn't make sleep easier for them. They still kept pistols at the ready next to their beds.

The Cumberland Iron Works was in a state of tension never before seen or felt by any of the supervisors or owners. Violence was coming—they all knew it—but they didn't know how or from where it would show itself.

....

It was into this climate of fear and uncertainty—on the part of all sides—that Deputy Sheriff Perkins rode to the main gates of the Cumberland Iron Works. He was met by two heavily armed guards who immediately demanded he state the purpose of his visit.

"I've important news of the abolitionists headed this way. I must see someone in charge right now. We haven't time to waste or all may be lost."

His words were overheard by two slaves, chained at the ankles, who were digging up stumps just yards from the gate. When the guards looked their direction, they kept about their work and pretended they had heard nothing. Just as the guards looked back at Deputy Sheriff Perkins, the larger of the slaves mouthed the word "tonight" to the other—and they doubled the pace of their work.

The short, squat guard holding a shotgun with neatly sawed off barrels pointed his weapon in the direction of Perkins and replied, "Wait here."

Then, turning to the other guard, he commanded, "You keep a tight eye to him, 'till I get back. Goin' to fetch Captain Jordan. He'll know what to do."

Perkins dismounted, walked his horse to a tree, tied off the reins, and sat on the ground to the side. The guard stayed by the gate and studied him carefully.

"I don't bite," Perkins finally said, laughing. "I'm here to help."

"We'll see," the guard said, patting the pistol in his belt. "Cap'n Jordan will know for sure."

"Then we'll wait for Cap'n Jordan," Perkins said, mimicking the guard's drawl.

It was just a few minutes later the guard with the shotgun and Captain Jordan appeared.

"My man here says you've news for me. I expect to hear it, but first, just who are you?"

"Not here," Perkins said, first showing his badge then motioning to the slaves hard at the stumps. "Too many ears. A place we can talk?"

Captain Jordan motioned him to several cords of firewood stacked next to the main gate. "Well," he said, finally. "I'm waitin."

"I'm Deputy Sheriff Perkins—on orders from my sheriff, Sheriff Bailey. Maybe you've heard of him—over to Rutherford?"

When Captain Jordan didn't respond, he continued, "He wanted me to warn you to double, maybe triple, your watch. We've definite confirmation the abolitionist Fairborne and a fair-sized group of men were spotted not a day's ride from here. Sheriff Bailey's positive their target is your Iron Works."

"We've already heard the rumors," Captain Jordan said, folding his arms tightly at his chest. "We're ready with a warm reception for him, if he shows. So, I thank you—and your sheriff—but I believe we have ...."

Perkins interrupted and said, curtly, "And that's exactly why that man has never faced the noose—misguided overconfidence."

"Your meaning, Sir?" Captain Jordan shot back, his words blending to anger. "How dare you...."

"Meant no disrespect, Captain Jordan. Believe me. But you didn't let me finish my news."

Captain Jordan stared intently at Perkins, paused briefly, unfolded his arms, then said, "Go on. I'm listening."

"Fairborne is tricky as they come. That's how he's never been caught. He's now disguised himself up as a slave catcher called Taggart. His men appear scruffy as lice, like trail-bums, so they fit in. We believe he plans to camp himself near here and offer his services to you in the event your slaves get unruly or run off. But what he'd really be up to is gettin' inside these walls to spy around. If he does, and you don't expect it, the wrath of Hell will surely follow. He's done these ruses b'fore, and even used this same exact one—pretendin' to be a catcher—to get slaves away by the dozens."

Before Captain Jordan could reply, he continued, "And never let it from your thoughts this Fairborne has also murdered innocent white women and children during his raids. I imagine you and the others likely to have family close to hand. Just thought you should know."

Captain Jordan looked down, kicked at the dirt, and said, "I see. Then please tell your sheriff I do appreciate his cautions, and if there's ever anything I can do to...."

"There is," Perkins interrupted. "He requests a trade of favors—to mutual benefit."

Motioning Captain Jordan to come closer, he said, "Sheriff Bailey's the best tracker I've ever known. I think we'll get to Fairborne first, and when we do, he has a trap thought up for him. This is where you can help us, and, in turn, Sheriff Bailey will be helping you as well—and filling your pockets deep with gold. He doesn't give a whit about Fairborne, and he can't accept the legal bounty on him because of his office in the law. It's Fairborne's right-hand-man he's after—not Fairborne. Fairborne's man shot Sheriff Bailey 'bout two years ago, and his arm hasn't been the same useful since. He wants his measure of justice for that. No, it isn't Fairborne he wants, but he'd give half his soul for this other man."

"And how do I play into this?" Captain Jordan asked, curiosity spreading across his face. "What am I expected to do?"

"First off, like I said, Sheriff Bailey knows of his ruses. We'll use that to trap him. Fairborne knows the Sheriff's face—but not mine. So, once we find him, I'll make friendly like and tell him I know you and can get him through the gates here to make a contract with you for his services. Don't believe he'll turn down an offer like that. Sheriff says he'll fall for this easy because he's done this same thing many times before. And, he'll figure this time'll be easier because he'll have a lawman to get him in. Once he's in here, he's trapped—we'll snare him. If you agree to our plans, Sheriff Bailey will be by and will explain the rest to you."

Captain Jordon was starting to smile, so Perkins continued, "Sheriff says you can keep him for the reward, which is now well to over two thousand. He'll also let you take all the praise, which'll make you a hero all through the South. All he wants is your word he can take the other men away to justice—and likely to a tree for one of 'em in particular."

Perkins studied Captain Jordan's face. "You can think it over long as you want, but I'm supposed to keep myself here until you give answer."

Captain Jordan stepped a few yards away and motioned his guards to gather close to him. After just a brief exchange, he returned and said, "Agreed—so long as I take all the reward. I'll keep Tucker here at the gate 'round the clock in case this really does come to pass, and I ain't totally convinced yet it will. Tucker'll recognize you and let you through. Tell him you're bringing in Mr. Taggart—to meet with me back to my office. He and another guard will follow you and get you there, but not before Tucker gives the signal for all to be at the ready. If this Fairborne shows, we'll have a nice surprise waiting for him once he steps into my office."

He paused and continued, "I hope you're right. Better not be just smoke and wind. This better work."

"It will," Deputy Perkins said, confidently. "You can bank on it. Of that, I'm positive."

Captain Jordan just stared at him and said, "We'll see. Yes, we'll see."

....

Chapter 25

Death to Abolitionists

DEPUTY PERKINS WAS AT THE back of the saloon and facing the door when Wilson Taggart entered, followed by two of his men.

Taggart walked right up to him, tapped his right hand rapidly on his pistol, and said, "My men here said you been lookin' for me all day. Well, I'm here. Start talkin'—and it better be to my liking or I'll gut you from throat to feet."

"I guess I know who you are," Perkins said, leaning back in his chair. "Please, sit. As I'm sure your men have told you, I've a proposition we need to...."

Taggart drew up his knife with his left hand and stabbed its point hard to the middle of the table. "I'll decide what's to be done. I take orders from nobody. Be clear on that b'fore I have to cut out your tongue."

"Won't be necessary," Perkins said, gulping sharply. "I intend no orders. Not for you. Just want to tell a plan. You'll decide if it's worthy enough."

"That's better. Now spill it before I use that."

"I understand you've been looking for this Fairborne for quite some time. Maybe I can help you get to the end of that trail."

"Stop jawin' and get to it. I'm not for conversation. If you got somethin' to say, now's the time while you still can."

Perkins pointed to the other men and said, "As I explained to these *gentlemen,* I can get you to him. All I want is a small token in return."

Taggart leaned over the table, his face inches away from the deputy, his hand curled around the knife. "Where is he?" Taggart asked, teeth clenched. "You better talk up—and now."

Perkins thought of stalling him, as Sheriff Bailey had instructed, but the second Taggart withdrew his knife from the table he thought better of it and decided to face him head-on.

"He's at the Iron Works—in the compound. I know exactly where he is in there because I saw him taken to quarters. He's pretending to be a slaver—to be your right-hand-man. Says he's waitin' for Taggart to show up to help him."

"You go over that again. Tell it plain. What are you talkin' about?"

"Think about it a minute. The Iron Works got slave trouble boilin', so the owners welcomed him, as one of your men, with open arms. They've heard of you and know your reputation. Who hasn't? What better to do at a time like this than to hire a famous slave catcher to be seen by those who are thinking of running off? When I was there the other day, I knew it was Fairborne right off when I saw him—from the posters that are everywhere—but didn't let on. No profit in it for me then. Had to have another way. Then I heard you were comin', and, well, here we are."

Perkins pulled the poster from his pocket, unfolded it, and placed it in the middle of the table before continuing, "He got himself hired as a slave catcher—no doubt so he could get himself inside the compound and make his plans ready for when the rest of his men show up. That's what I figure, anyway. So, if you're of a mind to share, say, $500 with me—I'm not greedy—I can get you inside the Works. They know me and will let me pass—and you also, if you're with me. You wouldn't be able to get inside by yourself. They're on alert and not lettin' anyone else cross in. If we do this on the quiet, I'll lead you right to him—and we'll be able to take him by surprise. I'd do it myself, but I know I'm no match for Fairborne. But, with you along, I know it can be done. Interested?"

Taggart, his expression cold, asked, "Why that no good.... Does he know I'm here?"

"Your men are everywhere, and they haven't exactly been bashful. I found them, didn't I? But so what if he does? He knows he's safe behind those walls. Guards are everywhere there now and aren't lettin' anyone else in. Don't see as how he could be more protected, which means he wouldn't be worried about you or anyone else."

Taggart drew his pistol and set it on the poster, the barrel aimed toward the deputy. "Could just shoot you now and save me that five hundred," he said, tapping the butt of the gun.

"I'll allow you could," Perkins said, placing his hands, slowly, palms down, on the table next to Taggart's weapon. "But if you do, they'll never let you pass, no matter what you say to the guards. Again, they know me and know I have business there. I can get in, and you can ride in with me. If you go rushin' in and make a ruckus, Fairborne will get away. So, look at it this way. You'll just be paying me five hundred to get you inside. Seems like a bargain to me, given the prize waitin' there."

Perkins hesitated, then said, "I've thought this through plenty. The guards will keep you from shootin' me after we take Fairborne, so I'm not too worried about an early grave just yet."

"Pretty sure of yourself, aren't you," Taggart grunted.

"This is my one chance to have enough of a stake to get myself away from that one-dog town I'm from—and a sheriff I'd just a soon gut as look at. I'll take this chance. Seems worth it to me. I need you for that—and you need me. Simple. We both get what we want."

"How you know I'll pay off? You sure 'bout that, too, little man?"

"Because I'll take the money now—before we go. I know you've got it. A man of your... reputation... always travels with a goodly sum."

Taggart picked up his pistol and returned it to the holster. "Maybe after this is done, you'll think on joinin' up with me. Could make it worth your trouble. Just lost my best man. Need someone to fall to that place. You ain't much of a man, but you do have thinkin'—and that's what these other lunkheads don't have a spit of. Idiots, all of 'em. You think on it some."

He next leaned forward and said, making each word sharp, "You'll have your money now, but if he's not there, I will shoot you—guards be damned. And, killin' you would be to my liking. Get me?"

Perkins nodded—and held out his hand and wiggled his fingers.

Taggart filled his palm with money.

....

Just as darkness was settling, Deputy Perkins, with Taggart and two of his men in tow, slowly approached the main entrance to the Iron Works.

"Evening, Tucker," Perkins said, smiling. "You can put the scattergun down. It's just me. I need to take Mr. Taggart here to see Captain Jordon. We've business to attend to."

"Kind of on the late side, ain't it, Deputy?"

"Never too late when a dollar's involved. Wouldn't you agree that's so?"

Tucker shrugged his shoulders heavily, which was the sign to the others laying in wait, and let them pass.

As soon as they were inside, Taggart, still looking straight ahead, asked, his words biting, "Deputy, where is he?"

"Hold on. See that building just ahead to the right, the one with just a low glow of a lamp inside? That's where he keeps himself of a night. He'll be there. Doesn't come out once he's settled. When we get there, I'll knock to the door and identify myself. He knows of me, so he'll open. Soon as he does, we'll charge in and take him before anyone's the wiser. After it's over, I'll explain all to the guards. You can depend on me."

Taggart grunted and checked his weapons. Then turning to his men, he barked, "I better feel your foul breath on my neck when we go chargin' through that door. If you hang back, you'll fall this night, too."

They didn't need to respond.

Perkins led them to a hitching rail across the lane and urged all to quietly tie off their mounts and follow him up the two steps to the landing in front of the door.

When all were all in position, Perkins drew his pistol, tapped gently at the door, and said, "It's me—Deputy Perkins. Captain Jordan sent me to fetch you. Seems like trouble tonight with the slaves, and he wants you by his side. Open up."

When the door opened just a crack, Perkins pushed it full open and charged in, Taggart and his men close at his heels. However, as soon as Perkins was two steps in, he quickly fell to the floor, leaving Taggart standing alone for an instant, leveling his gun back and forth across the room. A man hiding behind the door used the butt of his pistol to deliver a sharp blow to the back of Taggart's head. The instant Taggart hit the floor, he was out cold.

From the other side of the room, from pitch darkness, Captain Jordon called out to Taggart's men, "Drop your weapons or we'll fire!" Before they could move, the guards behind them poked gun barrels to their backs and urged them farther into the room. As they moved slowly forward, Taggart's men let their guns slip to the floor.

"We got him, Captain Jordan!" called out the man who had been hiding behind the door and who had knocked Taggart senseless.

It was John Fairfield, wearing large spectacles and most of his face hidden by a scruffy beard. A sheriff's star was pinned to his vest. He quickly tied Taggart's hands behind his back and gagged his mouth. "Don't want to soil the world with one more word from his filthy abolitionist mouth. Would slit his tongue if we had the time, but this'll have to do." Then, turning to Perkins, who was resting on the floor and smiling broadly, he said, "Bind those others—and gag 'em, too. We need to ride. Let's get movin'!"

Captain Jordon, his voice cracking with excitement, said, "Sheriff Bailey—we really do have him. It's him! Can't believe it. Wait 'till word gets out...."

"I'm sorry," Sheriff Bailey said, extending his hand to shake the Captain's, "but we do have to be off. I've my own judgment to give. As we agreed, I'll have them—and especially him—the tall one there. He's the cause of this arm of mine. I'll leave this... this monster there on the floor to your own devices. However, I'd suggest a strong taste of the whip for him. Be good for the slaves to see. No lesson like a bloody one."

He pointed at the taller of Taggart's men just before punching him violently in the pit of his stomach. The man, hands tied and mouth already gagged, let out a pitiful moan and dropped to his knees, his body wracked with pain. He tried to speak, but the words were unintelligible.

Captain Jordon turned up the lamp and ordered Tucker and the other guard to pick up Fairborne, take him out past the slave quarters, and tie him securely to a tree. "And then get the whips— all of 'em. I'll call out what supervisors I can round up and meet you there. It's time someone shows those darkies what'll happen to 'em if they don't settle down. And Sheriff Bailey here is right: there's no lesson like one with blood. That's exactly what they'll get this night."

Turning to face Captain Jordon one last time, Sheriff Bailey said, "Do what you must, but keep the body. No sense throwing the bounty away because of excitement. If you ask me, he's worth more dead than alive. That is, you'll get the bounty even if he's dead, but think of the value of the sight of his corpse when the slaves look upon it. Not tellin' you what to do. Just a suggestion is all."

"A good point," the captain replied. "I'll make sure there's at least some flesh left."

"Good luck to you, then," Sheriff Bailey said. "Thank you for your help."

Then, turning to Deputy Perkins, Sheriff Bailey commanded, "Get 'em outside and mounted. We've miles to go tonight."

"Goodbye, Captain," Perkins said, tipping his hat. "I also thank you."

"You're welcome," he replied, not really paying any more attention to either Sheriff Bailey or Perkins. Instead, he turned to Tucker and said, bruskly, "Well, what are you waiting for?"

Tucker and the other guard lifted up Taggart's still motionless body and carried it out into the night.

....

With their prisoners tied close behind, Jeremy Carstairs, deputy sheriff badge pinned to his vest, and John Fairfield headed directly west. Not five minutes from the Iron Works, they were startled by the faint but distinct sounds of gunshots. Turning to look back, they saw the tips of bright orange flames above what appeared to be the walls of the compound.

"What do you suppose?" Jeremy asked, peering back once again. "More trouble?"

"Likely so, Deputy Perkins," John replied. "And well deserved if you ask me. Hope the whole place burns to ashes."

"Deputy Perkins," Jeremy repeated, making a sideways glance at John. "I'm no actor, but I believe I pulled that off fair to well."

"You did just fine. You seemed a natural to me the first time you played an officer of the law. You might be useful to the cause yet."

They rode again in silence until John, after looking back one last time toward the Iron Works, leaned close to Jeremy and said, "The only thing that still bothers me is he'll never know I—that we—did that to him."

"Does it really matter all that much?"

John paused and said, "I suppose not. I suppose the justice, the satisfaction of it, will eventually be enough."

"And now, what about them?" Jeremy asked, pointing back to Taggart's men.

John knew their prisoners could hear them, so he said, flatly, "We kill them. But, let's do it when we're close to home because I don't want their smell fouling our trip back. I'm thinking a pistol—but if you'd rather practice your knife...."

John heard them groan loudly as Jeremy looked up, horrified. "We're going to do what? Did I hear you right?"

"You did," John said, turning and winking an eye so that Taggart's men couldn't see him doing so.

When Jeremy saw that, he started to laugh, covering his mouth just in time. "Don't you think that more than a bit cruel?" he leaned over and whispered. "They may die of fright before we get more than a mile from here now."

"They might at that," John replied, also in soft voice. "Actually wouldn't mind that at all. Still, I suppose they can't be held completely at fault, not with Taggart always poking his knife at 'em."

Then, raising his voice again so the men could hear, he continued, "They're still slave catchers, and it ain't no harm to kill 'em. Certainly wouldn't bother my conscience any."

More groans followed as the taller one teetered and nearly fell from his saddle.

"We'll talk more of this tonight after we camp," Jeremy said, again loud enough to be heard by all. "You haven't convinced me yet they deserve a shallow grave."

He turned to John and, hiding his face from the others, smiled. John shook his head and said, "I was right about you. You are well suited for this, aren't you?"

"Time will tell," Jeremy replied.

....

After John and Jeremy made camp and tied Taggart's men loosely to a dead oak tree, John was the first to speak.

"Well, I suppose we ought to talk about their fate," he said, pointing toward the men. "I still say we ought to kill 'em. And do it right now, no matter the stench the rest of the way back home. How you feel about it?"

"I'm still on the fence," Jeremy replied. "On the one hand, they are, as you say, slave catchers—and a death wouldn't be cheatin' anybody. On the other, I've always believed that souls can, at times anyway, be redeemed. There's even a passage from the Good Book to back it up, if I recall correctly."

Both men, still gagged, nodded their heads vigorously as Jeremy spoke of redemption and tried, in vain, to add a few words of their own.

"No, can't say I'm of that mind," John said, shaking his head. "Still think we ought to finish 'em off." John then tilted his head sideways and said, "Wait a minute. You hear that? Off there past the brush, down in the wash. Somethin' movin'. Might be we've been followed. They're bound good enough. Let's you and me get down there and look around. Get your rifle, and let's see what it's about."

John motioned Jeremy to follow him through the bushes and off into the darkness. When they were out of sight of Taggart's men but could still see into the camp, John took Jeremy's arm and held firm.

"This is far enough, I expect. Shouldn't take 'em long to throw off those ropes. I made the knots as loose as I could. I just hope they don't take my horse. I've grown rather fond of it."

"You planned this all along, didn't you?" Jeremy asked, grinning. "Why you.... you're terrible. That's what you are—absolutely rotten terrible. Those men about died from worry, you know."

"And they'd have deserved it if they had. I still stick by that much. Look! The first one's free. He's leaving his friend behind! Not even helping him." Laughing softly, he added, "At least he didn't take my horse. Wait a minute—I think that was yours!"

Jeremy looked intently ahead, saw his horse, and knew instantly he'd been had. "Very funny. Very, very funny. Don't forget, there's one more. Yours might be stolen yet. I sincerely hope so now."

"Oh you do, do you?" John replied. "Some friend you've turned out to be."

"There he goes!" Jeremy said, pointing to the other man. "Finally got loose. Bet he really gives it to his friend when he catches him."

"Whose horse did he take?" John asked, not looking ahead.

"Why, I believe it was yours. Imagine that."

"Imagine that, my foot," John replied. "You think I'd fall for that? Who do you think I am—you?"

"Okay, don't believe me. Doesn't bother me if you don't. Just know I'll buy you a good mount when I have the chance. I'll use this...."

He pulled the rolled up bundle of bills from his pocket and said, "This is the bounty I received for your sorry hide from Taggart. I figured, why not?"

"John shook his head and said, "I really did know it from the beginning. You'll do. You are suited for this. If I had any doubts before, I don't now."

Jeremy laughed. "I just have one more question for you— just one more thing I have to know. Why'd you let those men go? Aren't you worried they'll head right back to town and there might be a posse after us tomorrow?"

"Not worried in the least. Remember, Taggart was really Fairborne, which makes them abolitionists to everyone at the Works. If they're seen anywhere about, they're likely to suffer his same fate before they had two words out. No, I'm betting they won't stop riding until their mounts die, and then they'll continue running afoot until they drop as well. By that time, nobody'll care about 'em, and we'll be so far off it won't matter anyway."

"I see your point, and it's well taken. Still, when you first said it, I was fairly certain you really did mean to kill them."

"If I'd been by myself, I just might have. You'll never know for sure. And maybe I wanted to let them escape because I didn't want you all distracted tonight. We've still got much to talk about—about your future."

"My future? What about it?"

"It seems now that I'm dead, I've a chance to start a new life and take my talents elsewhere—and still help the cause. If I do that, someone needs to take my place up along the Underground

Railroad. That person might just be you. Think you might be interested in that?"

"I'll hear what you have to say first," Jeremy said, checking to see if John was being serious this time.

"Good. I was hoping you'd at least listen. When you hear everything, I judge you'll decide a new life wouldn't hurt you none, either. And what a life it would be, a life certainly like no other. And one well suited to you."

When they were finally back up the hill and reentered their camp, John saw his horse had, indeed, been taken. "I'll be damned," he said, slapping his leg.

"I've no doubt you will," John laughed, loudly. "No doubt at all."

....

Chapter 26

A New Dawn

St. Louis, Missouri

As soon as *Fairborne* had met with justice in the woods near Cumberland Furnace, there was still much work to do. After letting our prisoners escape, Jeremy and I rode directly to his home in Camden. I remained there for three days while I schooled him in the routes, the people, and the depots, of the Underground Railroad I most frequently used so he could assume the work I was leaving behind. He had talked the matter over at length with his wife, a strong woman of great resolve in all areas pertaining to the cause, and both were of a mind they were ready to move to the front of the fight. I had so strongly hoped they'd make that decision. Once they had, I felt better about my plans to move to the west.

While at his home, I also prepared letters for him to deliver on my behalf when he moved north. It was important that word of my death be spread far and wide, so I planned to let even many of my closest and dearest of friends believe I had met my end in Tennessee. However, I wanted two people—and only those—to know the truth of the matter. Therefore, I prepared one of the letters for Levi Coffin. In it, I asked him to do his best to promote my demise every chance that would present itself. Since Coffin was the President of the Underground Railroad and also one of the most "watched" of all abolitionists, I knew if he talked of it, those on both sides of the fight would receive the information.

I prepared the other for Lucius because I considered him the best friend I'd ever had and for a practical consideration: I knew he'd be invaluable to Jeremy as he began his work. But, other than those two, the true story of what happened at Cumberland Furnace would be known to no other, which, I prayed, would allow Cat and me to start our lives anew and the shadows of my past to dissipate once and for all.

Before leaving Jeremy, I also prepared a will of sorts, and dated it months earlier, that left him my properties in Canada and claim to all the rest of my worldly goods I had left behind at the settlement. I figured he'd need these to establish himself there and, at the same time, serve as something of an introduction to those he'd be living and working with.

In the remaining time at Jeremy's home, I did all I could to teach him the proper handling and concealment of weapons—everything from pistols to knives. He was an attentive student showing great aptitude. What I wasn't able to teach him, I was sure Lucius would in my stead. At the same time, I offered my best advice for "carrying a ruse" while living among people from whom slaves were going to be taken. This was not easily explained, but watching Jeremy serve twice as a deputy, and both times performing exceptionally well, made me believe he'd do just fine with a little practice. That is, he'd be fine if he survived his first few forays.

The whole time I visited with Jeremy, I felt as if I were, in a manner, living my own obituary. Each time I passed along to him knowledge I had gained and used in the cause, I felt a streak of unexplainable melancholy, as if I were actually leaving parts of my life and spirit behind me. I was going to badly miss those I had worked with for so long, but even I had to admit it was time for me to move along to new frontiers in the fight for equality for all. Still, the unknown of the future was now more frightening to me than any battle I had ever gotten myself into in the past. I was just going to have to trust I'd still feel useful, still be able to continue the fight—no matter where I eventually settled.

I knew Cat would be experiencing many of the emotions now passing through me. In order for our plan to work, there could be no suspicion of any kind that she had left Hanover to meet up with me. We had talked about it for quite a long time, and even though she said it wouldn't bother her in the least, one morning she would simply have to disappear without a trace. I had asked her to seek the assistance of Dr. Robertson—but not to tell him the full plan ahead.

We'd proceed under the assumption I'd survive the Tennessee venture, so when she did take her leave, she was also to meet along the way with Levi Coffin to secure additional funds for us to use in establishing our work in Kansas Territory. As I knew his house to be watched nearly all the time, this was the part of the plan I worried about most of all. Still, if anyone could sneak in and out of Levi's home without drawing attention, it would be Cat. Levi, after visiting with Cat and later receiving my letter, would be the only one to know of our whereabouts. I knew he'd never reveal this to anyone. Never.

When I felt my usefulness at Jeremy's home had reached conclusion, I left early on a Tuesday morning and headed toward St. Louis, taking back trails as much as I was able. The last time I was with Cat, I told her I had no idea, if all was successful in Tennessee, exactly when I'd be able to meet up with her in St. Louis. I asked her to take a room there and, each day at the noon hour, position herself close by the buildings of the Squire & Reed Iron Merchants, which were located on North Front Street, right along the bank of the Mississippi just east of the main district of commerce. I hated the thought of her sitting there day upon day until I arrived—*if* I arrived—but I could think of no better alternative.

....

I was never so scared in my life as I was during my journey from Camden to St. Louis. Truth be told, I had made just over fifty forays from north to south and back again in the name of the cause—delivering hundreds of passengers—and I had never felt half as nervous or frightened for my own safety as I did the last few days before I reached Missouri. I always figured I'd die one day during my efforts—and would have been happy to go down fighting. However, now that I was so close to meeting up with Cat and beginning our new lives together, I was worried some bounty hunter who hadn't heard of my demise would recognize me before I got to her—and all our dreams would go up in the smoke of a pistol or rifle shot. In many ways, I figured that was what I deserved anyway—that my violent past deserved a violent end. As I made my way to Cat, I saw what I imagined to be bounty hunters behind every tree and boulder on the back trails to St. Louis, but it all turned out to be nothing more than shadows of my past continuing to haunt me.

Even though I probably didn't need to, I kept to the side of caution and rode mostly at night. As I did so, I thought over and over the possibilities ahead for Cat and me in Kansas Territory, especially as related to our work with the cause. She and I had discussed the notion of building a general store where settlers moving west could be provisioned. I had pretended so many times before to be an agent for such a venture, I felt as if I already had all the knowledge needed to succeed at this. Plus, with Levi Coffin's help, some of those settlers passing through could have wagons with false bottoms, false bottoms which runaways could hide in as they were being transported to their freedom. Our general store could, therefore, serve as one of the westernmost— if not *the* westernmost—depots for the cause. At the same time, if I could find a forger of documents even half as skilled as Henry had been, we could create papers that would allow some of those seeking freedom to work at our store until such time they, too, moved along. The more I thought about it, the more I knew Cat and I could find reward, and true fulfillment, helping in this manner. On my second night of riding I vowed to do my best to sell the idea to her at first opportunity.

It was late of the morning on my fourth day out of Camden

I reached the Mississippi and took the ferry across to the landing just below where I was to meet Cat. Not quarter of an hour later I saw her, sitting in a wagon and peering out across the river, right alongside the southernmost building of the Squire & Reed Iron Merchants. She looked beautiful to me, her hair glistening in the early morning sun. At the same time, I could imagine from the look on her face she was growing quite weary of making this a part of her daily routine. I thought of sneaking up behind her and surprising her, but at the last minute I remembered the knife she always kept close at hand—and decided to make a frontal assault instead.

"Waiting for someone in particular?" I asked, riding into her line of vision.

I had kept a fairly healthy growth of mustache and beard, so at first she didn't recognize me. Then, after a few moments of confusion, she shouted, "John!" as she jumped from the wagon and ran to me, the base of her skirt swishing on the cobblestone the entire way.

No sooner had I dismounted than she was in my arms, our lips pressed together in an instant. Holding her close, feeling the warmth of her cheek and her breathing matching mine, I knew, at that moment, all would be well. I knew it with all my being.

"We've a long way yet to Kansas Territory," I said, slowly easing her away. "Don't know what eyes are here in St. Louis, so we best be on watch. We'll have plenty of time for this soon."

"You promise?" she said, stepping politely back even farther. "I'm going to hold you to that."

"And you'll have no trouble doing so. That I do promise. But for now, let's be away from this part of the city. Too many travelers here. Too many people to watch."

I stepped back and admired her handiwork. "The wagon looks sturdy, looks perfect. Supplies?"

"Got them—all of them. I've brought 'em every day," she said, pointing to the wagon's bed.

"Good. Then we won't waste a minute. If you're ready, let's be off. Plenty of day left. We'll drop south before carving to the west. We should be able to cover a goodly distance before nightfall."

I tied my horse at the back and then helped her up to the wagon seat again. When I climbed up beside her, she said, coyly, "We *could* make one stop first. The other day I just happened to meet a preacher not far from here. He's just in the direction we're going. That's a mighty coincidence, isn't it?"

"Yes," I replied, rolling my eyes. "A mighty one at that."

"So," she continued, "if you've a mind, we could stop by to visit with him for a few minutes. You know, just to have a proper send-off. We wouldn't have to stay long."

Before I could respond, she added, "And by the way, which name shall we go by?"

"Fairfield, I think. The name's always been a lucky one for me, and I have the feeling we'll need a touch more of that before we finally get settled in. So, think you could stand to be Mrs. John Fairfield?"

Cat immediately shot back, "You can call me Mrs. Flapjack for all I care—as long as we take the vows. But haven't you used that name too much before? You think it'll be safe?"

Fairfield, Fairborne, Fairchild—they're all dead now. Doesn't seem to me much to worry about in takin' the name of a dead man. No, Fairfield will do."

"I do like the name," she said, reaching for my hand. Then, after a few moments, she added, softly, "So, think we ought stop and take a minute with the preacher?"

"I do," I said, putting my arm around her. "Finally, at long last, I do. Still don't understand why you'd want to spend your life with a wretch like me, but I won't question it any more. If you think you can stand me, I'll just consider myself lucky and let it go at that."

She nudged even closer to me but didn't say a word. Out of the corner of my eye, I saw on her the biggest smile I'd ever seen before. I did love her so much, but I had been truthful when I said I hadn't a clue why she'd chosen me. However, her smile was all I needed to see. It told me I had her heart, for whatever reasons, and that was more than I deserved.

We rolled along in silence, passing by one merchant after another in this magnificent city as we made our way to the south. Just when the buildings were becoming fewer and far between, I heard an unmistakable sound, the sound of a whip reaching its mark, which was followed by a heart-wrenching wail.

Cat pointed to our right and said, "Look there—coming out of the barn."

Two men, both caked from head to toe with what appeared miles of trail dirt and muck, were dragging two black men, both chained from neck to feet, from the barn toward a small wagon. When the foot of the black man at the rear caught in a bush, the shorter of the two white men uncoiled his whip again and immediately sliced him twice. The black man didn't move an inch as his skin was peeled.

I pulled our horses up and said, "Whoa there, Mister. What's this about?"

The short man didn't reply at first. Instead, he coiled his whip, spit tobacco juice lazily to the side, some of it dripping to his boots, then said to me, "Don't see it none to your business— and if you don't want a taste of this here whip, you'll just ride along now."

"What about those men," I said, ignoring his warning. "Why are they chained? Where you taking them?"

Cat then whispered to me, "Remember what you said. We need to be miles from here yet today."

I looked at her blankly, turned back to the man, and continued, this time my voice even louder, "I'm waitin' for your answer."

The man studied me before spitting toward our wagon and responding, "Still don't see it none of your concern, but these here darkies run off from Memphis. Somehow got theirselves up to here. But we got 'em, though. Me and Jimson takin' 'em back for reward. Answer your nosiness, did I?"

"Oh, I see," I said, softening my words. "Sorry for bothering you, Sir. Didn't know they was runaways. You carry on now. Good to see justice being served."

He didn't reply. Instead, he uncoiled his whip and laced each of the slaves once again. The one to the front immediately rose up, tears streaming down his cheeks. The still one remained so, even when the other man kicked him sharply at the ribs.

"Riley, looks like this one's out cold. Have to carry him to the wagon, I expect."

"Then you do it," the short man said, curtly, spitting on the chest of the slave standing before him.

"Again, sorry to have bothered you," I said, tipping my hat. "Good luck to the both of you."

With that, we were off again, our wagon rocking back and forth with the stride of the horses. We had gone just a short distance when I looked over at Cat. Her mouth was full open, and she was shaking her head.

"Are you truly going to let that alone?" she finally asked. "We ridin' away from that?"

"What do you think?" I said, turning the horses and guiding the wagon behind a grove of trees off to our right. As soon as I was sure we couldn't be seen from the road, I urged the horses to halt. "They'll be by here shortly, mark my words. It's the quickest way back to Memphis. Since they're moving by wagon, we shouldn't have a problem keeping up with 'em and keepin' 'em in sight. I've been along here many times, and I figure we'll come to a forested area I've camped before in about two hours. That's where they could be taken."

Slapping her forehead, she said, "I should have known better."

"I think you did," I replied, smiling.

She shook her head again and said, "Well, what are you waitin' for? Let's go get 'em. I imagine those poor slaves will fit under the sacks in back. Might as well take 'em with us."

"And then, soon as we do, we're off to Kansas Territory," I said. "By the look of those catchers, this won't take long."

"No," Cat replied, evenly, leaning over to make sure I could see directly into her eyes. "Not to Kansas Territory. To the nearest preacher along the way first. *Then*, to the Territory. That's the order, Mr. Fairfield."

I just smiled, pulled her close again, and kissed her lightly. "Yes, Ma'am. I understand. I agree. I do."

"You had better," she said, pulling back as we heard a wagon rolling past.

"It's them," I said, picking up the reins again. "Just knew they'd be by. We'll give 'em a fair lead before we follow."

"While we're waitin'," Cat said, "tell me again about the Territory and what we're to do there. Tell me what's to our future."

"Adventure, the cause—and love," I said, drawing her close again. "Most of all—love."

And I meant it.

This time, I really did.

....

Epilogue

"With all his faults and misguided impulses, and wicked ways, he was a brave man; he never betrayed a trust that was reposed in him, and he was a true friend to the oppressed and suffering slave."
—*Levi Coffin (from Reminiscences), on John Fairfield*

I began this project knowing full well historians could not agree upon what eventually happened to John Fairfield after he suddenly disappeared from the high visibility he held while working for the cause of abolitionism. While a wealth of information existed about his efforts in the name of the cause, his last days were shrouded in mystery. This intrigued me immensely —and was one of the primary reasons I chose to begin my journey to shed additional light on this forgotten warrior in the fight for freedom and equality for all.

Initially, I decided to investigate a school of thought that held the abolitionist John Fairfield was actually a nom de guerre of an abolitionist by the name of James Cripps. Cripps had famously spent time in, and escaped from, the Bracken County Jail in Augusta, Kentucky, after being caught working to support the cause. After I gathered and reviewed all relevant data along this line, this theory did, indeed, seem plausible. I even made a pilgrimage to the Bracken County Jail, which still stands today, to conduct my own research into the possibility of Cripps and Fairfield being one and the same. While in that area, I read the *Autobiography of Adam Lowry Rankin* (written circa 1891-92). Adam was the son of Reverend John Rankin, whose home served as one of the most important depots on the Underground Railroad. In Adam's autobiography, he wrote of an abolitionist who hid out at his parents' home while recuperating from illness brought on by a stay in the Bracken County Jail. Adam Lowry Rankin stated:

> ...he was arrested on suspicion of being engaged in per-suading slaves to run away and was put in jail. The loss of twenty-one slaves in a radius of twenty miles in so few weeks made the people suspicious of strangers. One Saturday night he managed to break jail and started north, bringing with him, a few nights later, four more slaves, making twenty-five in all. His experiences in jail on bread and water had satisfied his ambition, and he went back to Canada with his last load, and we were thankful he did, for we were afraid he would make us trouble. He went by an alias, even with us, refusing to give his real name. While he was honest in his treatment of the fugitives, we were doubtful of him in other respects so were glad when he returned to his native land....

His information about "The Canadian," also believed by some in the Cripps' camp to be John Fairfield, did, at first review, seem to fit the same time period associated with Cripps' incarceration in Augusta and eventual escape. Therefore, it was assumed by many researchers and historians that Cripps and Fairfield ("The Canadian") were, indeed, the same man.

However, after working with Julie Huffman-klinkowitz, one of America's premier forensic genealogists, we were able to trace James Cripps' movements shortly after his release from the jail. We discovered Cripps moved to Albion, Iowa, where he remained the rest of his life. From his obituary (d. January 9, 1904) and other related documents, it became clear Cripps was *not* John Fairfield. James Cripps, originally of Pennsylvania, was a former schoolteacher and nurseryman who, in his younger days, worked tirelessly for the Democratic Party in Pennsylvania. He also spoke out against violence at every opportunity – and was deeply invested in temperance causes. In addition, the "time-line" of his life did not match with the known adventures of John

Fairfield. I came to the conclusion Cripps was, indeed, incarcerated for a time in the Bracken County Jail, but he was clearly not John Fairfield.

The second path I followed in determining what eventually happened to John Fairfield led toward the Cumberland Iron Works in Cumberland Furnace, Tennessee. It was none other than Levi Coffin, President of the Underground Railroad, whose writings initially led me to this line of inquiry. Coffin shared his story, at every opportunity, for years before finally setting it to print in his *Reminiscences* (first published 1876). In his Reminiscences, he "speculated" about how John Fairfield might have met his end. Coffin stated:

> The conjecture is that he was killed in Tennessee, near the iron-works, on the Cumberland River. It was reported through the papers that there was an insurrectionary movement among the slaves in that locality. .....It was reported that a white man, supposed to be the instigator of the movement and the leader of the negroes, was found among them, and that he was killed. He was a stranger in that neighborhood, and his name was not known. I have always supposed that this man was John Fairfield, and that in this way his strange career was ended by a violent death (p.446).

When I first read this, I immediately felt something amiss. Levi Coffin, from every bit of study I had conducted, was not a man to foster rumors or gossip. He was devout, many said to a fault, and always blunt and truthful. Therefore, I believe it highly unlikely he would have engaged in such speculation– unless it was to help cover the tracks of a man he both admired and admonished at the same time, a man he had worked with in the cause many times. There could not have been a more perfect cover story for the "end" of what many believed a "renegade abolitionist" than to have the story come from the mouth of the President of the Underground Railroad. I now believe this was

316 Ain't No Harm to Kill the Devil

Levi Coffin's true intent in presenting this story.

However, before I came to that conclusion, Coffin's speculation seemed, at first, to be supported by another document I discovered at just about the same time. This document was a letter written on December 25, 1856, by Mrs. George Lewis, wife of the main supervisor at the Cumberland Iron Works, to her parents (or, possibly, her husband's parents—this is unclear). Her letter provided a richly detailed account of the slave insurrection at the Works. In this letter, she provided background information about those reputedly responsible for the events – and shared her own fears about the safety of herself and her family:

> We are all more quiet this morning but the revelations of
> the negroes yesterday were awful. There would not have
> been a living white soul here at Clarksville on Christmas
> day and Aunt Dilsey (one of the slaves) consented to take
> your lives, mine and the children while we were all asleep,
> because none of our servents(sic) were willing, but they all
> knew it but darde(sic) not reveal at the risk of their lives.
> Only to think of us resting and secure with them all and
> they knowing about all the massacres....

Then, later in the letter, about those responsible for the uprising:

> They were under the impression that the Fremont men
> from the North would come on to their assistance and
> if they did not succeed entirely here, they were to fly as
> quickly as possible to Northern States and Fremont would
> protect them.

The "Fremont" reference made by Mrs. Lewis was most likely pointing to John Charles Fremont, another prominent abolitionist and the first candidate of the newly constituted Republican Party; he was a man feared by nearly everyone in the South, and many historians have suggested if he had been elected President in 1856, the Civil War would have started four years before it did. Still, John Fairfield was also known to use the name Fremont when moving slaves to their freedom, so which abolitionist was being referred to in the letter?

However, the more I studied this letter, and particularly her account of the atrocities performed and other information related to the slave insurrection, the more I believed John Fairfield would not have been involved in the action there. This theory simply did not seem to make sense. Such an adventure would have been completely out of character for the John Fairfield I was starting to know through my research. Fairfield, by all accounts, was meticulous in his planning for his adventures and ruses. While it is true he helped groups as large as fifteen to thirty-five (depending upon which account is believed), with the aid of Levi Coffin, to their freedom (the now famous "funeral procession" escape), he preferred serving as a Conductor for smaller numbers, in large part because of financial concerns (both cost and reward).

The Cumberland insurrection was ill planned and conceived, resulting in a very large number of individuals losing their lives (some accounts reported as many as nineteen slaves being hung and several white men incarcerated, or worse, as well). John Fairfield, a man known to be prone at times to over-planning, never would have been involved in something so haphazard and impromptu. He stayed alive for so long, even with the enormous price on his head, because he avoided just such ventures. Therefore, I believe, based upon all documents I had been able to uncover and study, the white man whipped to death in the woods outside Cumberland Furnace was not John Fairfield. At the same time, the following should also be noted: No word of the slave catcher Wilson Taggart was ever heard again after the Cumberland uprising....

A final point on this theory: I also made a journey to Cumberland Furnace to explore the terrain around the area. Something about the geography immediately struck me. Because of where the furnaces were situated at the time, and all the open ground around, it would have taken an army to burst in there and free that many slaves from their cruel lives. John Fairfield

worked with a very small number of close associates; he was simply not the "general" it would have taken for a successful rescue
of the slaves at the Works.

During my research I also came across a theory held by
many historians that Fairfield eventually moved west to Kansas
Territory (Kansas did not become a state until 1861) – and
helped further the cause from there. This line of thought made
the most sense to me because I had been able to uncover that
Fairfield knew John Brown's sons, who lived not that distant from
Ashtabula, Ohio, the port frequently used by John Fairfield to get
runaways by ship from America to Canada. At this same time,
John Brown was establishing his work in the Territory. Fairfield
would have known this and, therefore, known Kansas Territory
would have been a logical frontier in which to continue his work.
After studying this possibility at length, I again enlisted the aid of
genealogists and historians to see if records could be uncovered
to provide support for this theory.

I first looked at what I considered the most probable location
where a man of his talents might settle in the Territory: Salina.
Salina had become known for its trading posts offering goods
and supplies for westbound travelers, prospectors, hunters, and
area Native American tribes. In addition to this, it gained a reputation, not popular with all, as a locale ripe with depots for runaways making to the west. A detailed study of census records for
the surrounding areas revealed the following. In the 1860 census
for Arapahoe County, Kansas Territory, half way down the list a
name appeared—a name that sent a shiver down my back. The
name was John Fairfield. In the information provided about John
Fairfield were these details: he was thirty-five years of age and
originally from the state of Virginia. The age was perfect, and the
place of birth matched other documents. Everything fit.. Would
he have used this name in Kansas Territory? Most certainly – as
this was an alias of a dead man, a man who supposedly met his
demise in the woods outside of Cumberland Furnace, Tennessee.
Who would be looking for a dead man, especially in the Territory,

where homesteaders settled themselves to begin new lives? As I continued to study the census records, I felt I had, indeed, found the John Fairfield I'd been searching for all along.

One thing still bothered me, though. I didn't have a face for John Fairfield. No photographs are known to exist of him. Photography was just in its infancy when he was working with the cause, and pictures were not common at the time. On top of this, Fairfield never would have agreed to a photograph because of the large bounty that followed him everywhere he went. If a picture had been taken and circulated, those chasing after him would have had a decided advantage, an advantage a man of Fairfield's skills and talents could ill have afforded. Still, the entire time I was working on this project, I wondered what the man had looked like. Many who knew him and wrote about him offered physical descriptions of him that were quite different. This made sense, as he would have been required to change his appearance regularly to keep from being identified during his adventures. Still, I wasn't going to rest until I had an image to put with this warrior of the cause.

After collecting all the descriptions of Fairfield I could find, putting these together, and then visiting with nearly a dozen law enforcement agencies, I was finally put in contact with Suzanne Lowe Birdwell, Forensic Artist for the Texas Rangers' Evidential Art & Facial Identification division. I asked if she could create, using the information provided, an image of John Fairfield. Her duties with the Texas Rangers often involved the same type of work, and the images she created were used in the capture of a wide assortment of those who had broken the law. I felt she was a natural to take on this project, and the results of her work did not disappoint me. What she created, I believe, is as close to knowing what Fairfield looked like as that we'll ever have. That image is on the cover of this book, adding a final piece of the puzzle to my search for John Fairfield.

This search for John Fairfield was fascinating. I followed him through historical records, I visited Underground Railroad sites he'd used, and I retraced the routes he used in leading slaves to freedom. Additional details about the journey I conducted to obtain the background information for this book are chronicled in *Finding Fairfield: The Behind-the-Scenes story of Ain't No Harm to Kill the Devil: The Life and Legend of John Fairfield, Abolitionist for Hire.* I hope all will enjoy that story as well.

Did John Fairfield make it to Kansas Territory and continue the cause from there? While we may never know for sure everything related to his last days, I believe it isn't his "end" that is most important. What will live on is his legacy, one burned forever into the cause of abolitionism and the battle for freedom for all. He was, in the end, one of the most successful and creative of all Conductors of the Underground Railroad—a man who believed so strongly in the cause the phrase most attached to him for all-time will be "Ain't no harm to kill the Devil." A man like that should not be forgotten.

—JSC

Acknowledgments

This book could not have been written without the generous assistance of many wonderful people, all of whom gave freely of their time and knowledge.

First and foremost, I'd like to thank my wife, Linda, for traveling with me and for helping with the research at the many Underground Railroad and other historical sites visited while gathering background information for the story.

The many Research Librarians at the Library of Congress who helped source historical documents and records.

Betty Campbell, Director, and Suzannah West, Guide and Historian, of the Reverend John Rankin House in Ripley, Ohio, for sharing their knowledge of the Rankin family and the Underground Railroad in Ohio and Kentucky.

The Ohio State Historical Society, for providing the photo of the Reverend John Rankin.

Caroline Miller, Underground Railroad Historian, for sharing her knowledge of Ohio and Kentucky history—and for taking me on a tour of the Bracken County Jail and other historic sites of the area.

Georgeanne Reuter, Executive Director, The Kelton House Museum & Garden, Columbus, Ohio, for providing the pictures of Fernando and Sophia Kelton.

Maryjo Kepler, Trustee; Frank Sacha, Treasurer; and Kay Brown, Docent, of Haines House in Alliance, Ohio, for providing a wonderful tour of that important home and sharing biographical information about the Haines family. I'd also like to thank Martha McClaugherty, President of The Alliance Area Preservation Society, for permission to use the photograph of Jonathan and Sarah Haines.

Rod Chapman, Manager of the Spread Eagle Tavern and Inn, Hanoverton, Ohio, for allowing me to spend the night there and explore the building and grounds.

Jean Hendricks, Local Historian, Hanoverton, Ohio, for sharing her knowledge of the history of the area; Rian Bobby, Local Historian, Leetonia, Ohio, for providing detailed information about the Sandy and Beaver Canal (and for directions when I became lost there!).

Sterling R. Minnoch, Historian/Volunteer, the Hubbard House Underground Railroad Museum, Ashtabula, Ohio, for providing information about the Hubbards' involvement in the Underground Railroad.

Bob Frisbie, Director, and all the wonderful historians at the Ashtabula Maritime Museum, Ashtabula, Ohio, for sharing their knowledge of the history of the local area and of the shipping trade of the era.

Norma Waters, Research Librarian, Jefferson Historical Society, Jefferson, Ohio, for providing the photo of William Hubbard and for providing a wealth of information about the ship captains who put their lives in peril to help deliver runaways to Canada.

Stephen M. Charter, Head and University Archivist, Center for Archival Collections, Bowling Green State University, for permission to use the photo of Ashtabula Harbor.

Jason Stratman, Assistant Librarian, Missouri Historical Society Library and Research Center, for helping secure historical documents and newspaper articles related to the "slave trade" of the era.

Stan Lyle, Research Librarian, University of Northern Iowa, for his help in uncovering a wealth of information about the Underground Railroad.

Julie Huffman Klinkowitz, Forensic Geneologist, for

providing census records and biographical information about characters included in the story.

Dana Peiffer, User Services Lead Support Specialist, of the University of Northern Iowa, for providing the full range of technology support services.

Peggy Dillard, historian (known nationwide as "Rebel Girl"), for information related to the slave insurrection at Cumberland Furnace, and John Walsh, Owner of Fort Donelson Relics, for granting permission to use sections of Mrs. George Lewis' letter of December 25, 1856.

Mark Coplin, for sharing with me his knowledge of weapons of the time period

Chuck Cross, Barry Eastman, and Doug Davis of "Rudy's of Waterloo" for providing a splendid atmosphere for writing.

Suzanne Lowe Birdwell, Forensic Artist, Texas Rangers' Evidential Art & Facial Identification division (Chair, Forensic Art Subcommittee for the Int'l Assoc. for Identification).,for creating the image of John Fairfield used on the cover of this book.

The Abraham Lincoln Presidential Library and Museum for permission to use the photo of the "slave chains."

Jim Bubash, for sharing his literary skills and talents.

Shelley Terry, Staff Writer, Star Beacon (Ashtabula, Ohio), for her photographic expertise.

I'd also like to offer a special thanks to Kenneth Johnson, Writer and Director of "The Liberators"—a superb film about the early life of John Fairfield—for sharing his own research into the life and work of Fairfield.

Finally, I'd like to thank Rosemary Yokoi, truly the best editor and friend a writer ever had!

Thank you, and bless you all!

Photographs

*The Reverend John Rankin House, Ripley, Ohio
(across river, at very top of hill).*
Courtesy: Copeland Collection

The Reverend John Rankin House, Ripley, Ohio
Courtesy: Copeland Collection

Reverend John Rankin.
Courtesy: The Ohio State Historical Society.

Kelton House Museum & Garden, Columbus, Ohio.
Courtesy: Copeland Collection.

Fernando Cortez Kelton
Courtesy: Kelton House Museum & Garden.

Sophia Stone Kelton
Courtesy: Kelton House Museum & Garden.

Haines House, Alliance, Ohio.
Courtesy: Copeland Collection

Jonathan Ridgeway Haines, Sarah Haines.
Courtesy: The Alliance Area Preservation Society.

The Spread Eagle Tavern & Inn, Hanoverton, Ohio.
Courtesy: Copeland Collection

Dr. James Robertson Home (secret room upper level, far left)
Courtesy: Copeland Collection

Hubbard House Underground Railroad Museum, Ashtabula, Ohio.
Courtesy: Copeland Collection.

William Hubbard.
Courtesy: Jefferson Historical Society.

Ashtabula Harbor (c. 1856), Ashtabula, Ohio.
Courtesy: Center for Archival Collections, Bowling Green State University.

Author at the Cumberland Iron Works, Cumberland Furnace, Tennessee.
Courtesy: Copeland Collection.

John Fairfield.
Courtsey: Suzanne Lowe Birdwell